HUMAN RIGHTS IN EUROPE

HUMAN RIGHTS
IN EUROPE

being an account of the European Convention for the Protection
of Human Rights and Fundamental Freedoms signed in
Rome on 4 November 1950, of the Protocol thereto
and of the machinery created thereby:
the European Commission of Human
Rights and the European
Court of Human Rights

by

A. H. ROBERTSON
B.C.L. (Oxon), S.J.D. (Harvard)

MANCHESTER UNIVERSITY PRESS
U.S.A.: OCEANA PUBLICATIONS INC.

© 1963 A. H. Robertson

Published by the University of Manchester at

THE UNIVERSITY PRESS

316–324 Oxford Road, Manchester, 13

U.S.A.

OCEANA PUBLICATIONS INC.

40 Cedar Street, Dobbs Ferry

New York N.Y.

Printed in Great Britain by Butler & Tanner Ltd., Frome and London

CONTENTS

v

PREFACE

SEPTEMBER 3 1963 marks the tenth anniversary of the entry into force of the European Convention on Human Rights and the fifth anniversary of the date when eight European States had accepted as compulsory the jurisdiction of the European Court of Human Rights, an event which made it possible for the Court to come into existence. The European Commission of Human Rights was constituted in May 1954, so that its tenth anniversary will not be long delayed. As a result there is a story to be told of some interest—at least for international lawyers—about this new development in securing the international protection of human rights and fundamental freedoms and in establishing machinery which grants to individuals a status which has never previously been accorded to them in international law.

The purpose of this book is to tell that story and thus give an account of the major developments resulting from the conclusion of the European Convention on Human Rights, of the system of protection thus established for a number of civil and political rights and of the more important decisions of the Commission and the Court. This involves, moreover, a description of the European Social Charter and of its provisions designed to secure a number of rights of an economic and social character. In addition, reference is made to the wider political objectives underlying the activities of the Council of Europe in this domain and to their repercussions in other parts of the world.

Having published a number of articles and lectures on these subjects in recent years, I have naturally made use of that material in writing this book. Thus the first and last chapters are based on two of the Melland Schill Lectures delivered at the University of Manchester in 1961 and published by the Manchester University Press under the title of *The Law of International Institutions in Europe*; the chapter on the European Court of Human Rights reproduces in part an article published by the *American Journal of Comparative Law* in the autumn of 1959; and the chapter on the Lawless case is largely taken from two notes in the *British Yearbook of International Law* for 1960 and 1961. I have also drawn on the chapter on Human Rights in my book *The Council of*

Europe, 2nd edition, 1961, published by Stevens and Sons in the Library of World Affairs. My thanks are expressed for permission to republish this material; all of it has been revised and brought up to date, together with much that is new, in order to make a single book about the European Convention, the Commission, and the Court.

I have been assisted by a number of my colleagues and express my thanks to Monsieur J. Velu, Mr. A. B. McNulty, Monsieur H. Leleu, Mr. H. Golsong and Mr. F. Tennfjord who have read respectively Chapters 2, 3, 4, 5 and 8 and made a number of valuable suggestions.

In conclusion, as an international official, I wish to make the usual disclaimer and point out that any opinions expressed in this book are the views of the author and not of the organisation by which he is employed.

A. H. ROBERTSON

Strasbourg, 5 April 1963

FOREWORD

THIS is the sixth book on International Law produced by the Manchester University Press since 1957 and the second of Dr. Robertson's.

Dr. Robertson's academic record, his wide experience of international affairs and his years of practice in the day-to-day working of the Council of Europe, make him admirably qualified to explain the important arrangements made for the legal protection of Human Rights in a large part of Europe today, and this he does, making excellent use of *travaux préparatoires* and the evolving case-law.

Some Member States of the Council of Europe have accepted the jurisdiction of the European Court of Human Rights at Strasbourg; others have merely accepted the jurisdiction of the European Commission of Human Rights, but all states which have ratified the European Convention, as Dr. Robertson points out (see p. 17), have accepted Article 13. This article imposes on every ratifying state the international obligation to provide 'an effective remedy before a national authority . . .' when a breach of the Convention is committed. Some states of course provided in their courts effective remedies for foreigner and citizen alike, even before the Convention was concluded, but the Convention establishes norms and goes a long way towards making them enforceable by ratifying states—and not only in respect of their own nationals (p. 15).

This work may well prove to be one of the most important recent books for practitioners concerned to protect the interests of their clients of whatever condition of nationality or of statelessness, when they are in the countries of Free Europe. This book should also be a landmark for students of political science and of jurisprudence the world over. At last, what Holland called 'antecedent rights in rem', and what are often called 'natural rights', have been set out and clothed with extensive legal protection on an international basis.

This work is confidently submitted to the attention of every forward-looking person, layman or lawyer, interested in the future of human liberty.

B. A. WORTLEY

Law Faculty,
University of Manchester
July 1963

CHAPTER I

THE ORIGINS AND HISTORY OF THE CONVENTION

1. *Human Rights as the Guarantee of Democracy*

HUMAN rights have a very special place in the philosophy of the Council of Europe. The reason is not far to seek and may be stated quite simply: respect for human rights is the guarantee of democracy.

The preambles to treaties frequently constitute a rewarding object of study. We often tend to ignore them, on the ground that they have no legal effect and are little more than 'window dressing' for the operative clauses. But this is a mistake, because in many cases they reveal the political objectives of the Contracting Parties and enable us to place in perspective, that is to say in their historical context, the legal obligations that follow.

The Covenant of the League of Nations was drafted after the war of 1914–18 and the principal object of its authors was to prevent the repetition of such a catastrophe; their main concern was thus for the maintenance of international relations on a peaceful basis and this is reflected in the words of the Preamble: 'to promote international co-operation and to achieve international peace and security. . . .'

In 1945, the situation was broadly similar and the Preamble to the Charter of the United Nations is thus mainly concerned with international relations: 'to save succeeding generations from the scourge of war . . . to establish conditions under which justice and the respect for the obligations arising from treaties and other sources of international law can be maintained . . . to unite our strength to maintain international peace and security . . .'—and so on. But then something new is introduced in the second paragraph of the Preamble, which

Reaffirms faith in fundamental human rights, in the dignity and worth of men and women and of nations large and small.

Human rights are mentioned almost for the first time in an

international treaty,[1] presumably because the drafters of the
Charter were looking behind the facts of war to its causes, that
is to say to the existence of dictatorships which make wars
possible. An international order which can effectively secure human
rights is thereby taking the biggest single step towards the prevention of war.[2] This would have been a splendid objective for
the United Nations; but its accomplishment would, no doubt,
have been too much to expect in the near future. The Preamble
of the Charter 'reaffirms faith in fundamental human rights',
and Article 1 includes among the purposes of the United Nations:
'to achieve international co-operation ... in promoting and
encouraging respect for human rights and for fundamental
freedoms for all without distinction. ...' Later articles (particularly Articles 55, 56 and 76) contain undertakings to 'promote'
or 'encourage' respect for human rights and fundamental freedoms, but this still falls far short of an actual guarantee.[3]

It was left to the regional organisations in Europe to carry the
matter further by adding to the idea of respect for human rights,
which primarily concerns the individual, the further concept

[1] The treaties for the protection of minorities concluded after the First
World War related to the rights of special groups, but not to human rights
in general. Though the German-Polish Convention on Upper Silesia did
contain a provision (Article 4) for the international protection of the rights
of the individual even against the State of which he was a national.

[2] Cf. President Truman's closing speech to the San Francisco Conference
in which he said : 'Under this document (the Charter) we have good reason
to expect an international bill of rights acceptable to all the nations involved.
That Bill of Rights will be as much a part of international life as our own
Bill of Rights is a part of our Constitution. The Charter is dedicated to the
achievement and observance of fundamental freedoms. Unless we can attain
those objectives for all men and women everywhere—without regard to
race, language or religion—we cannot have permanent peace and security
in the world.'

[3] There is an extensive literature on the question whether the United
Nations Charter has created legal obligations for the Member States to
respect human rights and fundamental freedoms. See *inter alia* H. Lauterpacht,
International Law and Human Rights pp. 145–65 ; Hans Kelsen, *The Law of
the United Nations* pp. 27–50 ; M. Ganji, *International Protection of Human
Rights* pp. 113–39. The draft Covenants as approved by the Third Committee
of the General Assembly refer to 'the obligation of States under the
Charter ... to promote universal respect for, and observance of, human
rights and freedoms' (doc. A/C. 3/L. 978 of 25 September 1962) ; but, as
stated in the text, this is much less than an international guarantee.

which results from their projection on to the larger scale of the body politic, and so concerns the state itself, namely democracy and the rule of law. In the Brussels Treaty of 17 March 1948 the five signatories, after reaffirming their faith in the ideals proclaimed in the Charter of the United Nations, stated that they were resolved:

To fortify and preserve the principles of democracy, personal freedom and political liberty, the constitutional traditions and the rule of law, which are their common heritage.

The same ideas were reproduced, with a slight rearrangement, in the North Atlantic Treaty of 4 April 1949, in which the Parties declare:

They are determined to safeguard their freedom, common heritage and civilisation of their peoples, founded on the principles of democracy, individual liberty and the rule of law.

Another variant was enshrined in the Statute of the Council of Europe, which was signed in St. James's Palace on 5 May 1949. In the Preamble the Contracting Parties declare that they are:

Reaffirming their devotion to the spiritual and moral values which are the common heritage of their peoples and the true source of individual freedom, political liberty and the rule of law, principles which form the basis of all genuine democracy;

Thereafter come two important innovations. The first article of the Statute sets out the aim of the organisation as 'to achieve a greater unity between its Members' and then specifies various means by which this aim shall be pursued, including 'the maintenance and further realisation of human rights and fundamental freedoms'. Secondly, Article 3 of the Statute continues:

Every Member of the Council of Europe must accept the principles of the rule of law and of the enjoyment by all persons within its jurisdiction of human rights and fundamental freedoms, and collaborate sincerely and effectively in the realisation of the aim of the Council as specified in Chapter I.

It thus appears that the maintenance of human rights and respect for the rule of law are not only included among the general affirmations of faith which it is customary to insert in the Preamble to an international treaty; they are actually included among the objectives of the Council of Europe and also made a condition of membership. It was in this respect that the Statute went much further than any earlier treaty. But the matter was not left there. As soon as the Council met for its first session in August 1949, the Consultative Assembly put on its Agenda 'Measures for the fulfilment of the declared aim of the Council of Europe, in accordance with Article 1 of the Statute, in regard to the maintenance and further realisation of human rights and fundamental freedoms'; it then recommended that the Committee of Ministers should cause to be drawn up a Convention, providing a collective guarantee, and designed to secure the effective enjoyment of the rights and freedoms proclaimed in the Universal Declaration of Human Rights adopted by the General Assembly of the United Nations on 10 December 1948.

Why was the cause of human rights espoused so ardently by the Council of Europe? There were, it is believed, two main reasons. The first of these was the ideological conflict between East and West which surrounded its creation. It must not be forgotten that the post-war movement for European unity was not only the result of a conviction that this was a desirable political goal; it was also a reaction to the Communist threat which was very real at that time. The year which elapsed between the Hague Congress in May 1948, which led to the establishment of the Council of Europe,[1] and the signature of the Statute in the following spring witnessed also the seizure of power by the Communists in Czechoslovakia, the civil war in Greece and the Berlin Blockade. M. Spaak once remarked that the man who did most to bring about the union of Western Europe was Josef Stalin. It was when the European countries were acutely aware of the challenge of Communism that they felt the need to reaffirm the principles of their own political faith; it was the danger of dictatorship that made them conscious of the value of democracy. The Council of Europe was thus a peaceful association of democratic states (not, be it noted, a military alliance—that was NATO), which proclaimed their faith in the rule of law and 'their devotion to the spiritual and moral values which are the common heritage of their peoples'. This aspect of the matter was well summarised when the Convention on Human Rights was signed at the sixth session of the Committee of Ministers in Rome, in November

[1] See A. H. Robertson, *The Council of Europe*, Ch. 1, pp. 1–9 ; see also below pp. 6–7.

1950. Mr. Sean MacBride, the Irish Minister for External Affairs, said on that occasion:

The present struggle is one which is largely being fought in the minds and consciences of mankind. In this struggle, I have always felt that we lacked a clearly defined charter which set out unambiguously the rights which we democrats guaranteed to our people. This Convention is a step in this direction.

and M. Robert Schuman added:

This Convention which we are signing is not as full or as precise as many of us would have wished. However, we have thought it our duty to subscribe to it as it stands. It provides foundations on which to base the defence of human personality against all tyrannies and against all forms of totalitarianism.

This last remark is the clue to the second reason underlying the Council's devotion to the cause of human rights. 1949 was very close to 1945, when all of Europe was suffering from another form of tyranny. Many of the leading statesmen of the immediate post-war epoch had been in the resistance or in prison during the war and were acutely conscious of the need to prevent any recrudescence of dictatorship in Western Europe. They knew that as long as human rights are respected, democracy is secure and the danger of dictatorship is remote; but that the first steps towards dictatorship are the gradual suppression of individual rights—infringement of the freedom of the press, prohibition of public meetings, trials behind closed doors, and so on—and that once this process has started, it is increasingly difficult to bring it to a halt. What is necessary, therefore, is to lay down in advance what are the standards of rights and freedoms that must be respected in a democratic society and institute machinery to ensure that they are observed. If any member State should then start on the path which leads to dictatorship, the alarm would be sounded and international machinery put in motion to restore the rule of law. Monsieur Pierre-Henri Teitgen (a leader of the French Mouvement Républicain Populaire) expressed this graphically in a speech to the Consultative Assembly in August 1949:[1]

Many of our colleagues have pointed out that our countries are democratic and are deeply impregnated with a sense of freedom; they

[1] Consultative Assembly, *Official Reports*, August 1949, p. 1158.

believe in morality and in a natural law. . . . Why is it necessary to build such a system?

Democracies do not become Nazi countries in one day. Evil progresses cunningly, with a minority operating, as it were, to remove the levers of control. One by one, freedoms are suppressed, in one sphere after another. Public opinion and the entire national conscience are asphyxiated. And then, when everything is in order, the 'Führer' is installed and the evolution continues even to the oven of the crematorium.

It is necessary to intervene before it is too late. A conscience must exist somewhere which will sound the alarm to the minds of a nation menaced by this progressive corruption, to warn them of the peril and to show them that they are progressing down a long road which leads far, sometimes even to Buchenwald or Dachau.

An international Court, within the Council of Europe, and a system of supervision and guarantees could be the conscience of which we all have need, and of which other countries have perhaps a special need.

The provisions about human rights in the Statute of the Council of Europe, the obligations undertaken in the European Convention and the machinery of the Commission and the Court are thus designed primarily to preserve the rule of law and the principles of democracy in the member States and, should the danger arise, forestall any trend to dictatorship before it is too late.[1]

2. *The History of the Convention and Protocol*

The history of the Convention goes back to a period antedating the Council of Europe. The Congress of Europe convened by the International Committee of Movements for European Unity was held at the Hague, 8–10 May 1948; it included 713 delegates from sixteen countries[2] and observers (of whom a

---

[1] On the Convention in general see *inter alia* Lauterpacht, *op. cit.*, pp. 435–63 ; P. Modinos, ' La Convention Européenne des Droits de l'Homme', *European Yearbook* ,Vol. I, 1955, pp. 141–70, and 'Effects and Repercussions of the European Convention', *I.C.L.Q.*, October 1962, pp. 1097–1108 ; K. Vasak, 'Cour et Commission des Droits de l'Homme', *Juris-Classeur de Droit International*, Fascicule 155F, 1961 ; Faculté de Droit de Strasbourg, *La Protection internationale des Droits de l'Homme dans le Cadre Européen* ; McNair, *The Expansion of International Law*, pp. 9–28 ; Ganji, *op. cit.*, pp. 230–71 ; G. L. Weil, *The European Convention on Human Rights*.

[2] Austria 12, Belgium 18, Britain 140, Denmark 32, Ireland 5, France 185, Germany 51, Greece 18, Italy 57, Liechtenstein 3, Luxembourg 8, the Netherlands 59, Norway 12, Saar 5, Sweden 19, Switzerland 39.

number were refugees) from ten others.[1] The purposes of the Congress were to demonstrate the wide support for the cause of European unity, to provide fresh impetus to the movement and to make practical recommendations for the accomplishment of its objectives. The participants included a number of former prime ministers and foreign ministers, many members of parliament and leading citizens from different sectors of the community. A number of them were later to become prominent members of the Consultative Assembly. The President of Honour was Mr. Winston Churchill and the Chairmen of the three committees of the Congress were M. Ramadier of France, M. van Zeeland of Belgium and Professor de Madariaga, a Spanish exile. In the 'Message to Europeans' adopted at the final plenary session the delegates proclaimed:

We desire a united Europe, throughout whose area the free movement of persons, ideas and goods is restored;

We desire a Charter of Human Rights guaranteeing liberty of thought, assembly and expression as well as the right to form a political opposition;

We desire a Court of Justice with adequate sanctions for the implementation of this Charter;

We desire a European Assembly where the live forces of all our nations shall be represented;

And pledge ourselves in our home and in public, in our political and religious life, in our professional and trade union circles, to give our fullest support to all persons and governments working for this lofty cause, which offers the last chance of peace and the one promise of a great future for this generation and those that will succeed it.

The desire for a Charter of Human Rights and for a Court of Justice with adequate sanctions for its implementation subsequently formed the subject of more detailed study. Early in 1949 the International Juridical Section of the European Movement was set up under the Chairmanship of M. Pierre-Henri Teitgen, former French Minister of Justice, with Sir David Maxwell Fyfe (later Lord Chancellor Kilmuir) and Professor Fernand Dehousse of Belgium (later President of the Consultative Assembly) as joint rapporteurs. This group set to work to prepare

[1] Bulgaria, Canada, Czechoslovakia, Finland, Hungary, Poland, Roumania, Spain, U.S.A. and Yugoslavia.

a draft Convention in which the Contracting Parties would undertake to uphold the fundamental liberties of their citizens and establish a European Court to adjudicate in cases of alleged violation. The draft thus prepared was submitted to the Committee of Ministers of the Council of Europe in July 1949, with a recommendation that the matter should be placed on the Agenda of the First Session of the Consultative Assembly which was about to take place in the following month.[1]

The other progenitor of the European Convention was, of course, the *Universal Declaration of Human Rights*, proclaimed by the General Assembly of the United Nations on 10 December 1948. As is well known, this Declaration had no legal effect, though its authors intended it to have 'a moral value and authority which is without precedent in the history of the world';[2] it 'gave expression to what, in the fullness of time, ought to become principles of law recognised and acted upon by states members of the United Nations'.[3] Once the Declaration had been proclaimed, the General Assembly instructed the organs of the United Nations to give priority to the drafting of a Covenant of Human Rights, intended to give legal effect to the general principles enunciated in the Declaration; this work has been in progress ever since, but has not yet reached a successful conclusion.[4] But what is important in the present context is that, when the Council of Europe started work in this field, it found ready to hand the statement of general principles contained in the Universal Declaration.

In spite of the recommendation of the European Movement, the Committee of Ministers of the Council of Europe did not include the question of human rights on the draft Agenda which

---

[1] *The European Movement and the Council of Europe*, 1949, p. 114. The draft Convention worked out by the European Movement is to be found *loc. cit.* at pp. 115–19 ; and the draft Statute for the Court *loc. cit.* at pp. 184–98.

[2] The words quoted are from the speech of the Belgian delegate on the occasion of the adoption of the Declaration (A/PV 181 p. 47).

[3] Lauterpacht : 'The Universal Declaration of Human Rights', *B.Y.I.L.*, 25 (1948), p. 354.

[4] Though work on the United Nations draft Covenants has not yet been completed, more progress has been made with the Convention on Genocide, the Convention on the Status of Refugees, the Convention on the Status of Stateless Persons, instruments designed to secure Freedom of

it drew up for the first session of the Assembly in 1949.[1] The Assembly itself then proposed to include on its Agenda the study of 'measures for the fulfilment of the declared aim of the Council of Europe in accordance with Article 1 of the Statute in regard to the maintenance and further realisation of human rights and fundamental freedoms'.[2] The Committee of Ministers (whose consent was then required, in accordance with the original text of Article 23 of the Statute) approved the inclusion of this item on the Agenda and asked the Assembly to devote particular attention to the question of the definition of human rights.[3]

The Assembly held a general debate on the subject on 19 August 1949 and a formal proposal was made for the establishment of an organisation within the Council of Europe to ensure the collective guarantee of human rights.[4] This was referred to the Committee on Legal and Administrative Questions, presided over by Sir David Maxwell Fyfe, with M. Antonio Azara (Italy) as Vice-Chairman and M. Pierre-Henri Teitgen (France) as Rapporteur. The Report of the Committee[5] was presented to the Assembly by M. Teitgen and adopted on 8 September.[6] The Committee took as the basis of its work the Universal Declaration

Information, the Convention on the Political Rights of Women, the Conventions on the Abolition of Slavery and Forced Labour and Conventions on the Right to Organise and Collective Bargaining.

There is an immense literature on this subject. The following may be mentioned more particularly : The United Nations' *Yearbook on Human Rights*; *These Rights and Freedoms* (a U.N. publication); G. Bebr, 'International Protection of Human Rights and Freedoms', *Philippine Law Journal*, 29, 1954, p. 307 ; M. Moskowitz, *Human Rights and World Order* ; Egon Schwelb, 'International Conventions on Human Rights', *I.C.L.Q.*, 1960, p. 654 ; Paul Weis, 'The Convention relating to the Status of Stateless Persons', *I.C.L.Q.*, 1961, p. 255 ; Ganji, *op. cit.* ; C. W. Jenks, *Human Rights and International Labour Standards.*

[1] Consultative Assembly, *Minutes of Proceedings of the Second Sitting*, 11 August 1949, Appendix I.

[2] *Minutes of Proceedings of the Fourth Sitting*, 13 August 1949, Appendix I.

[3] *Minutes of Proceedings of the Fifth Sitting*, 16 August 1949, Appendices II and III.

[4] Motion of M. Teitgen, Sir David Maxwell Fyfe and others, *Documents of the Assembly*, 1949, doc. 3.

[5] *Documents of the Assembly*, doc. 77, 1949.

[6] Recommendation 38, *Texts adopted by the Assembly*, 1949, p. 49.

of the United Nations, and listed ten rights which it proposed should be the subject of a collective guarantee. It then considered how this guarantee should be established. In the first place, it proposed that all member States should bind themselves to respect the fundamental principles of democracy, and to hold free elections at reasonable intervals with universal suffrage and secret ballot; it was then to be left to each signatory state, subject to certain safeguards, to determine the rules by which the guaranteed rights and freedoms should be established and protected within its territory. The object of the collective guarantee was to ensure that the laws of each State in which are embodied the guaranteed rights and freedoms, as well as the application of these laws, are in accordance with 'the general principles of law as recognised by civilised nations' and referred to in Article 38(c) of the Statute of the International Court of Justice. Secondly, in order to implement the collective guarantee of human rights, it was proposed to create a European Commission for Human Rights and a European Court of Justice.

Member States might bring any alleged breach of the Convention before the Commission, which would endeavour to settle the matter by conciliation. A similar right was to be granted to private individuals or associations, after exhausting local remedies. If conciliation failed, the Commission itself, or a member State, might refer the matter to the European Court of Justice, though this right was not to be accorded to private parties. The Court would take decisions as to whether a violation had occurred; these would be transmitted to the Committee of Ministers of the Council of Europe, with which would rest responsibility for further action. This plan, then, to recapitulate, proposed for the first time the institution of an effective remedy for the citizen whose rights were infringed by a sovereign state: he would, in his individual capacity, have a direct recourse to an international organ (the Commission) and, though he could not himself appeal to the European Court, a state could be made answerable before the Court if the individual's case were championed by the Commission or by another signatory State.

Under the Statute of the Council of Europe, the Consultative Assembly is a deliberative organ, which has no powers of decision but makes recommendations to the Committee of Ministers; the latter, as the executive organ of the Council, then acts on them as it thinks fit.[1] Accordingly these proposals were submitted to the Committee of Ministers with a request that it should cause a Convention to be drafted which would give them the force of law.[2] The Ministers at their meeting in November 1949 decided to appoint a committee of governmental experts to prepare a draft Convention, 'due attention being paid to the progress achieved in this matter by the competent organs of the United Nations'. The Committee thus appointed met in Strasbourg in February and March 1950 and prepared a draft Convention, taking as the basis of its work the proposals of the Consultative Assembly. It made considerable progress, but was unable to reach agreement on certain questions (such as the problem whether the rights to be protected should be merely enumerated, or defined in detail) and did not attempt to reach agreement on others (including the creation of a European Court) which it considered to be of a political rather than of a legal character; it therefore submitted to the Committee of Ministers a report containing a number of alternative texts. The Ministers considered this report in April 1950 and decided to convene a meeting of senior officials to take the political decisions necessitated by the report of the Legal Experts. The Committee of Senior Officials met in June 1950 and prepared a draft Convention incorporating the greater part of the texts submitted by the Legal Experts. This draft adopted a compromise formula on the question of the enumeration or definition of human rights, and proposed the creation of a European Court with optional jurisdiction. It left undecided a certain number of questions of a largely political nature (such as the institution of a right of individual petition) which were referred for decision to the Ministers themselves.

The Committee of Ministers, during its fifth Session in August 1950, considered the report of the Senior Officials together with the comments thereon of the Assembly's Legal Committee.[3] On 7 August they adopted a revised text of the draft Convention; this was considerably weaker than the original proposals of the Assembly, since the right of individual petition was made conditional and the jurisdiction of the Court optional.

[1] The powers and functions of the Assembly and the Committee of Ministers are explained in Robertson, *op. cit.*, Chs. 3 and 4.

[2] Recommendation 38, *Texts adopted by the Assembly*, 1949, p. 49.

[3] *Documents of the Assembly*, 1950, doc. 6, Appendix 5.

This new draft was then submitted to the Assembly at its second session, and again considered by the Legal Committee, whose report was approved by the Assembly on 25 August 1950[1] and considered by the Committee of Ministers at its Sixth Session in Rome in November of the same year. Once more the Ministers brought with them their legal advisers, who reviewed the amendments proposed by the Assembly and undertook a final revision of the text. They were unable to reach agreement on accepting the majority of the amendments proposed, with the result that the Convention was finally signed on 4 November 1950 substantially in the form which had been approved by the Ministers in August.[2]

The Assembly's comments on the draft Convention in August 1950 included a recommendation to add three rights not included in the Ministers' draft. These were the right of property, the right of parents to choose the education of their children, and the so-called 'political liberties clause'.[3]

It was obvious that any clause designed to guarantee the individual's enjoyment of his possessions and protect them from arbitrary confiscation would be unacceptable to Socialist governments unless it was made quite clear that this would not prevent the state from nationalising private property. At the same time, it was a matter of some delicacy to draft a clause which would permit a democratic Socialist government to nationalise private property 'in accordance with the general interest' but would not allow a totalitarian government to confiscate private property in accordance with a policy which it claimed to be in the general interest, but which democratic countries would regard as discriminatory.

The right to education trod on equally delicate ground. In modern society, where the education of children is primarily— at least in most countries—the function of the state, the right of parents to choose the education to be given to their children might be held to involve as a corollary the duty of the state to furnish education in accordance with the individual convictions of its nationals. How far is this duty to be carried? Must schools of all denominations be provided in every village? If not, where

[1] Recommendation 24, *Texts adopted by the Assembly*, 1950, p. 33.

[2] The text of the Convention is given in Appendix I.

[3] Recommendation 24, *Texts adopted by the Assembly*, 1950, p. 33, paras. II, III and IV.

is the line to be drawn? These questions immediately evoke in many continental countries the long and bitter dispute between Church and State over education and the support of church schools. They also raised a newer, and even more controversial question: if parents have the right to choose the education to be given to their children, have communist parents in a non-communist state the right to have their children educated in the doctrines of Marx and Lenin?

The text on free elections also raised difficulties. Clearly, all member States of the Council of Europe are advocates of political liberties. The Statute of the Council of Europe reaffirms their 'devotion to the spiritual and moral values which are the common heritage of their peoples and the true source of individual freedom, political liberty and the rule of law, principles which form the basis of all genuine democracy'. Again, under Article 3 of the Statute 'every Member of the Council of Europe must accept the principle of the rule of law and of the enjoyment by all persons within its jurisdiction of human rights and fundamental freedoms'. It is however, quite a different question to draft a short paragraph which contains a legal guarantee of the political rights of individuals.

In view of these difficulties, when the Committee of Ministers came to consider the proposals of the Assembly on the three rights of property, education, and political liberty as part of a heavy Agenda at a two-day Session in Rome in November 1950, they did not find these texts acceptable in their original formulation, but decided to refer them for further study to their legal experts. They were then faced with the choice of deferring signature of the Convention until these proposals had been more carefully examined, or, on the other hand, of signing the Convention without them. In view of the extended negotiations which had already been necessary to produce the text of the Convention as it then was, there was unanimous agreement among the Foreign Ministers that it was preferable to sign it immediately without these additional articles and to conclude a Protocol at a later date, if agreement thereon proved possible.

In fact a series of meetings of the legal experts took place during the year 1951 and the Assembly's Legal Committee was consulted on two occasions about the progress of their work.[1]

[1] See Recommendation 15 of 8 December 1951.

A Protocol to the Convention covering the three further rights of property, education and free elections was duly concluded and signed on 20 March 1952.[1]

The first ratification of the Convention was that of the United Kingdom, which was deposited on 8 March 1951; its ratification of the Protocol followed on 3 November 1952. In other countries, where positive action by the Parliament was a pre-requisite to ratification, the procedure was slower; but the Convention entered into force on 3 September 1953, when the necessary ten instruments of ratification had been deposited. By the end of 1962 the Convention had been ratified by fifteen States, that is to say by all members of the Council of Europe except France.[2]

The Protocol entered into force on 18 May 1954, when the tenth instrument of ratification was deposited. By the end of 1962, it had been ratified by the same fifteen States as the Convention.[3]

[1] For the text of the Protocol, see Appendix 2. The rights contained in the Protocol are discussed below in Ch. II, Sec. 3.

[2] The dates of ratification are given at the end of the text of the Convention in Appendix 1.

[3] The dates of ratification are given at the end of the text of the Protocol in Appendix 2.

CHAPTER II

THE RIGHTS GUARANTEED BY THE CONVENTION

1. *General Considerations*

ARTICLE 1 of the Convention contains the undertaking that 'the High Contracting Parties shall secure to everyone within their jurisdiction the rights and freedoms defined in Section I of this Convention'. This is a very wide commitment and noteworthy in two respects.

In the first place, the category of persons who are to benefit from the provisions of the Convention has been drawn as liberally as possible. The undertaking of the Parties is not limited to securing these benefits to its nationals, nor—as might be expected in a multilateral treaty—to its own nationals and the nationals of the other Contracting Parties. Human Rights are to be secured 'to everyone within their jurisdiction' without distinction as regards nationality, race, religion or other criteria of that sort. The guarantee as regards non-discrimination is subsequently made explicit in Article 14.

Secondly, this undertaking is so formulated that individuals are the direct beneficiaries. The Parties do not undertake *inter se* to introduce legislation for the protection of human rights; they state that they will secure them to everyone within their jurisdiction. This is even clearer in the French text, which reads: 'Les Hautes Parties Contractautes *reconnaissent* à toute personne relevant de leur juridiction les droits et libertés définis au Titre I de la présente Convention'. Very important consequences flow from this in certain countries.

In the United Kingdom, international treaties have no effect in municipal law unless expressly enacted by Parliament. The same is true in Ireland, where the Supreme Court has held that the Convention on Human Rights does not form part of Irish law, since it has not been enacted by the *Oireachtas*, which alone, under Article 15 of the Irish Constitution, has the power to make or change the law; furthermore Article 29 of the Constitution specifically provides that international agreements shall not become part of domestic law, save as maybe determined by the *Oireachtas*.[1] But the situation is different in many continental countries where international treaties, once ratified, take precedence over provisions of municipal law and—in some cases—even over provisions of the Constitution. The European Convention on Human Rights in this way now forms part of the internal law, and is applied by the national courts in a number of Member States of the Council of Europe, including the Federal Republic of Germany, Belgium, the Netherlands, and Greece; the position is similar in principle, even though actual cases may not yet have occurred, in Italy, Turkey and Cyprus. The Scandinavian countries appear to be in the same situation in this respect as the United Kingdom, and in Iceland a decision is recorded to the effect that the Convention, not having been expressly enacted by the Althing, is not incorporated into municipal law. In Austria, the principle is recognised that international treaties have the force of law provided they have been approved by the Parliament and their provisions are sufficiently precise; nevertheless the Austrian Constitutional Court has held that Articles 5 and 6 of the Convention were not applicable in the Austrian courts.[2]

It thus appears that the practical effect of the European Convention is not limited to those cases which may come before the Commission and the Court in Strasbourg. In about half of the Member States of the Council of Europe the Convention receives direct application by the national courts;[3] a number of decisions in this sense have now been reported.[4]

[1] See the judgment in the Lawless Case, *Yearbook of the Convention*, Vol. II, 1958–9, p. 608.

[2] See H. Golsong, 'The European Convention on Human Rights before Domestic Courts', *B.Y.I.L.*, 1962.

[3] There is a growing volume of literature on this subject. See: Golsong, *op. cit.*; Golsong, 'The European Convention on Human Rights in a 'German Court', *B.Y.I.L.*, 1957, p. 317; C. H. M. Waldock, 'The European Convention on Human Rights', *ibid.*, 1958, p. 356; A. Susterhenn, 'L'Application de la Convention sur la plan du droit interne', *La Protection Internationale des Droits de l'Homme dans le cadre européen*, p. 303; Philippe Comte, 'The Application of the European Convention on Human Rights in Municipal Law', *J.I.C.J.*, summer 1962, p. 95; Mme. Janssen-Pevtschin, J. Velu and A. Vanwelkenhuyzen, 'La Convention des Droits de l'Homme et le Fonctionnement des Juridictions Belges', *Chronique de Politique Etrangère* (Brussels), June 1962, pp. 199–246.

[4] *Yearbook of the Convention*, Vol. 2, 1958–9, pp. 568–627; *ibid.*, Vol. 3, 1960, pp. 614–73; *ibid.*, Vol. 4, 1961, pp. 600–50.

Moreover, even in those countries where international obligations are not incorporated automatically into municipal law, there will still be an international obligation to ensure that municipal law affords an effective remedy for the breach of the provisions of the Convention, for Article 13 contains an express stipulation to this effect.

After this far-reaching first Article, Section I of the Convention then consists of seventeen articles (Articles 2 to 18) setting out the rights to be guaranteed and certain rules to be observed for their effective enforcement. Before commenting on them individually, it is necessary first of all to say something about the technique that was adopted when the Convention was drafted.

The Definition of Human Rights

The original proposals of the Assembly[1] listed for inclusion in the European Convention ten rights from the Universal Declaration of the United Nations. These rights, and the corresponding articles of the Universal Declaration, were the following:

1. Security of person (Arts. 3, 5 and 8);
2. Freedom from slavery and servitude (Art. 4);
3. Freedom from arbitrary arrest, detention, or exile and the right to a fair trial (Arts. 9, 10 and 11);
4. Freedom from arbitrary interference in private and family life, home, and correspondence (Art. 12);
5. Freedom of thought, conscience, and religion (Art. 18);
6. Freedom of opinion and expression (Art. 19);
7. Freedom of assembly (Art. 20);
8. Freedom of association (Art. 20, paras. i and ii);
9. Freedom to unite in trade unions (Art. 23, para. iv);
10. The right to marry and found a family (Art. 16).

When the Committee of Ministers approved the inclusion on the Assembly's Agenda of the item relating to human rights, it had requested that particular attention should be devoted to the question of their definition. The Assembly, however, contented itself with enumerating them and referring to the relevant articles of the United Nations Declaration. The question of defining the rights to be protected was, therefore, one of the first items discussed by the Legal Experts when they met in February 1950. Two conflicting views were then expressed. One school of thought

[1] Recommendation 38 of 9 September 1949 in *Texts Adopted*, 1949, p. 49.

favoured the method of 'enumeration' of human rights, as statements of general principle, which each Member Government would implement within its jurisdiction in accordance with its own law;[1] it was argued that it would be extremely difficult to codify human rights, and that if the attempt were to be made it would be better to await the conclusions of the United Nations Commission on Human Rights, which had already started on this work. The opposing point of view was that an essential pre-requisite to any Convention was the precise definition of the rights to be safeguarded and of the permitted limitations on those rights; unless this were done it would not be possible for a state to know whether its existing laws were consistent with the obligations imposed by the Convention, nor what amendments it should introduce. Moreover, it would be extremely difficult to decide whether a State had violated its obligations under the Convention if they were not precisely defined.

The legal experts were unable to agree on either of these conflicting principles as a basis for drafting the Convention. Consequently, they agreed to differ, and decided to submit two alternative texts: the first was based on an enumeration of general principles, reproducing verbatim the relevant texts of the United Nations Declaration; the second text contained detailed definitions of the rights and freedoms and of the limitations to which they might be subjected. When the Committee of Senior Officials met in June 1950, it decided in favour of a compromise solution. This involved amalgamating the two texts drawn up by the Legal Experts; the result was to start each article with a general statement of the right to be guaranteed and to set out in later paragraphs a more detailed definition of the restrictions which may be permitted. This compromise remained substantially unaltered in the final text of the Convention as signed in November.

The human rights and freedoms involved were the same as

[1] On the reluctance of the common lawyer to codify human rights, see S. A. de Smith, 'Fundamental Rights in the New Commonwealth', *I.C.L.Q.*, 1961 at pp. 83-9. 'The English lawyer finds political manifestoes out of place in a legal document, particularly when their philosophical foundations are insecure. He instinctively prefers brass tacks to noble phrases, pragmatism to metaphysics and obstinately insists that the proof of the pudding is in the eating. . . . When Dicey declared that the Habeas Corpus Acts were for practical purposes worth a hundred constitutional articles guaranteeing individual liberty, he spoke for the mass of English constitutional lawyers.'

those originally proposed by the Assembly in August 1949 and listed above. Their treatment, however, differed considerably. As a result of the method of definition that was adopted, some rights were spelt out in considerable detail, though for others this was not considered necessary. Thus freedom from torture (Article 3) and the right to marry and found a family (Article 12) each occupy only two lines. Again the Assembly included as three separate rights: freedom of assembly, freedom of association, and freedom to unite in trade unions. It was found possible to combine all three in the first paragraph of Article 11 of the Convention, which reads: 'Everyone has the right to freedom of peaceful assembly and to freedom of association with others, including the right to form and to join trade unions for the protection of his interests'.

Certain rights, on the other hand, required more detailed treatment. Article 9 of the United Nations Declaration reads: 'No one shall be subjected to arbitrary arrest, detention or exile'. The civilians proposed to incorporate this verbatim in the draft Convention. To a common lawyer it immediately implied the necessity of defining the circumstances in which detention is lawful. This meant listing the following cases: detention after conviction by a competent court or for non-compliance with the lawful order of a court; arrest or detention to bring a suspect before a magistrate; detention of minors; detention of persons of unsound mind or suffering from infectious diseases, etc. The result was to expand a phrase of two lines into a page of print, which may be found in Article 5 of the Convention. Similarly, the right to a fair trial, which is expressed in three lines in the United Nations Declaration, involved, when the subject of detailed definition, inclusion of the following: the presumption of innocence until guilt is proved; the public nature of the hearing, including admission of the press and definition of the circumstances in which it may be excluded; adequate time and facilities for the defence; free legal assistance; production and examination of witnesses; and, when necessary, interpretation (Article 6 of the Convention).

This method of detailed definition has, it is submitted, considerable advantages for those who have to apply the Convention. By reading the final text it is possible to have a much clearer idea of what rights are to be secured, and of what limitations are permitted, than is possible with the very general enumeration in the United Nations Declaration.[1] It is also to be observed that the United Nations Commission on Human Rights, in working out its draft Covenants, has introduced a far greater measure of precision than was to be observed in the original Declaration. Nevertheless, any attempt at exhaustive definition always carried with it the danger of unintentional omissions which may later be construed as deliberate exclusions. Only the future will show whether this pitfall has been successfully avoided.

2. *The Rights provided for in the Convention*[2]

ARTICLE 2: THE RIGHT TO LIFE

The Assembly had listed as one right 'security of person in accordance with Articles 3, 5 and 8 of the United Nations Declaration'. This became three separate articles (2, 3 and 13) of the European Convention. But the experts who drafted it did much more than merely restore the separate formulation in three different articles. Their work affords another illustration of the difference of technique between the 'enumeration theory' and the 'definition theory'—which was fundamentally a difference between the civil law approach and the common law approach. Article 3 of the United Nations Declaration reads simply: 'Everyone has the right to life, liberty and security of person'. In the European Convention, the right to life necessitated, in the first place, the affirmation that 'everyone's right to life shall be protected by law' and secondly a precise indication of the circumstances in which someone may be deprived of his life, that is to say: in the execution of the sentence of a court following a conviction for a crime which involves the death penalty; when deprivation of life results from the use of force, which is no more than absolutely necessary, in self-defence in order to affect a lawful arrest in quelling a riot, and so on. The results of this method of definition are to be found in Article 2 of the Convention.[3]

[1] The United Nations Declaration did include a provision (Article 29(2)) permitting limitations on the rights proclaimed 'for the purpose of securing due recognition and respect for the rights and freedoms of others and of meeting the just requirements of morality, public order and the general welfare in a democratic society'.

[2] Cf. G. Heraud, *Les Droits garantis par la Convention*, Strasbourg Recueil, 1961, pp. 107–126.

[3] The full text of each article is to be found in Appendix 1.

ARTICLE 3: FREEDOM FROM TORTURE

The text of the United Nations Declaration read in its Article 5: 'No one shall be subjected to torture or to cruel, inhuman or degrading treatment or punishment'. Article 3 of the Convention repeats this *verbatim*, except for the omission of the word 'cruel'. It does not appear from the *travaux préparatoires* why the word 'cruel' was omitted; but it may be supposed that it was thought tautologous and its meaning sufficiently covered by the word 'inhuman'.

The two applications brought by Greece against the United Kingdom in 1956 and 1957 relating to the situation in Cyprus both invoked Article 3 of the Convention. The first alleged that the legislation providing for the imposition of flogging and various forms of collective punishment was contrary to this Article; the second referred to the Commission forty-nine cases of 'torture or maltreatment amounting to torture' which were alleged to have occurred in Cyprus and for which the British Government was alleged to be responsible.[1] The Commission declared the first application to be admissible and the second admissible as regards twenty-nine of the alleged incidents.[2] But, as recounted in a later chapter, a political settlement of the Cyprus question was achieved and the cases withdrawn before any final decision was taken on these applications.[3]

The Commission has also considered whether a form of punishment under Austrian law known as 'sleeping hard' (hartes Lager) is inconsistent with Article 3. In a decision of 7 July 1959 it decided that the infliction of this punishment on a prisoner once every three months was not inhuman or degrading.[4]

ARTICLE 4: FREEDOM FROM SLAVERY AND SERVITUDE

Article 4 of the Convention corresponds to Article 4 of the United Nations Declaration, which reads: 'No one shall be held in slavery or servitude; slavery and the slave trade shall be prohibited in all their forms'. The Convention goes further than this, because, while omitting the reference to the slave trade, it adds a second paragraph to the effect that 'no one shall be required to

---

[1] *Yearbook of the Convention*, Vol. 2, 1958–9, pp. 174–80.

[2] *ibid.*, pp. 182–96.

[3] See below, Ch. III, Sec. 4.

[4] Application 462/59, *Yearbook of the Convention*, Vol. 2, 1958–9, p. 382.

perform forced or compulsory labour'. Having thus established the general rule, it goes on to set out in paragraph 3 what are the permitted exceptions, namely work done during imprisonment or detention, military service, service in the public interest during an emergency or service which forms part of normal civic obligations.[1]

ARTICLE 5: THE RIGHT TO LIBERTY AND SECURITY OF PERSON

The United Nations Declaration proclaimed in its Article 3: 'Everyone has the right to life, liberty and the security of person'. The Convention, having dealt with the right to life in Article 2, devotes Article 5 to the right to liberty. It starts off with the affirmation: 'Every one has the right to liberty and security of person' and then continues by defining the circumstances in which someone may be deprived of his liberty, provided this is done 'in accordance with a procedure prescribed by law'. These circumstances include the following cases:

a. detention after conviction by a court;
b. arrest or detention for non-compliance with the order of a court;
c. arrest or detention on reasonable suspicion or as a preventive measure;
d. the detention of minors;
e. detention for medical and similar reasons;
f. detention to prevent unauthorised entry into a country or to permit deportation or extradition.

The following paragraphs of Article 5 provide that anyone who is arrested or detained shall be informed promptly of the reasons therefor and shall be entitled to take proceedings to determine the lawfulness of his detention. Moreover, a person arrested or detained on suspicion or as a preventive measure shall be entitled to trial within a reasonable time or release pending trial.

It will be observed that this Article deals with two different questions: it defines in paragraph 1 the cases in which detention

[1] Early in 1963 the Commission began consideration of a case in which a Norwegian dentist, who had been fined for non-compliance with an order made under an Act of June 1956 to practise in the Far North of Norway (where dentists were required and otherwise unavailable), complained that this Act and his conviction were contrary to Article 4 of the Convention. *Council of Europe News*, March 1963, p. 2.

is permitted; secondly, it goes on to define the rights of a person thus detained.

One question which the Commission has been called on to decide is whether detention of an habitual criminal for an indefinite period (which is permitted by German law) is consistent with Article 5 (1)(*a*). It has held that this is not in violation of the Convention, provided the detention is lawfully ordered 'after conviction by a competent Court'.[1]

Probably the most important case to arise under Article 5 of the Convention was *Lawless v. Ireland*. One of the points which had to be considered both by the Commission and by the Court was whether the detention of Lawless without trial, on suspicion of belonging to an illegal organisation, was in conformity with Article 5 (1)(*c*). This sub-paragraph permits deprivation of liberty in the following case:

the lawful arrest or detention of a person effected for the purpose of bringing him before the competent legal authority on reasonable suspicion of having committed an offence or when it is reasonably considered necessary to prevent his committing an offence or fleeing after having done so.

The Irish Government argued that the arrest of Lawless constituted 'the lawful arrest or detention of a person . . . when it is reasonably considered necessary to prevent his committing an offence. . . .' as expressly authorised by this paragraph. In the proceedings before the Court, the delegates of the Commission argued that it was necessary to look at the whole of the paragraph, which authorised 'the lawful arrest or detention of a person *effected for the purpose of bringing him before the competent legal authority* . . .' Detention otherwise than for this purpose was therefore not consistent with Article 5. The Court held that the plain and natural meaning of the words was that given to them by the Commission; it also pointed out that the construction advocated by the Government would open the door wide to arrest and detention on suspicion without the requirement of bringing to trial —which would be contrary to the whole spirit of the Convention.[2]

[1] Application 99/55, *Yearbook of the Convention*, Vol. 1, 1955-7, pp. 160-61 ; Application 180/55, *ibid.*, pp. 1962-3 ; Application 138/55, *ibid.*, pp. 234-5.

[2] *Publications of the European Court of Human Rights. Series A : Judgments & Decisions :* 'Lawless' case (merits), July 1961 pp. 46-53. For a full account of the Lawless case see below, Ch. VI.

C

Article 6: The Right to a Fair Trial

This is based on Articles 10 and 11 of the Universal Declaration. The first paragraph of Article 6 (corresponding to Article 10 of the United Nations text) provides for 'a fair and public hearing within a reasonable time by an independent and impartial tribunal established by law' in both civil and criminal matters. The words 'within a reasonable time' have been added in the European Convention. The remainder of the paragraph, which is also new, defines the circumstances in which the press may be excluded from the hearing.

Paragraphs 2 and 3 of Article 6 (based on Article 11 of the United Nations text) contain the guarantees of a fair trial in a criminal case. First, and most important, is the principle that 'everyone charged with a criminal offence shall be presumed innocent until proved guilty according to law'. Then come five secondary guarantees: to be adequately informed of the charge, to have adequate opportunities to prepare the defence, to have legal assistance, to have the right to call witnesses and to cross-examine witnesses called by the prosecution, and to have the services of an interpreter if required.

The Commission has held that Article 6 paragraph 1 does not guarantee the right to be present in person at all civil proceedings but has indicated that it does imply the right to be present in certain classes of cases, such as 'where the personal character and manner of life of the party concerned is directly relevant to the formation of the Court's opinion on the point which it is called upon to decide'; and '. . . a case in which a parent, following upon a divorce, makes an application to the Court for a right of access to a child of the marriage is without doubt a case of this kind'.[1]

The Commission has also held that the provision in paragraph 2 of Article 6 that 'everyone charged with a criminal offence shall be presumed innocent until proved guilty according to law' does not apply to a request for a retrial by a person already convicted.[2]

Another decision of the Commission has interpreted paragraph 3(*a*) of Article 6, which provides that an accused person has the right 'to be informed promptly in a language which he

[1] Application 434/58, *Yearbook of the Convention*, Vol. 2, 1958-9, p. 354 at p. 370.
[2] Application 914/60, *Yearbook of the Convention*, Vol. 4, 1961, p. 372.

understands and in detail, of the nature and cause of the accusation against him'. 'It follows from this provision,' says the Commission, 'that as part of the right to a fair trial guaranteed by the provisions of Article 6 as a whole, an accused person has the right to be informed not only of the grounds for the accusation, that is not only the acts with which he is charged and on which his indictment is based, but also of the *nature* of the accusation, namely the legal classification of the acts in question'.[1]

It has also been held that the right to free legal assistance is limited to persons charged with a criminal offence and does not apply in civil proceedings.[2] Furthermore, that the right to call witnesses 'does not permit an accused person to obtain the attendance of any and every person and in particular of one who is not in a position by his evidence to assist in establishing the truth'. The Court is therefore entitled to refuse to call witnesses if it considers that they could not prove the accuracy of quite general statements made by the accused.[3] The Commission has also held that the requirement of paragraph 1 of Article 6 that 'judgment shall be pronounced publicly' applies in civil and criminal matters, but not in an administrative court determining a matter which is not a civil right.[4] Similar decisions have been taken by the Federal Administrative Court and the Federal Constitutional Court in Germany.[5]

ARTICLE 7: GUARANTEE AGAINST RETROACTIVITY OF THE LAW

This article is based on paragraph 2 of Article 11 of the United Nations Declaration. Its first paragraph sets out the general principle of non-retroactivity of the law: 'No one shall be held guilty of any criminal offence on account of any act or omission

[1] Application 524/59, *Yearbook of the Convention*, Vol. 3, 1960, p. 322 at p. 344.

[2] Application 250/57, *Yearbook of the Convention*, Vol. 1, p. 222 at p. 228. See also Application 134/55, *ibid.*, p. 232 ; Application 180/56, *ibid.*, p. 236 ; Application 265/57, *ibid.*, p. 192.

[3] Application 753/60, *Yearbook of the Convention*, Vol. 3, 1960, p. 310 at p. 320.

[4] Application 423/58, *Collection of Decisions of the Commission*, No. 1, January 1960.

[5] See Comte, *op. cit.*, p. 122, and J. Velu, 'Le Problème de l'Application aux Juridictions Administratives des Règles relatives à la publicité des Audiences et des Jugements', *Revue de Droit International et de Droit Comparé*, Brussels, 1961, pp. 129–71.

which did not constitute a criminal offence under national or international law at the time when it was committed.' It continues by providing that no heavier penalty shall be imposed than was applicable at the time when an offence was committed. Its second paragraph, however, has a saving clause:

This article shall not prejudice the trial and punishment of any person for any act or omission which, at the time when it was committed, was criminal according to the general principles of law recognised by civilised nations.

This saving clause was introduced in order to make it clear that the trial of war criminals for acts which were criminal according to the general principles of law recognised by civilised nations 'was not inconsistent with the Convention and not contrary to the general guarantee against retroactivity of the law'.

In the case of *De Becker v. Belgium,* one of the allegations of the applicant was that the penalty imposed on him after the war on account of his war-time activities as a collaborator, by which he was deprived of the right to exercise his profession as a journalist, was contrary to Article 7. The Commission held that the offence committed by the applicant clearly fell within the exception contained in the second paragraph of that article.[1]

The Government of the Federal Republic of Germany, at the time of ratifying the Convention, made a reservation as regards paragraph 2 of Article 7. It stated that it could only apply this provision within the limits of paragraph 2 of Article 103 of the Basic Law, which provides that an act can only be punished if the law declared it to be an offence before it was committed.[2]

ARTICLE 8: THE RIGHT TO PRIVACY AND TO FAMILY LIFE

This article, which is based on Article 12 of the Universal Declaration, guarantees to everyone 'the right to respect for his private and family life, his home and his correspondence'. It was recognised, however, that this right is not absolute and that there are circumstances in which the general interest requires that the State should be empowered to interfere with the right to privacy. Article 8 is therefore drafted in such a way—and a number of

[1] Application 214/56, *Yearbook of the Convention,* Vol. 2, 1958–9, p. 214 at p. 226. On the *De Becker* Case see below, Ch. III, Sec. 4.

[2] *Yearbook of the Convention,* Vol. 1, 1955–7, p. 41. See also below, Appendix 3.

later articles follow the same model—that the first paragraph contains the affirmation of the general principle and the second paragraph sets out the permitted exceptions. And it must be admitted that the net is widely cast. Paragraph 2 reads as follows:

There shall be no interference by a public authority with the exercise of this right except such as is in accordance with the law and is necessary in a democratic society in the interests of national security, public safety or the economic well-being of the country, for the prevention of disorder or crime, for the protection of health or morals, or for the protection of the rights and freedoms of others.

It has been argued that the German law which punishes homosexuality is an infringement of the right to respect for private life; but the Commission has rejected this contention on the ground that the public authorities are entitled, under paragraph 2, to limit the right in accordance with the law for the protection of health or morals.[1]

Article 8 has also been the subject of an interesting decision of the Federal Administrative Court in Germany. The Federal Republic is one of those countries where the terms of a treaty, once it is ratified, have full effect in municipal law. Consequently the Court set aside an order for the expulsion of an alien, who had been convicted and served a sentence of imprisonment, on the ground that it would break up the family in a manner contrary to the provisions of the European Convention.[2]

The Commission has also been called on to decide whether censorship of the correspondence of prisoners was inconsistent with the guarantee contained in Article 8. It stated that 'in the view of the Commission the measure commonly adopted in the law of democratic societies of permitting prison authorities to examine the correspondence of the prisoners under their charge clearly falls within the exceptions permitted in paragraph 2 of Article 8'.[3]

[1] Application 104/55, *Yearbook of the Convention*, Vol. 1, 1955–7, p. 228; Application 167/56, *ibid.*, p. 235.

[2] See Golsong: 'The European Convention on Human Rights in a German Court', *B.Y.I.L.*, 1957, pp. 317–21. See however the decision of the Belgian Supreme Court of 21 September 1959, *Yearbook of the Convention*, Vol. 3, 1960, p. 624.

[3] Application 646/59, *Yearbook of the Convention*, Vol. 3, 1960, p. 272 at p. 278.

ARTICLE 9: FREEDOM OF THOUGHT, CONSCIENCE AND RELIGION

The first paragraph of Article 9 is taken directly from Article 18 of the Universal Declaration and guarantees not only freedom of thought, conscience and religion but also freedom to practise and to change one's religion or belief. The second paragraph sets out the limitations on this freedom which are necessary in the public interest.

The Netherlands Supreme Court was called upon in 1962 to consider whether Article 184 of the Constitution of the Netherlands was in conformity with Article 9 of the Convention. Article 184 of the Constitution authorises the practice of all religions *inside* buildings and permits their exercise *outside* buildings only subject to the laws and regulations in force at the date of the adoption of the Constitution, that is to say in 1848, which meant in fact that religious processions which were already traditional at that date could continue, but that new ones would not be authorised. On 8 March 1951, the Court of Appeal of Arnhem held that Article 184 of the Constitution was in conflict with Article 9 of the European Convention, but the Supreme Court, on appeal, held on 19 January 1962 that the limitation on the free practice of religion in public places contained in Article 184 was intended to prevent possible tensions and demonstrations and was thus in the interests of public order—as permitted by the exceptions contained in paragraph 2 of Article 9.[1]

ARTICLE 10: FREEDOM OF EXPRESSION

This article guarantees freedom of expression, including freedom to hold opinions and receive and impart information and ideas without interference by public authority and regardless of frontiers. The text is based closely on Article 19 of the Universal Declaration, but contains the rider: 'This Article shall not prevent States from requiring the licensing of broadcasting, television or cinema enterprises'.

Once more the general affirmation of principle, contained in the first paragraph of the Article, is subject to the limitations and

---

[1] *Yearbook of the Convention*, Vol. 4, 1961, pp. 630 and 640. The Greek Supreme Court has held that the requirement of prior authorisation by the Minister of Public Worship for the construction of churches is compatible with Article 9—see Comte, *op. cit.*, p. 126.

exceptions set out in the second paragraph. In this case they are particularly extensive and may be quoted in full:

The exercise of these freedoms, since it carries with it duties and responsibilities, may be subject to such formalities, conditions, restrictions or penalties as are prescribed by law and are necessary in a democratic society, in the interests of national security, territorial integrity or public safety, for the prevention of disorder or crime, for the protection of health or morals, for the protection of the reputation or rights of others, for preventing the disclosure of information received in confidence, or for maintaining the authority and impartiality of the judiciary.

It was Article 10 of the Convention which was the principal basis of the case of *De Becker v. Belgium*, for it was in respect of Article 10 that the Commission had ruled the application admissible. De Becker was a Belgian journalist who had collaborated with the enemy during the war and was subsequently condemned— initially to death and, on appeal, to life imprisonment. In 1950, the sentence was reduced to 17 years' imprisonment, and in the following year he was released on giving an undertaking to reside abroad and not to engage in politics. He had been condemned under Article 123 *sexies* of the Belgian Penal Code which provided that persons sentenced to a penalty of more than five years' imprisonment for certain offences committed in time of war should be deprived for life of various rights including:

(*e*) the right to have a proprietary interest in or to take part in any capacity whatsoever in the administration, editing, printing or distribution of a newspaper or any other publication;

(*f*) the right to take part in organising or managing any cultural, philanthropic or sporting activity or any public entertainment;

(*g*) the right to have a proprietary interest in, or to be associated with, the administration or any other aspect of the activity of any undertaking concerned with theatrical production, films or broadcasting.

The Commission considered by eleven votes to one that these provisions of the Belgian Code 'in so far as they affect freedom of expression are not fully justified under the Convention. . . . They are not justifiable in so far as the deprivation of freedom of expression in regard to non-political matters, which they contain,

is imposed inflexibly for life without any provision for its relaxa-
tion when, with the passage of time, public morale and public
order have been re-established and the continued imposition of
that particular incapacity has ceased to be a measure "necessary
in a democratic society" within the meaning of Article 10, paragraph 2, of the Convention.'[1]

ARTICLE 11: FREEDOM OF ASSEMBLY AND ASSOCIATION

The Consultative Assembly, in its Recommendation 38 of 8
September 1949, listed as two separate rights freedom of assembly
and freedom of association. They were, however, the object of one
article—Article 20—in the Universal Declaration. Similarly, they
were grouped together in Article 11 of the European Convention.
The first paragraph affirms the right 'to freedom of peaceful
assembly and to freedom of association with others'—in words
which differ little from the U.N. text; but it then continues with
the words: '. . . including the right to form and join trade unions
for the protection of his interests', which relate to a right that is
dealt with separately in Article 20 of the Universal Declaration.
Then it is perhaps significant that the second paragraph of Article
20 of the Universal Declaration is omitted: 'No one may be com-
pelled to belong to an association'. No doubt this was done with
the 'closed shop' in mind. The Convention has instead a second
paragraph on the same lines as in the three previous articles,
permitting restrictions in the interests of national security,
public safety, for the prevention of disorder or crime and so
forth. A specific restriction is then introduced: 'This Article shall
not prevent the imposition of lawful restrictions on the exercise
of these rights by members of the armed forces, of the police or of
the administration of the State.'

ARTICLE 12: THE RIGHT TO MARRY AND FOUND A FAMILY

This right is set out succinctly as follows: 'Men and women of
marriageable age have the right to marry and to found a family,
according to the national laws governing the exercise of this
right'. This is based on Article 16 of the Universal Declaration,

---

[1] *Publications of the European Court of Human Rights*, Series A, 1962, De
Becker Case, p. 12. For a fuller account of this case see below, Chapter III,
Sec. 4.

but it omits certain provisions of the latter, including a prohibition of any limitation due to race, nationality or religion and the affirmation that men and women 'are entitled to equal rights as to marriage, during marriage and at its dissolution'. It was unnecessary to insert in Article 12 of the Convention a prohibition of discrimination, since a general prohibition is to be found in Article 14, which will be discussed shortly.

Articles 13 to 18 of the Convention then lay down a certain number of rules which are designed not so much to secure additional rights as to ensure the effective exercise of the rights enunciated in the previous articles. Before commenting on them, it will be convenient to deal with the first three articles of the Protocol, since they provide for three other rights which are additional to those covered by Articles 2 to 12 of the Convention itself.

3. The Rights provided for in the Protocol

ARTICLE 1: THE RIGHT OF PROPERTY

As explained in Chapter I, three additional rights were proposed by the Assembly for inclusion in the Convention in August 1950, at a time when the negotiations and the drafting were already far advanced.[1] The Committee of Ministers then decided in the following November to incorporate these in a Protocol, rather than delay signature of the Convention, to which they were then ready to proceed.

The first of these additional rights was the right of property. Once again the point of departure was the Universal Declaration of Human Rights, Article 17 of which proclaims very simply:

1. Everyone has the right to own property alone as well as in association with others.
2. No one shall be arbitrarily deprived of his property.

The kernel of the matter, of course, is the meaning of the word 'arbitrarily'; this text raised all the problems both of international and of municipal law which are latent in the nationalisation or confiscation of property. The right to nationalise private property had to be recognised—particularly having regard to the programme of the Socialist Government then in power in Britain. It was,

[1] Recommendation 24 of 25 August 1950 in *Recommendations and Resolutions Adopted by the Assembly*, August 1950, p. 33.

however—as pointed out in Chapter I—a matter of some difficulty to draft a text which would, on the one hand, assert the principle of the right to private property and, on the other hand, permit a Socialist government to nationalise private property by legislation legitimately adopted in a democratic society without, at the same time, condoning confiscation by an authoritarian government on grounds which would generally be regarded as discriminatory.[1]

The text finally incorporated in Article 1 of the Protocol reads as follows:

Every natural or legal person is entitled to the peaceful enjoyment of his possessions. No one shall be deprived of his possessions except in the public interest and subject to the conditions provided for by law and by the general principles of international law.

The preceding provisions shall not, however, in any way impair the right of a State to enforce such laws as it deems necessary to control the use of property in accordance with the general interest or to secure the payment of taxes or other contributions or penalties.

It will be observed that one of the limitations on the right of the state to deprive someone of his possessions is constituted by 'the conditions provided for . . . by the general principles of international law'. This provision was intended to guarantee compensation to foreigners for the expropriation of their property, even if compensation is not paid, or an inadequate compensation is paid, to nationals; it would make it impossible for a state which nationalises foreign property without adequate compensation to justify its action on the ground that the foreign owners of property were treated on a footing of equality with its own citizens. The rules of international law, however, do not apply to the measures taken by a state in relation to the property of its own nationals.[2]

In 1959, the Commission considered an interesting case arising under Article 1 of the Protocol. The Liability Equalisation Act of 1948 (*Lastenausgleichsgesetz*) of the Federal Republic of Germany imposed, as part of the financial reforms associated with the

---

[1] Further details of the problems considered in drafting the Protocol may be found in the author's note : 'The European Convention on Human Rights : Recent Developments', *B.Y.I.L.*, 1951, pp. 359–65.

[2] Decision of the Commission on Application 511/59, *Yearbook of the Convention*, Vol. 3, 1960, p. 394 at p. 424.

introduction of the Deutsch mark, a special levy on all capital and also a levy on gains accruing to mortgagors from the reduction of their mortgages under the financial reform. The applicant in this case was subjected to a 100 per cent levy on his mortgage gains. He argued that his assets had been reduced to ten per cent of their former value, whereas his liabilities had not been subjected to any diminution, and that his right to the use of his property had been infringed in that the legislation imposing financial reform deprived him of a substantial part of his capital. The Commission rejected this contention in the following decision:[1]

Whereas with regard to the Applicant's complaint of an alleged violation of Article I of the Protocol it is to be observed that the second sentence of paragraph (1) of that Article expressly contemplates, as an exception to the right to peaceful enjoyment of possessions, that a person may be deprived of his possessions 'in the public interest and subject to the conditions provided for by law and by the general principles of international law'; and whereas the Liability Equalisation Act was introduced by the competent authorities as a measure forming part of financial and monetary reforms in Germany after the Second World War, and considered to be necessary for establishing a sound economic basis for a new democratic society in that country; whereas, furthermore, it was an express purpose of the said financial and monetary reforms to ensure that the economic burdens arising out of the war and out of the changes in the value of German currency should be distributed proportionately amongst the citizens; whereas it follows that the financial measure of which the Applicant complains was introduced in the public interest and was administered to the Applicant subject to the conditions provided by the relevant law, namely the Liability Equalisation Act; whereas it follows that the measure in question complied with the conditions laid down in the second sentence of paragraph (1) of Article I of the Protocol, and was not inconsistent with the right to peaceful enjoyment of possessions guaranteed under Article I of the Protocol;

A somewhat similar problem arose in connection with Icelandic Law No. 44 of 3 June 1957, which provided for taxation on large properties and which imposed a special tax on the properties of individuals exceeding one million kronur (about $65,000). The tax was a progressive tax on capital, varying from 15 per cent to 25 per cent on the value in excess of the first million

[1] Application 551/59, *Yearbook of the Convention*, Vol. 3, 1960, p. 244 at p. 250.

kronur. The applicant claimed that this law amounted to a measure for the expropriation of property by reason of its provisions for excessive and discriminatory taxation (it applied to only 604 individuals, 674 limited companies and 20 co-operative societies out of the whole population); he claimed *inter alia* that this was unconstitutional, that the levy was not a tax within the generally recognised meaning of the word; that it was discriminatory; and that it violated Article 1 of the Protocol. The Commission rejected this contention. The following paragraphs are extracts from its decision:[1]

Whereas the tax complained of by the Applicants was levied in pursuance of Law No. 44 of 1957 for the express purpose of achieving monetary and economic stability within the State and was therefore clearly a measure introduced with a public purpose and considered by the Government to be in the public interest; whereas it is true that this tax took the form of a levy on capital assets; whereas, however, under Law No. 44, the maximum incidence of the tax could not exceed 25 per cent of the real value of the taxable assets and, further, it was permitted to pay the tax claim by instalments over a period of ten years; whereas, in view of the general purpose of the law, the maximum percentage and terms of payment affecting the particular category of taxpayers were not such, even in combination with other applicable fiscal legislation, as could deprive Law No. 44 of the character of a tax imposed with the view of furthering the public interest;

Whereas, accordingly, the taxes or contributions imposed by Law No. 44 of 1957 are in every way consistent with what are contemplated in paragraph one of Article I of the Protocol, as permissible interferences with a person's right to the peaceful enjoyment of his possessions;

Whereas, in any event, paragraph two of Article I of the Protocol expressly declares that the provisions of paragraph one shall not 'in any way impair the right of a State . . . to secure the payment of taxes or other contributions . . .'; and whereas it clearly emerges from what has already been stated that Law No. 44 of 1957 of which the Applicants complain, is a measure 'to secure the payment of taxes or other contributions' within the meaning of paragraph two of Article I; Whereas, accordingly, the taxes or contributions imposed by Law No. 44 of 1957 also fall within the power to levy taxes or other contributions which is expressly reserved to States in paragraph two of Article I of the Protocol . . .'

[1] Application 511/59, *Yearbook of the Convention*, Vol. 3, 1960, p. 394 at pp. 422–4.

ARTICLE 2 OF THE PROTOCOL: THE RIGHT TO EDUCATION

This was one of the articles which gave rise to most difficulty during the drafting of the Convention and Protocol. Article 26 of the Universal Declaration is very extensive; it provides not only that 'Everyone has the right to education' but also that elementary education shall be free and compulsory, technical and professional education generally available and higher education equally accessible to all on the basis of merit. It also stipulates that 'parents have a prior right to choose the kind of education that shall be given to their children'.

The text proposed by the Assembly in 1950 started off with the general statement: 'Every person has the right to education' and continued by providing that the State shall not encroach on 'the right of parents to ensure the religious and moral education and teaching of their children in conformity with their own religious and philosophical convictions'.[1] The government experts who drafted the Protocol were fearful that this text went too far. Did the right of every person to education impose a corresponding duty on the State to ensure that everyone is educated? While that is the policy of all Members of the Council of Europe, there are few countries where governments can make it completely effective. The second part of the text also raised problems. As far as religious convictions were concerned, it presented no particular problem, but the education and teaching of children in conformity with the religious *and philosophical* convictions of the parents raised many difficulties. The notion of 'philosophical convictions' is very elastic. Does it include vegetarianism, polygamy and nudism? Were governments to accept that children could be brought up as agnostics and atheists? The government experts proposed limiting this provision to 'the right of parents to ensure the religious education of their children in conformity with their own creeds'. A number of texts went back and forth between the Committee of Ministers and the Assembly's Legal Committee;[2] the parliamentarians insisted on the retention of the word 'philosophical'; and the governments finally agreed to the following formula:

[1] Recommendation 24, *Recommendations and Resolutions*, August 1950, p. 34.

[2] See my note 'The European Convention on Human Rights : Recent Developments', *B.Y.I.L.*, 1951, pp. 359–65.

In the exercise of any functions which it assumes in relation to education and teaching, the State shall respect the right of parents to ensure such education and teaching in conformity with their own religious and philosophical convictions.

But, as a result, several governments made reservations relating to this article at the time of signature or ratification.[1]

ARTICLE 3 OF THE PROTOCOL: THE RIGHT TO FREE ELECTIONS

This is one of the most important of all the rights guaranteed by the Convention and the Protocol. It was to be found in the Universal Declaration with the following formulation (Article 21 paragraph 3):

The will of the people shall be the basis of the authority of government; this will shall be expressed in periodic and genuine elections which shall be by universal and equal suffrage and shall be held by secret vote or by equivalent free voting procedures.

The Consultative Assembly in August 1950 proposed a text which differed somewhat in form but little in substance:[2]

The High Contracting Parties undertake to respect the political liberty of their nationals and, in particular, with regard to their home territories, to hold free elections at reasonable intervals by secret ballot under conditions which will ensure that the government and legislature shall represent the opinion of the people.

When the governmental experts came to examine this text, they discovered certain difficulties. In the first place, what would be the meaning of the undertaking by the Contracting Parties 'to respect the political liberty of their nationals'? If it was intended to relate to such rights as freedom of assembly, freedom of opinion and freedom of association, it was unnecessary, because these rights were already covered by separate provisions in the Convention itself. If, on the other hand, it was intended to relate

---

[1] Turkey, Greece, Sweden, United Kingdom. See Appendix 3. Early in 1963 the Commission had under consideration three applications concerning the linguistic arrangements for education in Belgium, in which the applicants complained that, in the absence locally of teaching in French, they were obliged either to give their children a Flemish education or to send them to a French-speaking school too far from home. *Council of Europe News*, March 1963, p. 2.

[2] Recommendation 24, *Recommendations and Resolutions*, August 1950, p. 34.

to other rights, it was imprecise and its meaning obscure. In the second place, the experts considered the phrase 'with regard to their home territories' to be unnecessary, since the whole Protocol would only apply to the metropolitan territories of the Contracting Parties in default of an express declaration extending its application to overseas territories. Thirdly, the expression 'under conditions which will ensure that the Government and legislature shall represent the opinion of the people' might be construed as a commitment to some form of proportional representation.

After a further exchange of texts between the Committee of Ministers and the Legal Committee of the Assembly, the definitive text was finally agreed as follows:

The High Contracting Parties undertake to hold free elections at reasonable intervals by secret ballot, under conditions which will ensure the free expression of the opinion of the people in the choice of the legislature.

It will be observed that the formulation of this right is different from that of those which have been discussed so far. The usual form is 'Everyone has the right . . .' or 'No one shall be held . . .' but in Article 3 of the Protocol 'The High Contracting Parties undertake to hold free elections . . . etc.' There is no provision to the effect that 'Everyone has the right to vote'. And in a case where an applicant complained that, when in prison, he was not allowed to vote in the Saar Plebiscite of October 1955, the Commission said:[1]

Although, according to this article, the Contracting Parties undertake to hold free elections, it does not follow that they recognise the right to every individual to take part therein; in other words, an individual's right to vote is not guaranteed by Article 3.

A similar decision was taken in a later case in which three Belgians who had long been resident in the Congo complained that they were not allowed to vote in elections in Belgium.[2]

4. *Articles relating to the Exercise of the Rights guaranteed*

To return now to the Convention itself, Article 13 provides that everyone whose rights as set forth in the Convention are

[1] Application 530/59, *Yearbook of the Convention*, Vol. 3, 1960, p. 184 at p. 190.

[2] Application 1065/61, *Collection of Decisions of the Commission*, No. 6, November 1961, p. 48 at p. 53.

violated shall have an effective remedy before a national authority, notwithstanding that the violation has been committed by persons acting in an official capacity. This is the guarantee against the so-called 'raison d'Etat', the protection of the private citizen against the Executive, against the governmental machine which in modern times interferes more and more with the private life of the citizen. When one reflects backwards on the pre-war authoritarian régimes in certain countries or whether one considers the enormous bureaucracy resulting from the post-war establishment of the welfare state, it is evident that the price of liberty of the citizen is eternal vigilance over the organs of the state. This was well put by the Rapporteur of the Legal Committee, M. Pierre-Henri Teitgen, in the Assembly on 19 August 1949, when he said:[1]

The first threat is the eternal reason of State. Behind the State, whatever its form, were it even democratic, there ever lurks as a permanent temptation this reason of State.

Montesquieu said: 'Whoever has power is tempted to abuse it.' Even parliamentary majorities are in fact sometimes tempted to abuse their power. Even in our democratic countries we must be on guard against this temptation of succumbing to reasons of State.

It is to be observed that Article 13 provides that there shall be an effective remedy *before a national authority* (in French, *devant une instance nationale*), an expression which is wider in its meaning than 'before a national court', and could include an administrative tribunal as well as a court of law. But, in order for the recourse to be effective, the court must be in a position of impartiality. The guarantee of an effective remedy, however, only applies to those whose rights under the Convention have been violated, and not to other persons.[2] In this respect it is narrower than Article 8 of the Universal Declaration which provides for an effective remedy 'for acts violating the fundamental rights granted . . . by the constitution or by law'. Moreover, the Netherlands Supreme Court has held that Article 13

[1] Consultative Assembly : *Official Report of Debates*, August 1949, Vol. 2, p. 404.

[2] Application 472/59, *Yearbook of the Convention*, Vol. 3, 1960, p. 206 at p. 212 ; Application 912/60, *Collection of Decisions of the Commission*, No. 7, March 1962, p. 128.

imposes on Contracting Parties the duty of ensuring that an effective remedy exists, but is not a provision which can be directly applied by national courts.[1]

Article 14 is a non-discrimination clause. It provides that the rights guaranteed by the Convention shall be secured without discrimination on any ground such as sex, race, colour, language, religion and so on. This text follows closely paragraph 1 of Article 2 of the Universal Declaration, but has added one new ground, which is 'association with a national minority'. The United Nations text itself recalls the Resolution on non-discrimination adopted at the first session of the Council of the United Nations Relief and Rehabilitation Administration at Atlantic City on 1 December 1943.[2]

In the same way that Article 13 is not a guarantee of an effective remedy for violation of all rights, but only of those guaranteed by the Convention, so Article 14 is not a general guarantee against non-discrimination but only of non-discrimination in respect of the rights set forth in the preceding articles and in the Protocol.[3] Moreover, the Commission has held that Article 14 does permit certain differences in the treatment accorded to men and women. It has rejected the contention that the punishment of male homosexuals but not of females is a contravention of this article.[4] Not all differentiation is discrimination.

Article 15 then provides for the possibility of derogation 'in time of war or other public emergency threatening the life of the nation'. In such circumstances, any High Contracting Party may take measures derogating from its obligations under the Convention 'to the extent strictly required by the exigencies of the situation', provided that such measures are not inconsistent with its other obligations under international law. It is to be noted, however, that under paragraph 2 of this article, no derogations may be made from Article 2 of the Convention (right to life) except in respect of deaths resulting from lawful acts of war,

---

[1] *Nederlandsche Jurisprudentie*, 1960, No. 483, p. 1121.

[2] Cmd. 6497, (1943) p. 8.

[3] Application 86/55, *Yearbook of the Convention*, Vol. 1, 1955–7, p. 198 ; Application 436/58, *ibid.*, Vol. 2, 1958–9, p. 386 at p. 390.

[4] Application 104/55, *Yearbook of the Convention*, Vol. 1, 1955–7, p. 228 ; Application 167/56, *ibid.*, p. 235.

D

nor from Article 3 (freedom from torture or degrading punishment), Article 4 paragraph 1 (freedom from slavery or servitude) nor Article 7 (protection against retroactivity of the law). Furthermore, paragraph 3 of Article 15 requires any High Contracting Party which avails itself of this right of derogation to keep the Secretary-General of the Council of Europe fully informed of the measures which it has taken and the reasons therefor.

The questions of compliance with Article 15 and of the rights and duties of the Commission and the Court when a Contracting Party has invoked this article were of cardinal importance both in the cases brought by Greece against the United Kingdom about Cyprus and in the Lawless case. These are discussed in later chapters.[1]

Paragraph 3 of Article 15 also raises the question of the duties of the Secretary-General when he has received a notice of derogation. This is also examined below.[2]

Article 16 is very short and makes it clear that Articles 10 (freedom of expression), 11 (freedom of association) and 14 (non-discrimination) do not prevent the Parties from imposing restrictions on the political activities of aliens.

Article 17 is important. It reads as follows :

Nothing in this Convention may be interpreted as implying for any State, group or person any right to engage in any activity or perform any act aimed at the destruction of any of the rights and freedoms set forth herein or at their limitation to a greater extent than is provided for in the Convention. . . .

This text is designed to prevent adherents to totalitarian doctrines from using the freedoms guaranteed by the Convention for the purpose of destroying human rights. This article was the basis for the rejection by the Commission in July 1957 of an application by the *German Communist Party*, which complained of a decision of the Federal Constitutional Court of 17 August 1956, that had declared the Party illegal, dissolved it and confiscated its assets. The Commission considered that the avowed aim of the Communist Party according to its own declarations, was to establish a communist society by means of a proletarian revolution and the

[1] Greece v. United Kingdom in Ch. III, Sec. 4. The Lawless case forms the subject of Ch. VI.

[2] Ch. IV, Sec. 1.

dictatorship of the Proletariat; that recourse to dictatorship would be inconsistent with the Convention, because it would involve the suppression of a number of the rights guaranteed thereby; and that the activities of the Communist Party therefore fell clearly within the terms of Article 17.[1]

There were certain features common to this case and to the later case of RETIMAG S.A. v. the Federal Republic of Germany, on which the Commission took a decision as to admissibility in December 1961. RETIMAG was a joint stock company registered under Swiss law in 1955. It owned property in Germany which included the local offices of the Communist Party in Mannheim, and a printing plant and publishing firm which worked partly for their account; also property in Munich allegedly intended to house the offices of a Communist newspaper. The penal chamber of the Federal Court of Justice at Karlsruhe in October 1959 ordered the confiscation of these two properties without compensation, on the ground that RETIMAG was a cover to conceal an organisation whose objects were to preserve the property of the outlawed Communist Party and to continue communist subversive activities. The company lodged an application with the Commission of Human Rights, claiming that this decision violated Article 1 of the Protocol, on the ground that it was made in circumstances not provided for by law and contrary to the general principles of international law. After an exchange of pleadings and oral hearings, the Commission declared the application inadmissible for non-compliance with the requirement of Article 26 on the exhaustion of local remedies.[2]

Article 17 of the Convention also came up for consideration in the Lawless Case. The Irish Government argued that Lawless, at the time of his arrest, was engaged in the activities of the Irish Republican Army, that these activities were of the type referred to in Article 17, and that therefore he could not rely on the provisions of the Convention at all. The Court's decision on this point was as follows.[3]

Whereas in the opinion of the Court the purpose of Article 17, insofar as it refers to groups or to individuals, is to make it impossible for

[1] Application 250/57, Yearbook of the Convention, Vol. 1, 1955–7, pp. 222–5.

[2] Application 712/60, Collection of Decisions of the Commission, No. 8, June 1962, p. 29.

[3] Publications of the Court, Series A, Lawless Case (merits), 1961, at p. 45.

them to derive from the Convention a right to engage in any activity or perform any act aimed at destroying ... any of the rights and freedoms set forth in the Convention; whereas, therefore, no person may be able to take advantage of the provisions of the Convention to perform acts aimed at destroying the aforesaid rights and freedoms; whereas this provision, which is negative in scope, cannot be construed *a contrario* as depriving a physical person of the fundamental individual rights guaranteed by Articles 5 and 6 of the Convention; whereas, in the present instance G. R. Lawless has not relied on the Convention in order to justify or perform acts contrary to the rights and freedoms recognised therein but has complained of having been deprived of the guarantees granted in Articles 5 and 6 of the Convention; whereas, accordingly, the Court cannot, on this ground, accept the submissions of the Irish Government.

Article 18, which concludes Section I of the Convention, provides that the restrictions permitted on the rights and freedoms guaranteed shall not be applied for any purpose other than those for which they have been prescribed.

Sections II, III and IV of the Convention relate to the Commission and the Court of Human Rights and will be discussed in the following chapters. Section V, consisting of Articles 57 to 66, contains the general clauses, which form the subject of Chapter VI.

CHAPTER III

THE EUROPEAN COMMISSION OF HUMAN RIGHTS

1. *The Composition and Functions of the Commission*

HAVING defined the rights to be guaranteed, the Convention then goes on to set up the international machinery which is to constitute their guarantee. The authors of the Convention were not satisfied with undertakings by the Contracting Parties to respect the different rights and freedoms: they required some further means of ensuring that these undertakings would be respected. In other words, national obligations were not enough; international machinery to reinforce them was also required. This same need has, of course, been felt both in the Council of Europe and in the United Nations; what has distinguished the negotiations has been the fact that the European States were able to agree quite quickly to set up the international machinery required—even though certain differences persisted about the extent of its jurisdiction, as will be recounted shortly—whereas such agreement has so far proved impossible in New York with the result that the work on the U.N. Covenants is still unfinished.

The Member Governments of the Council of Europe accepted the idea of the Assembly that a European Commission should be created for this purpose, as an impartial, international organ to which complaints could be made in the event that any Member State failed to secure to anyone 'within its jurisdiction' the rights and freedoms defined in the Convention. The principal function of the Commission is to investigate alleged breaches of the Convention, and to secure, if possible, a friendly settlement of the matter. The Assembly's proposals on the constitution and functions of the Commission were also accepted without major alterations.

The relevant provisions are contained in Section III of the Convention, which is constituted by Articles 20 to 37.

The Commission consists of a number of members equal to that of the High Contracting Parties. This meant on 31 December 1962 that the Commission had fifteen members, all Member States of the Council of Europe except France having become

Parties to the Convention. This provision is to be distinguished from the corresponding provision relating to membership of the Court; Article 38 provides that the number of judges shall be the same as the number of Members of the Council of Europe.[1]

There is no provision in the Convention about the nationality of the members of the Commission, except the sentence in Article 20 that no two members may be nationals of the same state. It would, therefore, be quite possible to elect persons who are not nationals of the Member States, though this has not so far occurred and, while legally possible, seems politically improbable. Curiously enough, there is also no provision in the Convention about the qualifications of the members of the Commission. This fact caused some heart-searching when the first election took place, as will be recounted shortly.

In the election, both of the Commissioners and of the judges, account has been taken of the fact that the Council of Europe consists of two organs, a Committee of Ministers representing the Governments and a Consultative Assembly representing the national parliaments; the procedure has been designed in such a way that the election is the result of the partnership of these two bodies. Under Article 21 of the Convention, the members of the Commission are elected by the Committee of Ministers on the proposal of the Assembly, while Article 39 provides that the judges are elected by the Assembly from a list of persons drawn up by the Member Governments.

For the election of the members of the Commission, each national group of Representatives in the Assembly puts forward three candidates, of whom at least two must be its own nationals. The Bureau of the Assembly then 'draws up' a list of names which is forwarded to the Committee of Ministers; the latter then elects the members of the Commission by an absolute majority of votes.

When the Bureau of the Assembly came to organise the first stage in the election procedure, after the Convention had entered into force on 3 September 1953, a number of problems arose which appeared not to have been foreseen when the Convention was drafted. In the first place, how many States were to participate in the procedure of electing the Commission: should it be all States which had signed the Convention, i.e., all Members of the Council of Europe, or only those which had ratified? Secondly,

[1] See further below, Ch. V, Sect. 2.

would the members of the Commission have a full-time job or only be required to sit intermittently; in other words, would membership of the Commission be compatible with the exercise of other occupations or must a person elected give up all outside activity, in which case the choice of candidates might be severely restricted? Thirdly, what role was to be played by the Bureau of the Assembly in 'drawing up' the list of candidates on the basis of the names put forward by the national groups of Representatives in the Consultative Assembly; was it merely to retype and transmit to the Committee of Ministers the lists of candidates received, or did it involve powers of discretion and judgment in choosing between the candidates proposed, establishing a balanced list and perhaps even indicating preferences in one way or another? Fourthly, what qualifications should be required of candidates: should they be lawyers, officials, politicians or what? Were certain of these professions additional qualifications for membership of the Commission, or, as was alleged in some cases, were they disqualifications?

In order to clarify these problems, the Bureau asked the opinion of the Assembly's Committee on Legal and Administrative Questions, on receipt of which it exchanged correspondence with the Committee of Ministers and then proceeded to draw up the list of candidates. This was duly submitted to the Committee of Ministers in May 1954 and the first European Commission of Human Rights was then elected.[1]

As regards the States whose representatives should participate in the election procedure, Article 20 called for a Commission consisting of 'a number of members equal to that of the High Contracting Parties'. Clearly, only those States which had ratified the Convention were 'High Contracting Parties'. It appeared, therefore, that a Commission of only ten members should be elected on the basis of names put forward by the Representatives of the ten States which had ratified at that time. On the other hand, if this procedure were adopted, the whole complicated machinery of election would have to be set in motion again each time an additional instrument of ratification was deposited, which would clearly be inconvenient and time-wasting. It was therefore decided that Representatives of all signatories should present their lists

[1] Fifth Report of the Committee of Ministers, *Documents of the Assembly*, 1954, doc. 237, paras. 47–8.

of candidates and that the Committee of Ministers would elect fifteen persons to be members of the Commission but that, as regards those persons elected in respect of States which had not ratified, their election would not take effect until their respective countries had become Parties to the Convention by depositing their instruments of ratification. In this way eleven members of the Commission were effectively elected (Turkey having ratified in the meantime) and four others designated as members subject to the condition precedent of ratification. The Committee of Ministers, however, recommended to the Commission that the four persons thus designated should, pending the assumption of their full functions, be allowed to participate in a consultative capacity in the preparatory work of the Commission and in drawing up its rules of procedure.[1]

As regards the intermittent or permanent nature of the functions of members of the Commission, it was, of course, impossible to determine in advance what would be the volume of the Commission's work. Nevertheless, it appeared questionable whether the Commission would have enough work to occupy all the time of its members, at least until it was empowered to entertain individual petitions; it was therefore agreed, subject to reconsideration of the matter whenever it should become necessary, to regard the duties of members of the Commission as intermittent and to fix their remuneration on a per diem basis.

This decision made it possible to elect to the Commission persons with other professional occupations. Since the Convention gave no indication of the qualifications required for membership of the Commission or as to whether certain occupations were incompatible with membership, it was not thought possible to lay down any rules to determine these points, though such considerations could, of course, be taken into account when the voting took place. In the event, the professions of the members elected at the first election were as follows: six judges or former judges, six law professors, two practising lawyers and one legal adviser. Three of the professors and the two practising lawyers were also members of parliament, one of them being an under-secretary for foreign affairs. Three of the original members of the Commission were women.

[1] Fifth Report of the Committee of Ministers, *Documents,* 1954, doc. 237, para. 49.

The last point which provoked preliminary discussion was the role of the Bureau of the Assembly in 'drawing-up' the list of names. It was argued that the fact that this task was entrusted to the Bureau of the Assembly and not to the Secretary-General of the Council of Europe meant that the preparation of the list was a political rather than a purely administrative or clerical function; consequently the Bureau should look into the merits and qualifications of the individuals proposed and try to produce a balanced list, having regard to a proper representation of various trends and types of experience on the Commission. On the other hand, the Convention itself contained no provision authorising the Bureau to interfere with, or even influence, the right of selection of the Representatives to the Assembly in presenting their candidates or of the Committee of Ministers in making their choice. No clear decision appears to have been taken on this point and the question what powers, if any, are possessed by the Bureau in 'drawing up' the list of candidates apparently remains unanswered.[1]

The first election took place on 18 May 1954.[2] The Belgian, Dutch, French and Italian members of the Commission, of course, could not participate in the substantive work of the Commission until their governments ratified the Convention; the Commission did, however, accept the recommendation of the Committee of Ministers that they should be allowed to participate in a con-

[1] The Assembly Committee on Legal and Administrative Questions was asked by the Bureau for its opinion on this subject in September 1953, and expressed the view that the Bureau had the right to list the candidates in the order of its selection ; also that candidates should possess, in addition to the requisite moral qualities, either an extensive knowledge of international law or a knowledge of legal practice (doc. AS/JA(5)19). In October 1955 the Committee on Rules of Procedure and Privileges expressed the view that membership of the Commission was not incompatible with membership of the Assembly (*Documents*, 1955, doc. 439). This view was subsequently endorsed by the Assembly in its Resolution 96 (*Texts Adopted*, April 1956).

[2] The following were elected members of the Commission :

M. M. Akbay	Turkish	Mme. I. Hansen	Danish
M. L. J. C. Beaufort	Dutch	Mme. G. Janssen-	
M. P. Berg	Norwegian	Pevtschin	Belgian
Mr. W. Black	Irish	M. I. Jonasson	Icelandic
M. F. M. Dominedo	Italian	M. G. Pernot	French
M. C. Th. Eustathiades	Greek	M. S. Petrén	Swedish
M. P. Faber	Luxembourg	M. A. Suesterhenn	German
Mme. I. Fuest	Saar	Mr. C. H. M. Waldock	British

sultative capacity in the preparatory work, and particularly in drawing up the Rules of Procedure.

The Commission held its first session in July 1954 and elected Mr. P. Faber of Luxembourg to act as its provisional President during the first sessions, when the Rules of Procedure were drawn up and adopted.[1] At its fourth session in December 1955, Mr. C. H. M. Waldock and M. C. Th. Eustathiades were elected President and Vice-President respectively; in July 1957 and again in June 1960 they were re-elected for another three years.[2] The members of the Commission hold office for a period of six years, though the terms of office of seven of the original members, chosen by lot, expired at the end of three years. A certain number of changes have taken place in the composition of the Commission, owing to death or resignation; a special case was that of Mme. Fuest who ceased to be a member on 1 January 1957, when the Saar was incorporated into the Federal Republic of Germany. On 6 April 1957, the other six members whose terms were due to expire were re-elected for a further period of six years. As a result of these and other changes, the membership of the Commission in February 1963 was as follows:

Mr. Sture Petrén, *President*	Sweden
Prof. C. Th. Eustathiades, *Vice-President*	Greece
Mr. Paul Faber	Luxembourg
Prof. L. J. C. Beaufort	Netherlands
Prof. Dr. A. Susterhenn	Fed. Rep. of Germany
Mrs. G. Janssen-Pevtschin	Belgium
Prof. Max Sørensen	Denmark
Prof. N. Erim	Turkey
Prof. F. Ermacora	Austria
Mr. Frede Castberg	Norway
Mr. G. Sperduti	Italy
Mr. J. E. S. Fawcett	United Kingdom
Mr. Sigurgeir Sigurjonsson	Iceland
Mr. Conor Maguire	Ireland

[1] At its first session in July 1954, the Commission entrusted the task of drafting its Rules of Procedure to a sub-committee of five members. The Rules were then adopted pursuant to Article 36 of the Convention, during the Commission's second session on 2 April 1955. After certain subsequent amendments had been made, the Commission adopted its revised Rules of Procedure during its 24th session from 1 to 5 August 1960. The full text of the Rules of Procedure is given in Appendix 4.

[2] On the resignation of Sir H. Waldock, Mr. S. Petrén was elected President of the Commission and took up his post on 10 January 1962.

After dealing with the membership of the Commission and the method of election, the Convention continues in Article 23 with a provision which is important, though perhaps self-evident, that the members of the Commission 'shall sit in their individual capacity' and therefore not as representatives of their governments; consequently they may not act on instructions from their governments but must take their decisions in full freedom as dictated by their own conscience.

Articles 24 and 25 then deal with the manner in which the Commission may be seised of a case. The first of these relates to inter-state action. 'Any High Contracting Party may refer to the Commission through the Secretary-General of the Council of Europe any alleged breach of the provisions of the Convention by another High Contracting Party.' This is the classic procedure well known to international law whereby one State may arraign another before an international tribunal for defaulting on its international obligations. Article 25, however, goes further and provides for the possibility that private individuals, groups of individuals or non-governmental organisations may also seise the Commission of alleged violations of the Convention; this provision is of such importance that it will form the subject of the next section of this chapter.

Article 26 introduces the well-known rule of exhaustion of local remedies. It provides that the Commission 'may only deal with a matter after all domestic remedies have been exhausted, according to the generally recognised rules of international law, and within a period of six months from the date on which the final decision was taken'. The words 'according to the generally recognised rules of international law' were added in order to refer to the jurisprudence according to which certain circumstances, such as unreasonable delay in granting redress or the inexistence of an effective remedy, dispense with the requirement of exhaustion of local remedies.

The remaining articles of Chapter III deal with the procedure of the Commission and the action to be taken on its report. They will, therefore, be considered in Section 3 of this Chapter.

2. *The Right of Individual Petition*

Several writers maintain that the Law of Nations guarantees to every individual at home and abroad the so-called rights of mankind without regarding whether an individual be stateless or not and whether he be a subject of a member-State of the Family of Nations, or not. Such rights are said to comprise the right of existence, the right to protection of honour, life, health, liberty, and property, the right of practising any religion one likes, the right of emigration, and the like. But such rights do not in fact enjoy any guarantee whatever from the Law of Nations, and they cannot enjoy such guarantee, since the Law of Nations is a law between States, and since individuals cannot be subjects of this Law.

So wrote Oppenheim in the first edition of his *Treatise on International Law* in 1905.[1]

One of the greatest achievements of the European Convention is that it demonstrates beyond any shadow of doubt that international law has developed from the position stated so lucidly by Oppenheim nearly sixty years ago to a point where an individual not only has rights under international law but can himself bring a case before an international organ, even against his own government. However, at the same time, it must be recognised that not all the European governments have so far been prepared to accept this revolutionary development.[2]

Under Article 24 of the Convention, as already related, any High Contracting Party may refer to the Commission, through the Secretary-General of the Council of Europe, any alleged breach of the provisions of the Convention by another High Contracting Party. The value of this provision, however, is limited. In international agreements which regulate the conduct of States inter se, it is, of course, highly desirable to provide for a tribunal before which one State can arraign another for non-compliance with the terms of the agreement. However, when the object of the agreement is to protect not States but individuals,

---

[1] Vol. 1, *Peace*, p. 346.

[2] An important step in this development was the opinion of the Permanent Court of International Law of Justice of 3 March 1928 on the competence of the Danzig courts, which held that the agreement between Danzig and Poland had created individual rights and obligations enforceable by national courts (*P.C.I.J.*, Series B, No.15, p. 17). Article 25 of the Constitution of the Federal Republic of Germany provides that rules of international law may 'create rights and duties directly for the inhabitants of the Federal territory'.

See Comte, 'The Application of the European Convention on Human Rights in Municipal Law', *Journal of the International Commission of Jurists*, summer 1962, p. 94 at pp. 96–106.

the real party in interest, if a breach of the agreement occurs, is the individual whose rights have been denied. It is therefore this individual who stands in need of a remedy, and the remedy he needs is a right of appeal to an organ which is competent to call the offending party to account.

It may be argued—and was indeed argued when the Convention was being drafted—that only States are recognised as subjects of international law. The weakness of this argument in relation to human rights is to be found in practical considerations of common sense. The object of the Convention on Human Rights is to protect the rights of the individual citizen; if his rights are violated, this will in all probability be done by his own government. Under the classic concept of international law, this individual has no *locus standi* on the theory that his rights will be championed by his government. But how can his government be his champion, when it is *ex hypothesi* the offender? It may be argued that another government can take up the cudgels on his behalf and lodge a complaint against his government. This is possible. But few foreign offices have the inclination gratuitously to pick a quarrel with an ally over the treatment accorded by the latter to one of its own nationals; nor are they likely to have the information necessary to do so, even if they should have the inclination. Moreover, if it is necessary for the individual whose rights are denied to seek the help of a foreign government, this has the result of transforming the complaint of an individual into a dispute between States—which is obviously undesirable.

For these reasons, the original proposals of the Assembly of August 1949 included an individual right of petition to the international Commission or, as the Legal Committee preferred to call it, 'a right of individuals to seek a remedy directly'. This right was made subject, of course, to the previous exhaustion of local remedies. During the negotiations, however, a difference of opinion arose as to the desirability of including the right of individual petition, the fear being expressed that this might easily lead to abuse, particularly in the interests of subversive propaganda. To guard against this danger two safeguards were introduced: a provision that 'nothing in this Convention may be interpreted as implying . . . any right to engage in any activity or perform any act aimed at the destruction of any of the rights and freedoms set forth herein . . .' (Article 17); and another provision to the effect that the Commission would not entertain petitions which were anonymous, manifestly ill-founded, or an abuse of the right of petition (Article 27). Nevertheless, the objections to the right of individual petition were maintained. The Legal Committee of the Assembly stressed that in its view it was essential that this right of individuals to seek a direct remedy should be preserved, but the Committee of Ministers in August 1950 was unable to reach agreement in this sense and decided, as a compromise solution, to make the right optional, that is to say, subject to an express declaration on the part of the government concerned that it recognises the competence of the Commission to receive petitions from individuals. It was, more-over, laid down that this procedure would only come into effect when six governments had made such declarations.

When the Assembly received the Ministers' draft Convention in August 1950, it was particularly concerned at this uncertain treatment of a right the maintenance of which it regarded as essential. In an endeavour to reinstate this provision, while taking account of the reluctance of some governments to accept it, the Assembly proposed that the procedure should be reversed and that the right of individual petition should obtain in all cases, unless the government concerned had made an express declaration to exclude it. The Ministers, however, found this amendment unacceptable and retained the formula which they had approved in August; the final text of Article 25 thus reads as follows:

1. The Commission may receive petitions addressed to the Secretary-General of the Council of Europe from any person, non-governmental organisation or group of individuals claiming to be the victim of a violation by one of the High Contracting Parties of the rights set forth in this Convention, provided that the High Contracting Party against which the complaint has been lodged has declared that it recognises the competence of the Commission to receive such petitions. Those of the High Contracting Parties who have made such a declaration undertake not to hinder in any way the effective exercise of this right.

2. Such declarations may be made for a specific period.

3. The declarations shall be deposited with the Secretary-General of the Council of Europe who shall transmit copies thereof to the High Contracting Parties and publish them.

4. The Commission shall only exercise the powers provided for in this Article when at least six High Contracting Parties are bound by declarations made in accordance with the preceding paragraphs.

Article 27, moreover, contains the provisions already referred to which exclude petitions which are anonymous, repetitive, manifestly ill-founded or constitute an abuse of the right of petition. Many guarantees are thus given to protect Member States against vexatious proceedings.

The need to accept the optional provisions of Article 25 was stressed by Sir David Maxwell Fyfe (later Lord Chancellor Kilmuir) when he was a member of the Consultative Assembly and Chairman of its Committee on Legal and Administrative Questions. In a speech to the Assembly on 25 August 1950, he said:[1]

Then I come to perhaps the most troublesome of our problems, the question of the right of individuals to petition the Commission . . .
. . . There are obvious dangers in leaving it to a State itself to decide whether or not it will be cited by an individual or group who complain of an infringement of human rights. . . .
There are certain rights which even in time of war or national emergency the Committee of Ministers do not suggest should be abrogated. They are the rights of safety of life, freedom from torture, and fundamental rights of that sort. Therefore, we took that as our guide, and we suggest that with regard to these rights there cannot be serious argument that the individual should not have the right to complain. If these rights are so fundamental that they must exist even in time of war, then surely they are equally fundamental from the point of view of the individual having the right to complain. . . .

A number of governments, however, have continued to hesitate to take a step which would permit their nationals and other persons within their jurisdiction to cite them before the European Commission. Recognising this fact, the Assembly made yet another proposal in October 1955 on the suggestion of M. Rolin, who had replaced Lord Kilmuir as Chairman of its Committee on Legal and Administrative Questions in 1951. This proposal took account of the fact that in cases where a State had not accepted the right of individual petition the only possibility of a complaint coming before the Commission rested on the

[1] *Official Reports*, 1950, Vol. 3, pp. 886–88.

willingness of some other State to present the complaint and thus champion the cause of the allegedly injured party. Other States, however, may be reluctant to take such action, not wishing to assume responsibility for what may be considered an unfriendly act. M. Rolin, therefore, proposed that the Council of Europe should follow the procedure adopted by the Council of the League of Nations in 1920 with a view to overcoming similar difficulties in relation to the protection of minorities, by arranging that individual petitions directed against States which had not recognised the competence of the Commission to receive them should be submitted to a commission of three members, consisting of the Chairman of the Committee of Ministers and two other members of the Committee selected by lot. This commission of three would then examine the petition and decide whether it should be referred to the Commission of Human Rights, by means of a collective application sponsored by the three governments.[1] If such action were taken, the individual concerned would see his case referred to the Human Rights Commission, but no individual government could be considered guilty of an unfriendly act. The Committee of Ministers, however, turned down this proposal. The right of individual petition therefore only exists in relation to those States which have made an express declaration stating that they are willing to accept this procedure.

The number of six acceptances of the right of individual petition was achieved by 5 July 1955, after the receipt of the declarations of Sweden, Ireland, Denmark, Iceland, the Federal Republic and Belgium. It then became possible for the Commission to entertain individual applications. Similar declarations were made subsequently by Norway (10 December 1955), Luxembourg (18 April 1958), Austria (3 September 1958) and the Netherlands (5 July 1960), so that this remedy is now available to nearly a hundred million Europeans. Ten Members of the Council of Europe having accepted this procedure—with their prestige in upholding the rule of law enhanced—it may be hoped that other Members will follow their example and thus render the Convention fully applicable in all the Member States.[2]

[1] Recommendation 83, *Texts Adopted*, October 1955.

[2] The official explanation for the refusal of the United Kingdom to recognise the right of individual petition is given below in Chapter V, p. 90.

3. *The Procedure of the Commission*[1]

When a petition has been lodged, the first duty of the Commission is to determine whether it is admissible. Article 27 of the Convention deals with admissibility and reads as follows:

1. The Commission shall not deal with any petition submitted under Article 25 which
   a. is anonymous, or
   b. is substantially the same as a matter which has already been examined by the Commission or has already been submitted to another procedure of international investigation or settlement and if it contains no relevant new information.
2. The Commission shall consider inadmissible any petition submitted under Article 25 which it considers incompatible with the provisions of the present Convention, manifestly ill-founded, or an abuse of the right of petition.
3. The Commission shall reject any petition referred to it which it considers inadmissible under Article 26.

The reference in the last paragraph to Article 26 relates to the rule on the exhaustion of local remedies. Other reasons for which an application may be declared inadmissible are that the events complained of took place before the entry into force, in respect of the Party concerned, of the Convention (*ratione temporis*); because the applicant has no personal interest or is otherwise not competent to make the application (*ratione personae*); because the application is against a State which is not party to the Convention or has not accepted the right of individual petition (also *ratione personae*); because the alleged violation is of a right not guaranteed by the Convention (*ratione materiae*); because no *prima facie* case is shown; because the application has not been filed within a period of six months from the date on which the final decision was taken, as required by Article 26; or for similar reasons.

The importance of the rules about admissibility will appear from the fact that, up to the end of 1962, more than 95 per cent. of

[1] On this subject see particularly : H. Rolin, 'Le Rôle du Requérant dans le Procédure Prévue par la Commission Européenne des Droits de l'Homme', *Revue Hellénique de Droit International*, 1956, pp. 3–14 ; A. B. McNulty and M.-A. Eissen, 'The European Commission of Human Rights—Procedure and Jurisprudence', *Journal of the International Commission of Jurists*, Vol. 1, No. 2, pp. 198–219 ; M.-A. Eissen, 'Le Nouveau Règlement Intérieure de la Commission Européenne des Droits de l'Homme', *Annuaire Français*, 1960, pp. 774–90.

E

the individual applications submitted to the Commission were declared inadmissible.

Under Rule 45 of the Rules of Procedure, an individual application is referred by the President of the Commission to a group of three members, which has the task of making a preliminary examination of its admissibility. If the group of three is unanimous that the application appears to be admissible or if the Commission itself so decides, the State against which the claim has been made is informed and is invited to submit its observations in writing on the question of admissibility. In all cases, the Commission itself takes the decision on this question, after obtaining the views of the respondent Government in writing, if required. Oral hearings on the question may also take place.

If the Commission accepts a petition as admissible, its first duty under Article 28 is to ascertain the facts and, for this purpose, to examine the petition together with representatives of the parties. It may proceed to an investigation, for which purpose the States concerned undertake to furnish all necessary facilities.

Under Article 29 of the Convention, these functions are to be performed by a Sub-Commission, which discharges its functions by calling for and examining written pleadings and, if it deems necessary, by oral hearings. It may summon witnesses and experts. In the case brought by Greece against the United Kingdom in 1956 arising out of the situation in Cyprus, the Sub-Commission carried out an investigation on the spot in the island in January 1958, during which a considerable number of witnesses were heard.

A Sub-Commission which discharges these functions consists of seven members. Each of the parties concerned may appoint a person of its choice as a member of the Sub-Commission; the remaining members are chosen by drawing lots, for which, under Rule 18 of the Rules of Procedure, the President is responsible with the assistance of the Secretary of the Commission.[1]

[1] In 1961, as the result of several years' experience, the Commission recommended to the Committee of Ministers of the Council of Europe that the system of Sub-Commissions should be abolished and that the functions set out in Article 28 should be discharged by the plenary Commission. The Committee of Ministers referred this proposal to the Committee of Experts on Human Rights (see below, Ch. IX) which expressed its agreement and drafted a Protocol to the Convention containing the necessary amendments. See Appendix 7.

When a Sub-Commission has ascertained the facts—if necessary, after conducting an investigation—its second duty is, under paragraph 2 of Article 28, 'to place itself at the disposal of the parties concerned with a view to securing a friendly settlement of the matter on the basis of respect for Human Rights as defined in this Convention'. If such a friendly settlement is achieved, Article 30 requires that a Report shall be drawn up, containing a brief statement of the facts and of the solution reached, which shall be sent to the States concerned, to the Committee of Ministers of the Council of Europe, and to the Secretary-General for publication. Clearly such a friendly arrangement is preferable to other forms of settlement, if it proves possible; nevertheless, up to the end of 1962 no instances of such friendly settlement had been recorded.

If a friendly settlement is not reached through the good offices of the Sub-Commission, the case is referred to the full Commission which, under Article 31, is required to draw up a Report on the facts and state its opinion whether they disclose a breach by the State concerned of its obligations under the Convention. The opinion of all members of the Commission may be stated in the Report. The Commission is required to transmit the Report to the Committee of Ministers of the Council of Europe and to the States concerned, which shall not be at liberty to publish it; the Commission may make such proposals for the settlement of the issue as it thinks fit.

It will be noted that the duties of the Commission are to ascertain the facts, if necessary to investigate, to lend its good offices and to draw up a Report setting forth its opinion. It may even make proposals, but it cannot determine the issue. That function is left either to the Committee of Ministers of the Council of Europe or to the European Court of Human Rights; the way in which they are to discharge it will be examined below.[1]

The remaining articles of Section III of the Convention are of a purely procedural nature. They provide that the Commission shall meet in camera; that it shall take decisions by a majority of members present and voting;[2] that it shall meet as circumstances

---

[1] For the Committee of Ministers, see Ch. IV. For the Court, see Ch. V.

[2] Decisions of a Sub-Commission are also taken by a majority of its members.

require; that it shall draw up its own Rules of Procedure; and that its secretariat shall be provided by the Secretary-General of the Council of Europe. More detailed provisions on these and similar matters are of course contained in the Commission's Rules of Procedure.[1]

One last point to be mentioned in this section is that some interesting problems relating to the procedure of the Commission arose during the first case that came before the Court of Human Rights, *Lawless v. the Government of Ireland*. These concerned particularly the relations between the Commission and the Court and the right of the Commission to communicate its report to an individual applicant. They will be discussed below in Chapter VII, which is devoted to the Lawless case.

4. *The Work of the Commission*

Once the right of individual petition had entered into force, the work of the Commission began. Between July 1955 and December 1962 it received over one thousand seven hundred applications. The very great majority were declared inadmissible, on grounds such as the failure of the applicant to exhaust his local remedies, because the events complained of took place before the entry into force (in respect of the Contracting Party concerned) of the Convention, because the alleged violation was of a right not guaranteed by the Convention, because no *prima facie* case was shown, or for similar reasons.[2]

By the end of 1962, only twenty-seven individual applications had sufficient appearance of admissibility that they had been referred to the respondent governments for their observations on the question of admissibility. Only seven individual applications had actually been declared admissible.

It would be beyond the scope of this book to attempt to give a comprehensive account of the work of the Commission.[3] Quite a number of its decisions have been referred to in the preceding chapter. What follows contains a summary of the three inter-State cases that have been considered by the Commission and

[1] Appendix 4.

[2] Statistics on the work of the Commission are given in the *Yearbook of the Convention*, Vol. 2 at pp. 522–5 ; Vol. 3 at pp. 470–3 ; Vol. 4 at pp. 426–9.

[3] Further information may be obtained in the *Yearbook of the Convention*, a large part of which is devoted to decisions of the Commission.

of the seven individual applications that have been declared admissible. In those cases where the affair has been referred to the Committee of Ministers or the Court of Human Rights, the proceedings there are also explained, in order to avoid interrupting the continuity of the narrative.

GREECE *v.* THE UNITED KINGDOM

Two inter-State applications were dealt with by the Commission in 1957, 1958 and 1959. They were both brought by Greece against the United Kingdom, and related to the situation in Cyprus. In its first application of 7 May 1956, the Greek Government alleged that the Government of Cyprus had violated the Convention by introducing certain exceptional legislative and administrative measures in the island—even though the United Kingdom had, in accordance with Article 15 of the Convention, notified the Secretary-General of a state of emergency, as a result of which it was temporarily suspending certain of the rights guaranteed. The application was declared admissible; a Sub-Commission was then appointed and held twelve sessions, including four hearings of the parties, and in January 1958 it carried out an investigation in Cyprus in order to judge on the spot as to the existence and extent of the state of emergency. On the basis of its findings, the Commission submitted its report to the Committee of Ministers in October 1958.[1] However, before this report could be examined, the Zurich and London Agreements settling the Cyprus question were concluded, so that, on 20 April 1959, the Committee of Ministers, on the joint proposal of the Greek and United Kingdom Governments, decided: 'In accordance with Article 32 of the European Convention for the Protection of Human Rights and Fundamental Freedoms, no further action is called for'.[2]

Though we now accept this procedure as normal under the terms of the Convention, it should be noticed how very much further it goes in the direction of international control than anything previously known under international law. The well-known provisions of paragraph 7 of Article 2 of the United

---

[1] The proceedings are summarised in *Yearbook of the Convention*, Vol. 2, 1958-9, pp. 174-8. The decision on admissibility is given *ibid.*, pp. 182-6.

[2] *Resolution* (59) 12 of the Committee of Ministers, *ibid.*, p. 186.

Nations Charter affirm the principle that: 'Nothing contained in the present Charter shall authorise the United Nations to intervene in matters which are essentially within the domestic jurisdiction of any State. . . .' Nevertheless, at a time when Cyprus was still a British colony, the Government of the United Kingdom, in compliance with the terms of the European Convention, not only appeared before the Commission to answer the charges of the Greek Government but actually afforded all necessary facilities for a Sub-Commission to visit the island to satisfy itself about the existence of an emergency within the meaning of Article 15 and examine the responsible officials on the spot. A special law was even enacted to grant diplomatic privileges and immunities to members of the Commission and their official staffs when exercising their functions on the island.[1]

In its second application of 17 July 1957, the Greek Government cited forty-nine cases of alleged torture or ill-treatment for which it said the Government of Cyprus was responsible. The Commission declared the application admissible in respect of twenty-nine of the alleged incidents. This application was still pending before the Sub-Commission set up to ascertain the facts when the Zurich and London Agreements were concluded.[2] At the request of the Greek and United Kingdom Governments, the Commission decided to terminate the proceedings without pronouncing upon the merits of the case. This decision was announced in a report submitted to the Committee of Ministers in July 1959. During their twenty-fifth Session on 14 December 1959, the Committee of Ministers, taking note of the report and of the reasons why the Commission had decided, at the request of the Parties, to terminate the proceedings, resolved that 'no further action is called for'.[3]

AUSTRIA v. ITALY

The third inter-state application made to the Commission was lodged by Austria against Italy on 11 July 1960. It concerned the

---

[1] Statute Law of 8 January 1958. *Yearbook of the Convention*, Vol. 2, 1958–9, p. 198.

[2] The proceedings are summarised *ibid.*, pp. 178–80. The decision on admissibility is given *ibid.*, pp. 186–96.

[3] Resolution (59) 32 of the Committee of Ministers, *Yearbook of the Convention*, Vol. 2, 1958–9, p. 196.

sentences passed successively by the Assize Court of Bolzano (16 July 1957), the Court of Appeal of Trent (27 March 1958) and the Italian Court of Cassation (16 January 1960) on six young men of the village of Fundres/Pfunders (Upper Adige) accused of mudering a customs officer, named Falqui, during the night of 15–16 August 1956.

The Austrian Government alleged that certain irregularities occurred in the trial procedure, constituting a violation of the European Convention on Human Rights and particularly of Article 6, which sets forth the principles governing a fair administration of justice.[1]

An exchange of pleadings first took place on the question of admissibility and the Commission gave its decision in April 1961. It declared the application admissible in so far as the Austrian Government alleged violations on the part of the Italian Government of Article 6, paragraph (2) of the Convention (presumption of innocence) and Article 6, paragraph (3)(d) (hearing of witnesses for the defence under the same conditions as witnesses for the prosecution) and also of Article 14 (non-discrimination).[2]

On the other hand, the Commission declared that the application was inadmissible in regard to the allegation of a violation of Article 6, paragraph (1) (right to a fair hearing) based on the composition of the Courts of Bolzano and Trent, because the convicted persons had not in that respect exhausted all the domestic remedies available to them, as required by Article 26 of the Convention.

A number of interesting points came up for consideration by the Commission before it gave its decision on the admissibility of the application. The Italian Government claimed that it was inadmissible *ratione temporis*, because Austria had only become a Party to the Convention on 3 September 1958 and the trial of the six young men at which it was alleged that irregularities had occurred had taken place in July 1957 and, on appeal, in March 1958. It was only the final appeal to the Court of Cassation in Rome in January 1960 which was subsequent to the Austrian ratification of the Convention, and no complaint had been made about the procedure on that occasion. The Commission rejected

---

[1] *Yearbook of the Convention*, Vol. 3, 1960, p. 168.

[2] The decision of the Commission on admissibility is given in *Yearbook of the Convention*, Vol. 4, 1961, pp. 116–82.

this contention on the ground that the whole conception of the Convention was to provide a collective guarantee of the rights and freedoms set forth therein, which the Contracting Parties undertake to secure 'to everyone within their jurisdiction' without condition of reciprocity; consequently 'it follows that a High Contracting Party, when it refers an alleged breach of the Convention to the Commission under Article 24, is not to be regarded as exercising a right of action for the purpose of enforcing its own rights, but rather as bringing before the Commission an alleged violation of the public order of Europe'.[1]

A second point considered by the Commission was the extent of application of the rule about the exhaustion of domestic remedies. The Austrian Government, while admitting the full application of the rule in relation to individual petitions under Article 25 of the Convention, argued that it did not apply to inter-State applications under Article 24; it drew a distinction between individual petitions, for which the applicant cannot prove violation of the Convention until he has exhausted domestic remedies, and inter-State applications to which this condition should not apply, because, it was said, the applicant State does not normally have access to the national courts of the respondent State. The Commission rejected this argument, holding that the provisions of Article 26 of the Convention applied equally to inter-State and individual applications; in so doing, it followed its own precedent in the Cyprus case, where it had rejected a part of the Greek Government's application on the ground that domestic remedies had not been exhausted.[2]

The Sub-Commission appointed under Article 29 to examine the case met early in 1962 and duly reported to the full Commission. The latter examined the report of the Sub-Commission and heard witnesses nominated by the Parties in November. The proceedings had not been completed by the end of 1962.

LAWLESS v. IRELAND

Gerard Richard Lawless was arrested on 11 July 1957 and detained without trial in a military detention camp until 11 December of that year, as being a suspected member of the Irish

[1] *Yearbook of the Convention*, Vol. 4, 1961, p. 140.

[2] *Ibid.*, pp. 150-2.

Republican Army, which had been declared an illegal organisation in Ireland. This action was taken by virtue of the Offences Against the State (Amendment) Act, 1940, which empowered the Government to arrest and detain persons without trial, when it considered that the exercise of such powers was necessary to preserve peace and public order and after it had made a proclamation to that effect. Such a proclamation had, in fact, been made a few days before Lawless' arrest.

In September 1957, Lawless instituted *habeas corpus* proceedings in the High Court. The commandant of the prison camp opposed the motion for a *habeas corpus* order, relying on the detention order made by the Minister of Justice. On 11 October 1957, the High Court upheld the cause of detention and rejected the prisoner's application. Three days later Lawless appealed to the Supreme Court of Ireland, invoking not only the Constitution and the laws of the Republic but also the provisions of the European Convention on Human Rights. The Supreme Court dismissed the appeal.[1] Lawless thereupon filed an application with the Commission of Human Rights.

This was the first case to be subjected to the full procedure laid down in the European Convention of consideration by the Commission and subsequently by the Court. Many issues arose of importance not only in relation to the particular facts of the Lawless case but also affecting the procedure of those two organs and the relationship between them. A separate chapter of this book has therefore been devoted to this case.[2]

De Becker *v.* Belgium

The facts of this case were as follows:

On 31 August 1940, a Belgian journalist, R. de Becker, founder of the newspaper *L'Esprit Nouveau*, became head of the administrative and editorial departments of the daily newspaper *Le Soir*, which had been confiscated by the Nazis.

In December 1940 he was appointed general editor and served the Nazi policies in Belgium. In 1943, however, he opposed the German plan to federate Belgium. As a result of this attitude he

---

[1] The judgment of the Supreme Court of Ireland is given in *Yearbook of the Convention*, Vol. 2, 1958–9, pp. 608–26.

[2] See below, Ch. VII.

was dismissed and placed under house arrest, first in Belgium and then in Germany, until 1945.

After the liberation of Belgium a Legislative Decree on crimes and offences against the external security of the State, dated 6 May 1944, was added to the Belgian Penal Code as Article 123 *sexies*. On the basis of this article, De Becker was sentenced to death by the Brussels *Conseil de Guerre* in July 1946, for collaborating with the enemy. On appeal to the Military Court, his sentence was commuted to one of life imprisonment by judgment of 14 June 1947. In 1950, this sentence was reduced to 17 years as a measure of clemency. Finally, on 22 February 1951 he was released by the Minister of Justice on condition that he would not engage in politics and that he would take up residence abroad within one month of his release.

Successive amendments to Article 123 *sexies* of the Penal Code, dated 19 September 1945, 14 June 1948, and 29 February 1952, altered the nature of the penalty without, however, exempting De Becker from its application.

De Becker took up residence in Paris in 1951 and filed an application with the Belgian judicial authorities for the restoration of his right to exercise his profession in Belgium. He obtained no satisfaction other than permission by a note issued by the Minister of Justice on 13 October 1953 to establish his legal domicile in Belgium without the possibility of effective residence. On 1 September 1956 he lodged an application against Belgium with the European Commission of Human Rights. He claimed that:

a. the undertaking which he had given to reside outside Belgium in order to obtain his provisional freedom was equivalent to exile and thus contravened Article 5 of the Convention;

b. the deprivation of his right to take part in the management, editorship, publication or distribution of a newspaper or any other publication was contrary to Article 7 of the Convention which prohibits retroactivity of the law, since it constituted punishment for actions performed before the Penal Code was amended in 1944;

c. the Belgian law in respect of which he was condemned, was contrary to Article 10 of the Convention which guarantees freedom of expression.

On the first two points the Commission ruled in July 1957 that De Becker's application was inadmissible. On the third point, after further written and oral pleadings by the parties, the Commission ruled in June 1958, that the application was admissible.[1] A Sub-Commission was then established on 22 July 1958 and proceeded to examine the substance of the application.

Having ascertained the facts, this Sub-Commission attempted to bring about a friendly settlement of the matter in accordance with Article 28 of the Convention. When this attempt failed, the Commission as a whole drew up a report, which was submitted to the Committee of Ministers on 1 February 1960. On 29 April of that year, the Commission, exercising its right under Articles 32 and 48 of the Convention, referred the matter to the Court.[2]

The Court's first hearing of the case took place in July 1961, but was adjourned in view of the promulgation of the Belgian law of 30 June 1961 modifying the section of the Penal Code which was the object of the application. A second hearing was held on 5 October 1961.

In addressing the Court, the principal delegate of the Commission referred, on the one hand, to the opinion which the Commission had expressed in its report on the case, and, on the other hand, to the Belgian law of 30 June 1961, which considerably modified Article 123 *sexies* of the Belgian Penal Code. Being of the opinion that the new Belgian law was in conformity with the requirements of the Convention, the Commission asked the Court to decide whether, during all or part of the period between the entry into force of the Convention with respect to Belgium (14 June 1955) and that of the law of 30 June 1961, De Becker had been the victim of a violation of Article 10 of the Convention.

The representative of the Belgian Government invited the Court to state that there was no incompatibility between Article 123 *sexies* of the Belgian Penal Code as amended by the law of 30 June 1961, and the provisions of the Convention; and to find, as regards the former Article 123 *sexies* of the same Code, that there was no longer any ground in the changed circumstances to render judgment on any of the submissions that had been made.

After the closure of the public hearings, the Court was informed by the delegates of the Commission that the Applicant had com-

---

[1] *Yearbook of the Convention*, Vol. 2, 1958–9, pp. 214–54.

[2] *Yearbook of the Convention*, Vol. 3, 1960, p. 488. For the Commission's opinion on the compatibility of the Belgian law with Article 10 of the Convention, see above, p. 29.

municated to them a declaration in which he made it known that he had no further claims to pursue and had withdrawn from the case.

Further hearings took place on 19 February 1962 at which the Commission, in its final submissions, suggested *inter alia* that the Court should strike the case off its list. The Belgian Government, in its own final submission, made the same request.

The Court gave its judgment on 27 March 1962. It accepted the submissions of the two Parties appearing before it, mainly on account of two factors:

the promulgation of the Belgian Act of 30 June 1961 amending Article 123 *sexies* of the Belgian Penal Code;

De Becker's memorandum to the Commission, dated 5 October 1961, in which, finding that his application before the Commission had been met by the Act of 30 June 1961, he stated that he regarded it as 'unnecessary further to proceed with this case' and that he withdrew his application.

As regards the first point, the Commission had emphasised in its final submissions of 30 June 1961 that the Act was in conformity with the Convention. The Belgian Government, in its turn, having maintained throughout that even the former legislation was in conformity with the Convention, declared itself in agreement with the Commission.

In its Judgment, the Court recalled that to those submissions was added the above-mentioned statement by De Becker, dated 5 October 1961, but the Court emphasised that the said declaration had not come from a Party represented before the Court and could not, therefore, possess the legal character or produce the effects of a notice of discontinuance of the proceedings. The Court nevertheless agreed that the Commission had the right to take the statement into account as a means of clarifying the issue before the Court.

On the basis of these facts and submissions, the Court considered that the proceedings brought before it no longer served any purpose and that, on general principles, it was now time to grant the request that the case be struck off the list. The Court nevertheless emphasised that it had been invested by the Convention with a particular responsibility and that its functions could not be compared with those of ordinary civil or criminal courts.

The Court had therefore satisfied itself as to whether there were any other grounds such as might, from the human rights point of view, oppose striking the case off the list. The Court had so satisfied itself in regard to the two following questions:

a. as to whether De Becker was the victim of a violation of the Convention between the entry into force of the Convention with respect to Belgium and the entry into force of the Act of 30 June 1961;

b. as to De Becker's freedom of expression in the light of the provisions of Article 123 *sexies* of the Penal Code as amended by the Act of 30 June 1961.

In its reply to these two questions, the Court emphasised that there was nothing to oppose removal of the case from the list, having regard to the effective protection of human rights.[1]

The competent Chamber of the Court reached its decision by six votes to one. Judge A. Ross (Denmark), availing himself of his right under the Rules of Court, annexed his dissenting opinion to the effect that the Court, notwithstanding the amendment of the Belgian Law, and without basing itself on De Becker's memorandum of 5 October 1961, should have embarked on a thorough investigation of the case.

There is one particularly interesting aspect of the De Becker case. The typical situation in which the Convention on Human Rights is likely to be invoked is one where it is necessary to protect the private citizen against arbitrary action by the Executive; the Lawless Case is a good example of such circumstances (even though the action of the Irish Government was finally upheld). The special danger which may be feared from the executive branch of the government is indeed recognised in Article 13 of the Convention, which provides as follows:

Everyone whose rights and freedoms as set forth in this Convention are violated shall have an effective remedy before a national authority notwithstanding that the violation has been committed by persons acting in an official capacity.

A second type of case is that where the Convention is invoked to protect the private citizen against irregularities on the part of the judiciary. Here Article 6 comes into play, containing guarantees

---

[1] *Publications of the European Court of Human Rights*, Series A, 1962, De Becker Case.

of a fair trial. But the De Becker case represents yet another kind of situation. Here there was no suggestion of improper action by the Executive or the Judiciary: it was an act of the Legislature itself which was in question. And while the proceedings were running their normal course, the Belgian Government asked the Parliament to amend the law, and the Parliament agreed to do so, in order to bring it into conformity with the provisions of the European Convention. It thus appears that all three branches of Government are subject to this measure of control, which is perhaps the strongest proof of the efficacy of the system initiated by the Council of Europe.

NIELSEN v. DENMARK

On 17 July 1954 the High Court in Copenhagen sentenced Mr. Bjørn Schauw Nielsen to life imprisonment for robbery, attempted robbery and homicide. More exactly, the jury had found him guilty of planning these offences and instigating, by various means of influence including hypnotic suggestion, their commission by another person, a certain Hardrup, in 1951. The Danish Supreme Court upheld the verdict of the lower Court on 18 November 1955. The Special Court of Complaint, which was petitioned for the re-opening of the case, dismissed the request on 29 June 1957. While agreeing that the charge of hypnosis had not been satisfactorily proved (Hardrup had withdrawn his allegation in December 1955), the Special Court did not consider that there was a sufficiently strong probability that the jury had wrongly assessed the other evidence produced.

On 23 December 1957, Nielsen lodged an application with the European Commission of Human Rights.

After an exchange of written observations between the Danish Government and Counsel for the Applicant, the Commission in July 1959 declared certain parts of the application inadmissible and, in regard to the remainder, invited the parties to make oral explanations on admissibility. This was done at a hearing from 31 August to 2 September 1959.

According to the applicant, several clauses of the Convention had been infringed, mainly those in Articles 5 and 6 which guarantee the right to liberty and security of the person and the right to a proper administration of justice. The Applicant's Counsel submitted *inter alia* that the period of preventive detention undergone by the Applicant (two and a half years) exceeded the limits authorised by Article 5, para. (3), whereby everyone placed in preventive detention 'shall be brought promptly before a judge or other officer authorised by law to exercise judicial power and shall be entitled to trial within a reasonable time or to release pending trial...' He further submitted that the charge of hypnosis was not contained in the indictment and that Nielsen had not subsequently been informed 'promptly... and in detail, of the nature and cause of the accusation against him', as required by Article 6, para. (3)(*a*). He added that the Copenhagen High Court had not given his client's case 'a fair hearing', 'within a reasonable time' (Article 6, para. (1)) and had allowed the psychiatrists to play a decisive part in the proceedings. Finally, he expressed his astonishment that the Special Court of Complaint, when seised of the matter after Hardrup's retraction, did not re-open the case even though it dismissed the charge of hypnosis.

The representatives of the Danish Government claimed as a preliminary argument that the Applicant had not observed the period of 6 months 'from the date on which the final decision was taken' as stipulated in the Convention. The application was first lodged on 23 December 1957. But the 6-month period should be held to run from the date of the order by the Supreme Court (18 November 1955) and not from that of the judgment by the Special Court of Complaint (29 June 1957), since it was not among the general principles of international law that there should be an appeal to the latter Court. They further maintained that the application was inadmissible *ratione temporis* in so far as it related to acts prior to the entry into force of the Convention. But their principal position was that the application was inadmissible by virtue of Article 27(2) of the Convention as being 'manifestly ill-founded'. No violation of the rights protected by the Convention had, in their view, occurred. The long period spent by Nielsen in preventive detention was justified by the need to make a thorough examination of his mental state and that of Hardrup. So far as the charge of hypnosis was concerned, the criminal investigation had allowed the applicant to wait until it was brought up before the High Court, particularly as the experts heard during the trial had submitted written reports on the subject during the investigation. According to the Danish Government representatives, the Copenhagen High Court gave Nielsen a fair trial; in particular, the opinions expressed before it by the psychiatrists had been purely of a medical character. Finally, the Special Court of Complaint had not been guilty of a miscarriage of justice by refusing to re-open the case, for, apart from the suggestion of hypnosis, there was sufficient proof that Nielsen had been the instigator of the crimes committed by Hardrup.

The Commission announced its decision on the admissibility of the application on 9 September 1959.[1] By this decision, the Commission:

i. rejected the contention of the Government of Denmark that the application was inadmissible on the ground that it was not filed within a period of six months from the decision of the Supreme Court on 18 November 1955 dismissing the applicant's appeal from the judgment of the High Court of Eastern Denmark;

ii. declared inadmissible that part of the application which related to an alleged violation of Article 6, paragraph 2, of the Convention (presumption of innocence);

iii. declared inadmissible that part of the application which related to an alleged violation of Article 5, paragraph 3, and Article 6, paragraph 1 (right to trial within a reasonable time);

iv. declared admissible that part of the application which related to an alleged violation of Article 6, paragraph 3, of the Convention (right to be informed promptly and in detail of any charge and of its nature);

v. declared that that part of the application which related to an alleged violation of Article 6, paragraph 1 (right to a fair hearing), was in some degree inter-connected with the part in (*iv*) above which has been held to be admissible and that the question to what extent it should be considered to be well or ill-founded must be decided after hearing the arguments of the Parties on the merits in regard to these two parts of the application, and that, in consequence, it should not be rejected under Article 27, paragraph 2, of the Convention.

A Sub-Commission was then appointed to ascertain the facts relevant to that part of the application which had been declared admissible and to endeavour to secure a friendly settlement.

---

[1] *Yearbook of the Convention*, Vol. 3, 1960, pp. 412–72.

After an exchange of pleadings, the Sub-Commission met in July and again in September 1960. It then reported to the full Commission, which drew up a report that was transmitted to the Committee of Ministers of the Council of Europe on 28 April 1961. At the beginning of June, it was announced that the Commission had decided not to refer the case to the Court of Human Rights, which meant that the Committee of Ministers had to decide, in accordance with Article 32, whether or not there had been a violation of the Convention. On 25 October 1961 the Committee of Ministers decided that no such violation had occurred, and in January 1962 the Committee decided to authorise publication of the Commission's report. The essence of the Commission's conclusions, which were endorsed by the Committee of Ministers, is contained in the following extract from the latter's resolution:[1]

Whereas the Commission, having rejected part of the application as inadmissible, retained as admissible, with the purpose of establishing the facts and formulating an opinion regarding them, the following two issues:

i. Whether the applicant had been informed in detail of the nature and the cause of the accusation against him, within the meaning of Article 6, paragraph (3)(a) of the Convention;

ii. Whether the applicant had been granted a fair hearing within the meaning of Article 6 of the Convention, in the Danish Courts, viz.:

a. the High Court and the Supreme Court;

b. the Special Court of Revision of Denmark;

Whereas the Commission in its Report unanimously expressed the following opinion on these two issues:

i. that the applicant was informed of the nature and cause of the accusation against him in sufficient detail and that in this respect there was no violation on the part of the respondent Government of Article 6, paragraph (3)(a) of the Convention;

ii. that

a. considered as a whole, the criminal proceedings brought against Nielsen in the Danish Courts (the High Court and the Supreme Court) 'do not fall short of the standard required by Article 6, paragraph (1) as to the right of every accused to have a fair trial';

---

[1] *Yearbook of the Convention,* Vol. 4, 1961, p. 590. The Commission's Report is published *ibid.* at pp. 494–588.

b. the findings as regards the proceedings before the Special Court of Revision in Denmark 'disclosed no breach of the Convention';

Having considered the case;

Voting in accordance with the provisions of Article 32, paragraph (1) of the Convention;

Decides that in this case there has been no violation of the Convention for the Protection of Human Rights and Fundamental Freedoms.

Four Applications lodged against Austria

The other four individual applications which had been declared admissible by the end of 1962 were all lodged by Austrian citizens against their own government, alleging that the Austrian Code of Criminal Procedure, in certain of its provisions governing appeal proceedings, violated the rules laid down in Article 6 of the Convention on the proper administration of justice.

The two cases of *Ofner v. Austria* and *Hopfinger v. Austria* were very similar. Ofner had been condemned to four years' imprisonment on six charges of fraud and misappropriation and appealed against the judgment, entering at the same time a plea of nullity. The Supreme Court heard the appeal and the plea at a non-public hearing, in the absence of both parties, but having 'heard' the Attorney-General, to the extent of taking note of his formal agreement to the draft decision. The Court dismissed the plea of nullity, but allowed the appeal and reduced the sentence.[1] Hopfinger had been sentenced to seven years' imprisonment for having defrauded his employers of a sum equivalent to nearly £3000. He appealed against his conviction and also entered a plea of nullity. He claimed *inter alia* that the Court had only heard the witnesses for the prosecution and had refused to call witnesses whose attendance had been requested by the defence; also that the sentence was excessive. Again, the Supreme Court heard the appeal at a non-public hearing in the absence of the parties, but having 'heard' the Attorney-General; it dismissed the appeal and the plea of nullity.[2]

In the case of *Pataki v. Austria*, the applicant had been sentenced to three years' imprisonment on several charges of theft and fraud. He stated that he was not allowed to call medical evidence

[1] Application 524/59, *Yearbook of the Convention*, Vol. 3, 1960, p. 322.

[2] Application 617/59, *Yearbook of the Convention*, Vol. 3, 1960, p. 370.

in his defence, which would have shown that there were extenuating circumstances, but he did not appeal since the Court took such circumstances into account and fixed a lighter sentence than would have been normal. The Public Prosecutor, however, did appeal, and the Court of Appeal increased the sentence from three to six years' imprisonment. Again, the hearing was not in public, the applicant and his lawyer were not present, but the Public Prosecutor was present and was heard.[1]

In *Dunshirn v. Austria*, the applicant was convicted on several charges of larceny and sentenced to fourteen months' imprisonment, the Court taking into account as an extenuating circumstance that he had made restitution as to 90 per cent. of the money stolen. The Public Prosecutor appealed against the sentence and the Court of Appeal, stating that it did not accept the existence of extenuating circumstances, increased the sentence from fourteen to thirty months' imprisonment. Once again, the Court of Appeal heard the Public Prosecutor *in camera*, without the presence of the applicant or his lawyer.[2]

Paragraph 3 of Article 294 of the Austrian Code of Criminal Procedure reads as follows (translation):

3. After the rejoinder has been submitted, or after the expiry of the prescribed time-limit therefor, all the documents in the case shall be laid before the Court of Second Instance which, sitting *in camera*, shall give judgment on the appeal after hearing the Public Prosecutor.

There is a similar provision in Article 296 relating to the Supreme Court.[3] Were these consistent with Article 6 of the Convention, which provides in its first paragraph for 'a fair and public hearing' (subject to certain stated exceptions which are not relevant in this connection); and in its third paragraph that the accused has the right 'to defend himself in person or through legal assistance . . .'?

During 1962 the Commission completed its examination of the cases of Ofner and Hopfinger and in December transmitted its

---

[1] Application 596/59, *Yearbook of the Convention*, Vol. 3, 1960, p. 356.

[2] Application 789/60, *Yearbook of the Convention*, Vol. 4, 1961, p. 186.

[3] Article 296 provides for hearings by the Supreme Court, when there is a plea of nullity 'at a non-public hearing, after hearing the Attorney-General'.

report to the Committee of Ministers, as required by Article 31 of the Convention. By the end of the year it had not yet completed its work on the other two applications.

In July 1962 the Austrian Parliament approved a bill submitted by the Government which amended Articles 294 and 296 of the Code of Criminal Procedure. Under the amended text, both parties are present or represented at appeals and the proceedings are public. When introducing the bill to the Parliament, the Government made specific reference to the European Convention on Human Rights and to the cases then pending before the Commission.

CHAPTER IV

THE RÔLE OF THE COMMITTEE OF MINISTERS

THE Committee of Ministers is the executive organ of the Council of Europe. This results from Article 13 of the Statute, which describes the Committee as 'the organ which acts on behalf of the Council of Europe'. The Consultative Assembly, as a parliamentary body, is the 'deliberative organ' of the Council which presents its conclusions, in the form of recommendations, to the Committee of Ministers (Article 22 of the Statute). The Committee of Ministers decides, on the recommendation of the Assembly or on its own initiative, what action shall be taken 'to further the aim of the Council of Europe', which, under Article 1 of the Statute, is 'to achieve a greater unity between its Members, for the purpose of safeguarding and realising the ideals and principles which are their common heritage, and facilitating their economic and social progress'. The action to be taken may include 'the conclusion of conventions or agreements and the adoption by governments of a common policy with regard to particular matters' (Article 15 of the Statute). The first convention so concluded was, as related in Chapter I, the Convention on Human Rights. Subsequently, nearly thirty other conventions and agreements have been concluded, providing for measures of European co-operation in other fields within the competence of the Council of Europe.[1]

The members of the Committee of Ministers are, in accordance with Article 14 of the Statute, the Ministers for Foreign Affairs. Nevertheless, when unable to be present, a minister may be replaced by someone else and, for the greater part of their business,

---

[1] These have included three agreements on social security and assistance; two conventions about patents; a general Cultural Convention; three conventions about university studies; conventions on the following legal questions: establishment, peaceful settlement of disputes, extradition, travel without passports, insurance of motor vehicles, mutual assistance in criminal matters; two agreements on medical subjects, and two about the exchange of television programmes. For further details see my *The Council of Europe, op. cit.*, p. 28 and Appendix 2.

the ministers are in fact replaced by officials of the foreign ministries known as the Ministers' Deputies.[1] Under Article 20 of the Statute, various decisions of the Committee of Ministers on procedural, administrative and financial matters can be taken by a majority vote; but such important decisions as recommendations to the Member Governments require unanimity.

The Committee of Ministers has had, and continues to have, an important rôle in relation to the Convention on Human Rights. In the first place, as recounted in Chapter I, it was the Committee of Ministers which approved the Assembly's proposals for the conclusion of the Convention, instituted the inter-governmental negotiations and finally approved the text and decided to open it for signature. Secondly, the Committee of Ministers is vested with certain specific functions by the Convention and has a definite rôle to play in ensuring the proper functioning of the machinery established for its implementation. Thirdly, the protection of human rights is not considered by the organs of the Council of Europe as something which has been effectively accomplished and therefore requires no further action; on the contrary, the Assembly is constantly making new proposals to improve the machinery already established or to secure the protection of additional rights; certain such proposals have also been made by the Commission and the Court. It is then for the Committee of Ministers—as the executive organ of the Council— to decide what action shall be taken on these proposals; it has in fact caused them to be studied by a committee of governmental experts and, as a result of their work, will be called upon to take important decisions about the conclusion of several protocols to the Convention. Further information on this subject is given in Chapter IX below.

It is the functions of the Committee of Ministers specifically arising out of the Convention itself which will form the subject-matter of the present chapter. These functions may be divided into two categories: those which relate to the administration of the organs set up by the Convention and those of a judicial or quasi-judicial character.

[1] For further information on the Committee of Ministers of the Council of Europe, *ibid.*, pp. 24–40.

1. *Administrative Functions of the Committee*

The first administrative function of the Committee of Ministers is in relation to the election of the members of the Commission. Article 21 of the Convention provides that they shall be elected by an absolute majority of votes from a list of names drawn up by the Bureau of the Consultative Assembly. The rôle of the Bureau in establishing this list has been mentioned above.[1] On receipt of this list, the Committee of Ministers effects the election. Since the proceedings of the Committee of Ministers take place behind closed doors in secrecy, no information is available as to the procedure which is followed when these elections take place; only the results are published—in communications of the Committee of Ministers to the Assembly and, when considered necessary, in press communiqués.[2]

The second administrative function of the Committee of Ministers is in relation to the election of the members of the Court. Article 39 of the Convention provides that they shall be elected by the Consultative Assembly from a list of persons nominated by the Members of the Council of Europe. The procedure for election in the Assembly is described below.[3] While it is true that Article 39 does not refer to the Committee of Ministers as such, it calls for nominations by the 'Members of the Council of Europe'. Since it is in the Committee of Ministers that the representatives of the Member States meet for the purpose of transacting business relating to the Council of Europe, it is in fact in the Committee of Ministers that the nominations are made, and it is the Committee of Ministers which draws up the list for transmission to the Assembly. Indeed, in its communication to the Assembly of 15 December 1958 transmitting the first list of candidates for the Court, the Committee of Ministers as such deliberately and consciously intervened in the procedure, as evidenced by the following extract from their letter:[4]

[1] Ch. III, Sec. 1.

[2] The results of the first election were published in the Fifth Report of the Committee of Ministers to the Consultative Assembly of 20 May 1954, *Documents of the Assembly*, 1954, doc. 237, para. 48.

[3] See below, Ch. V, pp. 92–4.

[4] Letter from the Chairman of the Committee of Ministers to the President of the Assembly of 15 December 1958, *Documents of the Assembly*, 1958, doc. 918.

... Although the Convention makes no express stipulation to that effect, the Committee of Ministers has itself decided to combine into a single list, as specified in the aforesaid Article 39, the fifteen lists submitted by the Governments of Member States.

The Committee of Ministers has unanimously recognised that the judges will sit in a purely individual capacity and will enjoy, in the exercise of their high office, the complete independence implied by the Convention. It considers that in this respect the candidates presented offer the fullest possible guarantees, together with all the qualifications required by Article 39, paragraph 3.

The last point illustrates the fact that the Committee of Ministers provides a forum in which all the High Contracting Parties are represented and in which they can conveniently examine matters arising out of the Convention which are not within the competence of the Commission or the Court. The Committee of Ministers may thus discuss questions of uncertain interpretation of the treaty—other than those, of course, which arise during proceedings before the other two organs. An example of this occurred in 1956 in relation to Article 15.

After providing for the possibility of derogation in time of war or other public emergency threatening the life of the nation, Article 15 provides in its paragraph 3:

Any High Contracting Party availing itself of this right of derogation shall keep the Secretary-General of the Council of Europe fully informed of the measures which it has taken and the reasons therefor. It shall also inform the Secretary-General of the Council of Europe when such measures have ceased to operate and the provisions of the Convention are again being fully executed.

The first such derogations were made by the United Kingdom in May 1954, when the British Government reported to the Secretary-General that states of emergency had been proclaimed in the Federation of Malaya and Singapore, in Kenya and in British Guiana.[1] This was followed in October 1955 and April 1956 by two similar communications relating to Cyprus.[2] On 7 May 1956 the Greek Government brought its first case against the United Kingdom in relation to the emergency measures in Cyprus, and did so in ignorance of the fact that the United Kingdom had

[1] *Yearbook of the Convention,* 1955–7, pp. 48–9.

[2] *Ibid.,* pp. 49–50.

made two derogations under Article 15. The question then arose whether the Secretary-General should have communicated to all Contracting Parties the notices of derogation which had been deposited by the British Government.

On the one hand, it could be argued that all Contracting Parties should be informed when a derogation had been made since it modified to some extent their mutual obligations. On the other hand, it was pointed out that Article 15 imposed no duty on the Secretary-General to notify the Contracting Parties of communications made to him, whereas Articles 25 (on the right of individual petition), 46 (on the compulsory jurisdiction of the Court), and 66 (on ratification) specifically provided for such notification; it must be presumed that this difference in drafting was intentional, in which case there was no duty to notify to other Parties communications made under Article 15. The Secretary-General referred this question to the Committee of Ministers for a decision and the latter, in September 1956, adopted its *Resolution* (56) 16 to the effect that 'any information transmitted to the Secretary-General by a Contracting Party in pursuance of Article 15, paragraph 3, of the Convention must be communicated by him as soon as possible to the other Contracting Parties and the European Commission of Human Rights'.[1] Subsequently the Consultative Assembly asked the Committee of Ministers to decide that the Secretary-General should also communicate such information to the Chairman of the Committee of Ministers and the President of the Assembly.[2] The Committee of Ministers replied in the following February that there was nothing to prevent his doing so, but the Committee was not prepared to take a formal decision that he must, since the Convention said nothing about communicating other declarations, notifications, etc. to those officers; consequently, a decision relating to Article 15, paragraph 3, 'might either appear to create a precedent or else give rise to arguments *a contrario*'.[3]

Another administrative function of the Committee of Ministers in relation to the Convention concerns the secretariat. Article

[1] Resolution (56) 16 of the Committee of Ministers, Supplementary Report of the Committee of Ministers, *Documents of the Assembly*, 1957, doc. 624.

[2] Resolution 103, *Texts adopted by the Assembly*, October 1956.

[3] *Documents of the Assembly*, 1957, doc. 624.

37 of the Convention provides that 'the secretariat of the Commission shall be provided by the Secretary-General of the Council of Europe'. Since, under Articles 37 and 38 of the Statute of the Council, the Secretary-General is responsible to the Committee of Ministers and has to submit to the Committee his budgetary requirements, this means that it is the Committee of Ministers which votes the credits for—and thus determines the size of—the secretariat of the Commission.[1]

The position is generally similar, though slightly different, for the Court. The Convention makes no provision for the secretariat or registry of the Court. The Rules of Court provide that the Court itself elects its Registrar and Deputy Registrar and that 'the President shall request the Secretary-General of the Council of Europe to provide the Court with the necessary staff, equipment and facilities'.[2] Since the Court has in fact elected as Registrar and Deputy Registrar officials of the Directorate of Human Rights in the secretariat of the Council of Europe, and since the Secretary-General has placed other members of the Directorate at the disposal of the Court, this means in fact that the Registry of the Court is provided by the Secretary-General of the Council of Europe and therefore that the Committee of Ministers has the ultimate control. This arrangement, though not required by the Convention, is obviously convenient, since the Directorate of Human Rights in the Council's secretariat already contains a number of officials conversant with the subject matter; it is also economical because it permits the use of the general facilities already available at Strasbourg.

2. *Judicial or Quasi-Judicial Functions of the Committee*

The more important functions of the Committee in relation to the Convention are under Article 32. This deals with the situation where the Commission has drawn up a report stating its opinion whether the facts in a particular case disclose a breach by the State concerned of its obligations under the Convention. Article 32 then provides as follows:

[1] At the end of 1962 this secretariat consisted of 6 officials of administrative grades and 5 of other grades. In addition, it could avail itself of the general facilities of the Council of Europe : interpretation, translation, reproduction of documents, etc.

[2] Rules 11, 12 and 13 of the Rules of Court.

1. If the question is not referred to the Court in accordance with Article 48 of this Convention within a period of three months from the date of the transmission of the Report to the Committee of Ministers, the Committee of Ministers shall decide by a majority of two-thirds of the members entitled to sit on the Committee whether there has been a violation of the Convention.

2. In the affirmative case the Committee of Ministers shall prescribe a period during which the High Contracting Party concerned must take the measures required by the decision of the Committee of Ministers.

3. If the High Contracting Party concerned has not taken satisfactory measures within the prescribed period, the Committee of Ministers shall decide by the majority provided for in paragraph (1) above what effect shall be given to its original decision and shall publish the Report.

4. The High Contracting Parties undertake to regard as binding on them any decision which the Committee of Ministers may take in application of the preceding paragraphs.

In such circumstances, therefore, the Committee of Ministers has a judicial or quasi-judicial function, for it has to 'decide . . . whether there has been a violation of the Convention'. This will only arise, however, if the matter has not been referred to the Court in accordance with Article 48, that is to say by the Commission itself or by a High Contracting Party concerned in the case, and only then if the Party against which the complaint has been made has accepted the jurisdiction of the Court—either by a general declaration under Article 46 or in the particular case. There are thus two procedures which are possible after the Commission has drawn up its report: decision by the Committee of Ministers or decision by the Court. The Convention is silent as to the criteria which should be applied in choosing between them. A logical criterion would be the test whether the issue involved is predominantly legal or political; if it is a legal matter, the Court would seem the more appropriate forum, whereas the Committee of Ministers would seem to be indicated for a basically political problem, since the Committee consists of the foreign ministers of the member States and is essentially a political organ.

In fact, however, the Convention leaves it to the choice of the Parties and of the Commission, and reference to the Court is only possible with the consent—either general or particular—of the defendant State. Moreover, it may be expected that States would normally prefer the forum of the Committee of Ministers to that of the Court, because the opinion of four judges is sufficient for an adverse decision of the Court (since the Court hears cases in a Chamber of seven judges) while eleven adverse votes would be necessary before the Committee of Ministers could decide that a State had defaulted on its obligations.

It will be observed that the Committee of Ministers can take decisions under Article 32 of the Convention *by a two-thirds majority* of the members entitled to sit on the Committee, whereas its more important decisions under the Statute of the Council of Europe require, as mentioned above, unanimity.

In 1959 and again in 1961 the Committee of Ministers gave some consideration to the procedure it should adopt when dealing with reports of the Commission referred to it under Article 32 of the Convention. It wisely decided to consider the question *in abstracto* at a time when it was not seised of any particular case, so that the matter could be examined with complete objectivity. Five rules were adopted, the effect of which is as follows:[1]

1. If the Chairman of the Committee of Ministers should happen to be the representative of a State which is party to a dispute referred to the Committee he would relinquish the Chairmanship during the discussion of the Commission's Report.[2]

2. The parties to the dispute will nevertheless retain the right to take part in the vote of the Committee of Ministers on the question whether there has been a violation of the Convention.

3. The next point considered was whether a member of the Committee of Ministers who is the representative of a State which has not ratified the Convention should be entitled to take part in the vote on the question whether there has been a violation of the Convention. It will be recalled that a member State of the Council of Europe which has not ratified the Convention does not have one of its nationals as a member of the Commission,[3] but does have one of its nationals as a judge on the Court.[4] Now Article 32

---

[1] *Yearbook of the Convention*, Vol. 4, 1961, p. 14.

[2] The Chairmanship of the Committee of Ministers is, under Article 6 of its Rules of Procedure, held in turn by the representatives of the member States in alphabetical order. The term of office is usually for about six months.

[3] See Ch. III, Sec. 1.

[4] See Ch. V, p. 92.

of the Convention provides for consideration of the reports of the Commission by the Committee of Ministers as such, and not by a committee of representatives of the High Contracting Parties. It was therefore decided that all members of the Committee of Ministers are entitled to take part in its proceedings under Article 32, irrespective of the question whether their countries have ratified the Convention.

4. The next question which arose was the procedure to be followed to permit States parties to the dispute to submit their observations on the Commission's report and for the subsequent exchange of pleadings. In this respect the following rule was adopted:

The Chairman of the Committee shall obtain the opinion of the representatives of the States parties to the dispute in regard to the procedure to be followed and the Committee shall specify, if necessary, whether and in what order and within what time-limits any memorials, counter-memorials or other documents are to be deposited.

5. The last point considered was that of obtaining additional information from the Commission during the course of proceedings before the Committee of Ministers. Here it was decided simply that 'the Committee may, if it deems advisable, request the Commission for information on particular points in the Report which it has transmitted to the Committee'. It will be observed that this provision is limited to requests for information and does not extend to the opinion or observations of the Commission on points which may be raised during the proceedings before the Committee of Ministers.

The Committee of Ministers has not yet been called on to take a decision under Article 32 in a contentious matter. As recounted in the previous chapter, two inter-state applications by Greece against the United Kingdom were brought before the Committee in 1959 but the two governments concerned requested that the proceedings should be terminated after a political settlement of the Cyprus question had been achieved, with the result that the Committee of Ministers decided that no further action was called for.[1] Only one report arising out of an individual application had been considered by the Committee of Ministers by the end of 1962. This was the case of *Nielsen v. Denmark.*

---

[1] See above, Ch. III, pp. 59–60.

The Commission was unanimously of opinion that no violation of the Convention had occurred; and the Committee of Ministers endorsed that conclusion in its decision.[1]

The Committee of Ministers has another important function under Article 54 of the Convention, which is to supervise the execution of judgments of the Court. Under the terms of Article 53, 'the High Contracting Parties undertake to abide by the decision of the Court in any case to which they are parties'. Article 54 then provides that 'the judgment of the Court shall be transmitted to the Committee of Ministers which shall supervise its execution'.

This presumably means that the Committee of Ministers would take steps to be kept informed whether a Member State had complied with a decision of the Court. Should it fail to do so, the Committee has no powers of coercion, but it would undoubtedly have strong persuasive authority. In the last resort it would have as a sanction the power of suspension from membership of the Council of Europe under Article 8 of the Statute; this expressly empowers the Committee to suspend a Member which has seriously violated Article 3, providing for acceptance of the principles of the rule of law and of the enjoyment of human rights and fundamental freedoms.

[1] See above, Ch. III, pp. 68–72. A further report by the Commission arising out of an individual application was referred to the Committee of Ministers in December 1962. This was the case of *Ofner and Hopfinger v. Austria*, which was still *sub judice* at the time of writing. See above, pp. 62–3.

CHAPTER V

THE EUROPEAN COURT OF HUMAN RIGHTS

1. *General Considerations*

THE first draft of the Convention prepared by the International Juridical Section of the European Movement[1] envisaged the creation of both a Commission and a Court of Human Rights, but with rather different functions from those conferred on the two organs that were finally established. Both States and individuals were to have the right to petition the Council of Europe in respect of any infringement of the rights guaranteed by the Convention; and these petitions were to be dealt with by the Commission, which could decide by a two-thirds majority to conduct an enquiry on the territory of the State concerned. If the Commission decided that the Convention had been infringed, it was to make a recommendation to the State in question with a view to obtaining redress. A case could be referred to the Court by the Commission, or by a State or (with the authorisation of the Commission) by the individual party 'for the purpose of determining any relevant question of fact or point of law coming within the jurisdiction of the Court'. The Court was to consist of nine judges, elected by the Committee of Ministers and the Consultative Assembly of the Council of Europe (by a procedure rather similar to that for the election of the members of the International Court of Justice) from a list of names put forward by the Contracting Parties to the Convention. The Court was to have extensive powers:

The Court may either prescribe measures of reparation or it may require that the State concerned shall take penal or administrative action in regard to the persons responsible for the infringement, or it may demand the repeal, cancellation or amendment of the act.

If a State failed to comply with a judgment of the Court, the matter was to be 'referred to the Council of Europe for appropriate action'.

It is interesting to compare these original proposals with the

[1] See above, Ch. I, Sec. 2.

provisions that were finally adopted; in doing so one notes inevitably how the powers which were to be conferred on the international organs (the Commission and the Court) were gradually watered down and the traditional rights of sovereign States asserted. The result, of course, was to make the Convention a less effective instrument than had been originally envisaged. The right of individuals to petition the Commission was made subject to an express declaration of the governments that they accepted this procedure; the right of individuals to bring a case before the Court was suppressed entirely; the power of the Commission to 'make recommendations to the State concerned, with a view to obtaining redress' was reduced to 'placing itself at the disposal of the parties concerned with a view to securing a friendly settlement', and, if that failed, expressing an opinion to the Committee of Ministers. Finally, the powers of the Court (ordering reparation, cancellation of the act, and punishment of the offender) were reduced to 'affording just satisfaction to the injured party', while its very existence was made conditional on the deposit by eight States of a declaration recognising the jurisdiction of the Court as compulsory.

The Assembly's proposals of September 1949 were already— as the result of discussions in the Legal Committee—somewhat less bold than the original plan of the European Movement. They included the creation of both a Commission and a Court of Human Rights; the Commission was to be open both to States and to individuals; but only States and the Commission itself might refer matters to the Court. (The European Movement had proposed that 'any affected party' might have access to the Court, provided it obtained the authorisation of the Commission.) Moreover, the function of the Commission was clearly stated as one of conciliation and that of the Court as 'judicial decision', but there was no provision that the Court could require States to take remedial action or demand the repeal or cancellation of their acts. As regards membership, the Assembly proposed a Court of nine judges (there being at the time twelve members of the Council of Europe[1]), the intention being apparently to show clearly that its members were independent judges and in no way representatives of the member States. A provision was also inser-

[1] Belgium, Denmark, France, Greece, Ireland, Italy, Luxembourg, Netherlands, Norway, Sweden, Turkey and the United Kingdom.

ted to the effect that the Parties could refer a matter to the International Court of Justice instead of the Court of Human Rights if they preferred.[1]

As explained in Chapter I, a serious difference of opinion arose during the negotiations on the fundamental question whether a European Court of Human Rights should be created at all. Since the proposal to create a Court with compulsory jurisdiction did not receive the support of the majority, it was not included in the draft Convention. A compromise solution was then sought, which would involve an option, whereby the Court would have jurisdiction only in respect of those states which expressly accepted it. For this purpose they might make a declaration by which they would agree to accept the jurisdiction of the Court as compulsory in all matters arising out of the Convention. As regards its membership, it was decided to set up a European Court with as many judges as the number of member States, which would all participate in the election of the judges and in the expenditure involved; moreover, since a Court consisting of twelve to fifteen judges would be inconveniently large,[2] it was decided that cases should be heard by Chambers of the Court consisting of seven judges.

The decision to make the Court an organ of all member States but with optional jurisdiction led to the need for specifying the minimum number whose acceptance of the jurisdiction would be required to make it effective. It would obviously be absurd to create a European Court in whose constitution fifteen States would be partners if its jurisdiction were only to be accepted by two or three. Considerable discussion took place as to the minimum number required, and the Committee of Ministers in August 1950 fixed on the figure of nine.[3]

---

[1] This was inserted at the request of Prof. Rolin, who wished 'to maintain a monopoly of competence for the Hague Court'—see speech of M. Teitgen, in *Official Reports*, 8 September 1949, p. 1282.

[2] The number of member States increased from twelve to fifteen while the Convention was under negotiation by the accession of Iceland, the Federal Republic of Germany and the Saar. (The last two were Associate Members ; the Federal Republic became a full member in April 1951.)

[3] The draft Convention proposed by the Committee of Ministers in August 1950 is to be found in *Documents of the Assembly*, 1950, doc. 11, Appendix A.

G

The same divergent opinions were apparently expressed in the Assembly's Legal Committee, and the compromise was accepted by the Assembly that the Court should only be set up when a sufficient number of member Governments had agreed to accept its jurisdiction as compulsory.[1] The Assembly asked, however, that the number required should be reduced from nine to eight, which would represent a simple majority of the fifteen member States.[2] This proposal was accepted by the Committee of Ministers and incorporated in the final text of Article 46 of the Convention as signed on 4 November 1950.[3]

These differences of opinion about the compulsory jurisdiction of the Court reflect, of course, divergent views on the basic issue: to what extent it is either necessary or desirable to have international machinery for the reinforcement of national obligations under international law. Traditionally, it has been the duty of States to comply on the national level with the obligations they assume internationally, but it has been their prerogative to do so in sovereign independence without supervision or control by some outside authority. Until 1919, when one State failed to comply with its international obligations, the only remedy available to another State was one of diplomatic representation, and eventually, by special agreement, of arbitration. Since then, it has been possible to bring an offending Party before the Hague Court. But this procedure is slow, complicated, and expensive. And it has the further disadvantage that what may be in essence a minor issue affecting the rights of an individual is thereby turned into an inter-State dispute, with all the consequences that that involves.

Various attempts have therefore been made in recent years to work out other methods for the international enforcement of national obligations which would be simpler to use and therefore, in many cases, more effective than an action before the Hague Court. One of these is the procedure evolved by the International Labour Organisation for the implementation of International Labour Conventions, whereby a permanent Committee on the

[1] The Assembly Committee's opinion is to be found in Document 93 of 24 August 1950.

[2] Recommendation 24, *Texts Adopted*, 1950.

[3] For the text of the Convention see Appendix 1.

Application of Conventions meets at regular intervals and examines the way in which, and the extent to which, they are applied in the different member States. This procedure makes it possible to examine informally and without publicity any allegations that certain States are not complying with their obligations; comparatively minor matters can thus be settled before they have become aggravated; if this procedure is unsuccessful, they can, if necessary, form the subject of recommendations to the International Labour Conference and thus of official approaches to the government concerned, but all this—be it noted—without involving an inter-State dispute before an international tribunal.[1] Something of a similar character, though on a more modest scale, is provided for in the Council of Europe's *Convention on Establishment*: this is a Standing Committee which will have the function of settling differences that may arise in the application of the Convention and generally of making proposals for its implementation or revision.[2] Similar functions were exercised by the Council and the various Boards of OEEC in relation to the obligations of members to one another under the terms of the Convention on European Economic Co-operation, the Code of Liberalisation of Trade, the European Payments Union and so on.[3] And the question of the need for international machinery to supervise its implementation led to sharp differences of opinion during the drafting of the *European Social Charter*, which is intended to be complementary to the Convention on Human Rights in the economic and social fields.[4]

The 'system of supervision and of guarantees' which was in

[1] The Constitution of the ILO also provides in Articles 26–31 for a procedure whereby a State may file a complaint that another State is not observing a convention to which they are both parties. The Governing Body may appoint a Commission of Enquiry, which is to report and make recommendations. If the Parties do not accept the proposals of the Commission, the matter may be referred to the International Court of Justice for a final decision. But this procedure has only recently been used for the first time. See McNair : *The Expansion of International Law*, p. 33.

[2] The Convention was signed on 13 December 1955 (*European Treaty Series*, No. 19) but has not yet entered into force. Its provisions are summarised in Robertson, *The Council of Europe, op. cit.*, pp. 185–8.

[3] See A. B. Elkin, 'The OEEC—its Structure and Powers', *European Yearbook*, Vol. 4 (1958), pp. 96–140.

[4] See below, Ch. VIII.

fact set up by the Convention on Human Rights represented a compromise, because it accepted the principle of an international organ to reinforce national obligations relating to human rights; but it was limited to the Commission and to inter-State proceedings, except for those Parties which voluntarily accepted the more extensive system of supervision represented by the right of individual petition and the Court.

The British attitude to the international guarantee was stated by the Under-Secretary of State for Foreign Affairs in the House of Commons on 25 June 1959 in reply to a speech by Mr. Elwyn Jones, M.P., who urged that the United Kingdom should accept the right of individual petition and the compulsory jurisdiction of the Court.[1] Mr. Robert Allan stated:[2]

The main burden of what the hon. and learned member said concerned the right of individual petition under the Convention. This is a question that has been raised and considered on many occasions since the Convention was signed.

It has been the policy of successive Governments since then to accept the procedure of application by States, but not to accept the right of individual petition. This was a decision made, among others, by the last Labour Government. We signed the Convention because we were prepared to accept an application by States, but it has always been clear that the British Government would not accept or concede the right of individual petition; and this decision is in full accordance with the belief that these petitions rest properly with the State.

By virtue of certain treaties it may be, of course, that certain individuals obtain benefits. They would apply in the case of commercial treaties, but it does not follow that the enforcement of the application against a State should be a matter to be placed in the hands of the individual. In principle, the enforcement of international obligations is a matter to be settled between the States on whom they rest.

and he continued:

If I may say a word or two about the Court, which the hon. and learned Member mentioned, the point there is that procedure by way

[1] Hansard, 26 June 1959, col. 1546.

[2] *Ibid.*, col. 1553. A debate in the House of Lords was held on the same subject on 18 November 1958, when Lord Layton urged the Government to accept the right of individual petition and the compulsory jurisdiction of the Court and the Lord Chancellor gave similar reasons for refusing to do so. *House of Lords Official Reports*, 18 Nov. 1958, cols. 601–30.

of the Commission is compulsory. The acceptance of the jurisdiction of the Court is entirely optional, so there is nothing wrong in choosing the Commission rather than the Court. The procedure by way of the Commission, in the absence of a friendly settlement, leads to proceedings in the Committee of Ministers, which may result in a binding decision . . . We are perfectly entitled under the Convention to take this view, but we do not thereby show any disrespect either for the Court or those States which have accepted its compulsory jurisdiction. Indeed the fact that we nominated such distinguished candidates for election goes to show that we wanted to see the best possible court for those who think it should be the ultimate arbiter.

It is clear, then, that the idea of the international reinforcement of national obligations is making headway, but that opinions differ as to what is the best machinery for the purpose and that the most important single step—recognition of the individual's right of access to the international forum—receives only limited support.

2. *The Creation of the Court*

Once the Convention had been signed and ratified, the next problem was to obtain the acceptance of its optional provisions. On the date of entry into force (3 September 1953), only three states had accepted the right of individual petition (Denmark, Ireland and Sweden) and two the compulsory jurisdiction of the Court (Denmark and Ireland). Much remained to be done, therefore, to bring these optional provisions into effect. The Assembly of the Council of Europe, as usual, took the initiative in urging the governments to take the necessary action and in its Recommendation 52 of 24 September 1953,[1] while expressing its satisfaction at the entry into force of the Convention, asked all member Governments to accept both the right of individual petition (in order to avoid 'transforming the complaint of an individual into a dispute between States') and the jurisdiction of the Court (in order that 'any complaint which the Commission considers legitimate, and which it is not able to settle by conciliation, should be referred to a judicial rather than a political organ').

By 5 July 1955, six States had accepted the right of individual petition.[2] The compulsory jurisdiction of the Court, however,

[1] *Texts Adopted*, September 1953.
[2] See above, Ch. III, Sec. 2.

took longer. By the summer of 1955, only five States had made declarations under Article 46 of the Convention accepting this jurisdiction as compulsory: Belgium, Denmark, the Federal Republic of Germany, Ireland and the Netherlands, of which the last-named had accepted the jurisdiction of the Court but not the right of individual petition. It was only in 1958 that three further acceptances were received, those of Luxembourg, Austria, and Iceland, the last two being deposited with the Secretary-General of the Council of Europe at a ceremony in the Council of Europe pavilion at the Brussels Exhibition held on 3 September 1958 to commemorate the fifth anniversary of the entry into force of the Convention on Human Rights.[1]

Once the eight acceptances of the compulsory jurisdiction of the Court had been received, the procedure for the election of the judges was put in motion. Under Article 39 of the Convention, the judges are elected by the Consultative Assembly of the Council of Europe from lists of persons nominated by the member States; each member is required to nominate three candidates, of whom two at least must be its nationals. This repeats in reverse the procedure for the election of the members of the Commission of Human Rights, who, under Article 21, are elected by the Committee of Ministers from a list of names drawn up by the Bureau of the Consultative Assembly on the basis of the lists proposed by the national delegations, each of which puts forward three candidates. The participation of both organs of the Council of Europe is thus secured in the election of both the Commission and the Court.

The Court consists of a number of judges equal to the number of Members of the Council of Europe and no two judges may be nationals of the same State (Article 38). This is another respect in which the Court differs from the Commission, since the latter consists of 'a number of members equal to that of the High Contracting Parties' (Article 20); as a result there was at the end of 1962 a French judge on the Court, though no French member of the Commission, since France had not yet ratified the Convention.

---

[1] The proceedings at this ceremony, including an interesting statement on the work of the Commission of Human Rights by its President, Professor C. H. M. Waldock, are published as a separate booklet by the Council of Europe.

The members of the Court must 'be of high moral character and must either possess the qualifications required for appointment to high judicial office or be jurisconsults of recognised competence' (Article 39). This reproduces almost textually the qualifications required of the judges of the International Court of Justice under Article 2 of its Statute, though it omits the final words in the phrase 'jurisconsults of recognised competence *in international law*'. In this respect, the judges of the Court differ from the members of the Commission of Human Rights, who are not required to be lawyers, though the majority of them in fact are. A comparison is to be found in the Court of Justice of the European Economic Community, set up by the Treaty of Rome of 25 March 1957, whose judges are similarly required to 'fulfil the conditions required for holding the highest judicial office in their respective countries or be jurists of recognised competence' (Article 167), a condition that was not required of the judges of the Court of the European Coal and Steel Community.[1]

On 17 October 1958, the Consultative Assembly in its Recommendation 183 asked the Committee of Ministers that the list of candidates required under Article 39 of the Convention should be submitted by the member States, without delay, and in its Order 129, decided to place the question of the election of the members of the Court on the Agenda of its next part-session. The Committee of Ministers approved the list of candidates at its Twenty-Third Session in December[2] and the election was set down on the Assembly's Order of Business for 21 January 1959.

Before the election could take place, however, a question of procedure had to be settled first. Article 39 of the Convention provides that the members of the Court shall be elected by the Consultative Assembly *by a majority of the votes cast*. Does this mean an absolute or a simple majority? Mr. Lannung of Denmark, Chairman of the Assembly's Legal Committee, argued that the

---

[1] Some of the judges of the Court of the E.C.S.C. were deliberately chosen for economic or trade union rather than legal experience. However, the Court of Justice of the E.C.S.C. has now been replaced by a single Court which acts as the judicial organ of all three of the Six-Power Communities : the E.C.S.C., the European Economic Community and Euratom. *Convention relating to Certain Institutions common to the European Communities* of 25 March 1957, Sec. 2. See *European Yearbook*, Vol. 5, p. 590.

[2] *Documents*, 1959, doc. 918. See also above, Ch. IV, Sec. 1.

Assembly should, in the absence of any clear provision in the Convention, apply its ordinary rule of procedure relating to elections (Rule 35(*b*)) which requires an absolute majority of the votes cast at the first ballot and a relative majority at the second ballot. Mr. Lynch of Ireland, a Vice-President of the Assembly, on the other hand, argued that only one ballot should be held, at which a simple majority would suffice for election; he based this contention on the fact that Article 21 of the Convention states explicitly that an 'absolute majority' is required for the election of the members of the Commission and that Article 10 of the Statute of the International Court explicitly requires an 'absolute majority' for the election of the judges. Since Article 39 of the Human Rights Convention only speaks of 'a majority of the votes cast', it must be supposed that its authors had deliberately omitted the word 'absolute' and therefore intended that a relative or simple majority should suffice. The Assembly first voted on this procedural question and decided to apply its normal rule, requiring an absolute majority at the first ballot and a relative majority at the second.[1]

The judges were then elected. In fact, fifteen candidates obtained an absolute majority on the first ballot, so that the Court was thus complete and no second ballot was required. The judges elected were the following:[2] Prof. Herman Mosler (Federal Republic of Germany); Prof. Alf Ross (Denmark); Prof. Fikret Arik (Turkey); Prof. Alfred Verdross (Austria); M. René Cassin (France); Judge Terje Wold (Norway); Mr. Richard McGonigal, S.C. (Ireland); Prof. Ake Holmback (Sweden); Lord McNair (United Kingdom); Prof. Georges Maridakis (Greece); Prof. Balladore Pallieri (Italy); Prof. van Asbeck (Netherlands); Judge Eugène Rodenbourg (Luxembourg); Judge Einard Arnalds (Iceland); Prof. Henri Rolin (Belgium).

The judges are elected for a period of nine years but, in order to secure a certain rotation without changing the whole court at one time, the terms of office of four judges expire at the end of three years and those of four more at the end of six years (Article 40). Lots were drawn by the Secretary-General of the Council at a public sitting of the Assembly immediately after the results

[1] *Consultative Assembly : Official Report of Debates*, 21 January 1959.

[2] The names are given in the order of the number of votes cast for the different candidates.

of the election were proclaimed, in order to determine which judges should retire at the end of these shorter periods, with the result that the following had three-year terms: Judge Arnalds; M. Cassin; Mr. McGonigal; Prof. Ross; and the following will retire at the end of six years: Prof. Balladore Pallieri; Prof. Holmback; Lord McNair; Prof. Mosler.[1]

A point of some interest that was discussed informally before the judges were elected was that of incompatibility of the office of judge with certain other functions. Article 16 of the Statute of the International Court of Justice provides explicitly that 'no member of the Court may exercise any political or administrative function, or engage in any other occupation of a professional nature'. A similar rule applies to the judges of the Court of the European Economic Community.[2]

This could not apply, however, to the members of the Court of Human Rights, because it is not expected to be in continuous session and, under Article 42 of the Convention, the judges are only to be remunerated on a daily basis when actually engaged on the business of the Court. Since they must, therefore, engage in other activities—at least in the majority of cases—it became necessary to consider what other activities were permissible.

There were five types of other activity which the candidates for election were likely to exercise: those of judge, practising lawyer, law professor, official, or member of parliament. The prevailing view was that there was no incompatibility between the first three professions and the function of judge; on the other hand, it seemed to be the prevailing view that the occupation of a national official (for example, that of legal adviser in a government department) was incompatible with the independence required of a member of the Court. The case of a member of parliament was more difficult. On the one hand, it could be argued that he

---

[1] On 26 September 1961 Judges Arnalds, Cassin, McGonigal and Ross were re-elected for a further period of nine years and Mr. Zekia was elected as a judge in respect of Cyprus, which had recently become the sixteenth Member of the Council of Europe.

[2] Article 4 of the Protocol to the Rome Treaty containing the Statute of the Court of Justice provides : 'The judges may not hold any political or administrative office. They may not engage in any paid or unpaid professional activities, except by special exemption granted by the Council'. The text of the Protocol may be found in *European Yearbook*, Vol. 5, pp. 439–53.

might be required, as part of his parliamentary duties, to take sides on a question which might subsequently come before the Court and that the two functions were therefore incompatible; on the other hand, the likelihood of this happening was small and if an individual was otherwise a suitable candidate it might be unwise to exclude him for purely hypothetical considerations. It was, moreover, evident that a member of the Court could not also be a member of the Commission; since the latter may refer to the Court a case which it has already examined itself.

These questions were discussed informally before the election took place, but no decisions taken or formal rules laid down. Indeed, the Assembly and its organs had no power to take decisions on matters arising out of, but not settled by, the Convention. It was therefore left for individual Representatives to consider the compatibility or otherwise of the office of judge with the exercise of other professions when they came to decide for which candidate they would vote.

The question of incompatibility was subsequently considered by the Court itself when it came to settle its rules of procedure. Rule 4 reads as follows:

A judge may not exercise his functions while he is a member of a Government or while he holds a post or exercises a profession which is likely to affect confidence in his independence.
In case of need the Court shall decide.

It goes without saying that the judges exercise their functions in complete independence and are in no way representatives of the States of which they are nationals or of particular parties to a dispute. Rule 3 contains the following provision:

1. Before taking up his duties, each elected judge shall, at the first sitting of the Court at which he is present after his election, take the following oath or make the following solemn declaration: 'I swear'—or 'I solemnly declare'—'that I will exercise my functions as a judge honourably, independently and impartially and that I will keep secret all deliberations.'
2. This act shall be recorded in the minutes.

In accordance with this rule, the judges each took the oath or made the solemn declaration at the ceremonial sitting of the Consultative Assembly held on 20 April 1959 to commemorate the tenth anniversary of the Council of Europe, in the presence of the Speakers or Presidents of the national parliaments, the Foreign Ministers of the member States, and the French Prime Minister.[1]

3. *The Jurisdiction of the Court*

As explained above, the function of the Commission, under Article 28, is to secure a friendly settlement of a case, if possible. It is only if the attempt to reach a friendly settlement fails that the other provisions of the Convention come into play. Even then, the matter is not brought automatically before the Court. The Commission is required to draw up a Report containing a statement of the facts and of its opinion as to whether a breach of the Convention has occurred; the Commission may also make proposals for a settlement, but is not bound to do so (Article 31). This Report is transmitted to the Committee of Ministers of the Council of Europe, which has to decide, by a two-thirds majority, whether there has been a violation of the Convention, *unless* the matter is referred to the Court within a period of three months from the date of transmission of the Report.

It will be seen, therefore, that the Court only has jurisdiction to consider a case when someone has specifically decided to refer the matter to the Court rather than to the Committee of Ministers. Who may take this decision?

Article 48 of the Convention provides that the following may bring a case before the Court:

a. the Commission;
b. a High Contracting Party whose national is alleged to be a victim;
c. a High Contracting Party which referred the case to the Commission;
d. A High Contracting Party against which the complaint has been lodged.[2]

---

[1] These proceedings are described and the speeches summarised in *Council of Europe News*, May 1959. On the functions and procedure of the Court, see R. Cassin, 'La Cour Européenne des Droits de l'Homme', *European Yearbook*, Vol. 7, 1959, pp. 75–92, and Eissen, *idem*, *Annuaire Français*, 1959, pp. 1–41.

[2] Article 44 also provides that only the High Contracting Parties and the Commission shall have the right to bring a case before the Court. It is curious that the two articles are to some extent repetitive.

Furthermore, this may only be done if the Contracting Party or Parties concerned have accepted the jurisdiction of the Court. Such acceptance may take place in different ways. Under Article 46 any High Contracting Party 'may at any time declare that it recognises as compulsory *ipso facto* and without special agreement the jurisdiction of the Court in all matters concerning the interpretation and application of the present Convention'. Such declarations may be made unconditionally or on condition of reciprocity. Independently of this, however, any State may consent to the jurisdiction of the Court in a particular case, either as plaintiff or defendant. All Members of the Council of Europe are therefore 'members' of the Court—in the sense of participating in its creation and maintenance—and all Parties to the Convention may avail themselves of its jurisdiction, even if only a limited number accept it as compulsory.

An individual or group of individuals who (or which) has brought a case before the Commission against a State which has recognised the right of individual petition has no access to the Court. Except for the unlikely possibility that a State which did not bring the matter before the Commission feels subsequently disposed to bring it before the Court, the only chance of an individual petition reaching the Court is if the Commission itself decides on this procedure.

The jurisdiction of the Court is therefore very much of a contingent remedy. It cannot come into play unless three conditions are fulfilled:

1. there is a failure to achieve a friendly settlement; and
2. one of the States concerned, or the Commission, opts for a judicial rather than political forum; and
3. the State or States concerned have either agreed to accept the jurisdiction of the Court as compulsory or have agreed to it *ad hoc* in the particular case.

It seems on the whole unlikely that inter-State disputes will often come before the Court. There are several reasons for this. In the first place, they are likely to arise very seldom. Of the seventeen hundred applications received by the Commission by the end of 1962, only three arose out of inter-State disputes: the two Greek complaints against the United Kingdom relating to the emergency measures in Cyprus and the case brought by

Austria against Italy.[1] Secondly, eight Member States out of sixteen had not yet accepted the compulsory jurisdiction of the Court. And thirdly, a State against which a complaint has been lodged is always likely to prefer the jurisdiction of the Committee of Ministers to that of the Court, for the simple reason that the chances of an adverse decision are much smaller. This is because eleven Foreign Ministers, deciding perhaps on political grounds, will naturally be reluctant to take a decision unfavourable to one of their colleagues; whereas four judges (in a Chamber of seven), deciding on legal grounds, are unlikely to feel the same hesitation about rendering a judgment against a State to which they have obligations of judicial impartiality but not of political friendship.

The bulk of the work coming to the Court is therefore likely to arise out of individual petitions to the Commission. Yet even in these cases, the individual applicant has no right to refer his case to the Court if the attempt at friendly settlement fails. He must in all probability depend on a decision of the Commission that the Court should be seised of the matter. It is therefore primarily to decisions of the Commission that a case is more suitable for judicial decision than for political settlement that we must look for the business of the Court. The Commission may take the view that, if it is unable to reach a friendly settlement, the normal course should be reference to the Court if the State concerned has accepted its jurisdiction as compulsory. Only the future can show.

One complication which may arise in connection with the jurisdiction of the Court results from the terms of Article 46 of the Convention. This provides that the declarations accepting the compulsory jurisdictions of the Court 'may be made unconditionally or on condition of reciprocity on the part of several or certain other High Contracting Parties or for a specified period'. If a Party has accepted the compulsory jurisdiction of the Court on condition of reciprocity, can the Commission then refer a case brought against the Party to the Court? This question was discussed at some length by the Committee of Legal Experts which undertook the final revision of the text on the eve of the signature of the Convention in 1950. On the one hand, it was argued that in the case of the Commission no reciprocity exists and that therefore, since this condition is unfulfilled, no jurisdic-

[1] See above, Ch. III, Sec. 4.

tion lies. On the other hand, it was asserted that the condition of reciprocity only relates to cases brought by other High Contracting Parties, and does not affect the ability of the Commission to bring a case before the Court, since the Commission is *sui generis*, and the right of the Commission to refer cases to the Court is an essential part of the procedure established by the Convention which cannot be excluded in default of a clear intention to do so.[1]

If this case arises, the issue must be settled by the Court itself, since Article 49 of the Convention provides:

In the event of dispute as to whether the Court has jurisdiction, the matter shall be settled by the decision of the Court.

In the meantime, it is cause for satisfaction that the rules relating to the jurisdiction of the Court seem clear and that no reservations have been made (except as regards time and reciprocity) in the declarations made accepting its jurisdiction as compulsory. In this respect, the Court of Human Rights seems more fortunate than the International Court of Justice, Article 36 of whose Statute (the optional clause) is more complicated in its provisions and hedged round with reservations to such an extent that the Court spends a large part of its time in dealing with objections to the jurisdiction.[2] It is to be hoped that the arguments of this sort heard at The Hague will not find their echo in Strasbourg.

4. *Procedure and Judgments*

The Convention on Human Rights contains some very brief provisions about the procedure of the Court, but there are no detailed texts established by treaty comparable to those contained in the Statute of the International Court[3] or in that of the Court of the Economic Community.[4]

The principal procedural matter regulated by the Convention is that each case shall be considered by a Chamber of seven judges. Article 43 reads as follows:

[1] See further below, Ch. IX, Part 2.

[2] Cf. C. H. M. Waldock, 'The Decline of the Optional Clause', *B.Y.I.L.*, 1955, 244–87.

[3] Articles 39 to 64.

[4] *European Yearbook*, Vol. 5, 1959, pp. 439–53.

For the consideration of each case brought before it the Court shall consist of a Chamber composed of seven judges. There shall sit as an *ex officio* member of the Chamber the judge who is a national of any State party concerned, or, if there is none, a person of its choice who shall sit in the capacity of judge; the names of the other judges shall be chosen by lot by the President before the opening of the case.

In addition, Article 51 provides that reasons shall be given for the judgments of the Court and that dissenting opinions may be delivered. Apart from these two questions and from a provision that the Court shall elect its President and Vice-President for periods of three years, it was left to the Court to settle its own procedure in accordance with a general authorisation conferred by Article 55 of the Convention.

The first business of the Court was therefore to work out its own Rules. This was done at a series of meetings during the spring and summer of 1959; the Rules were then adopted in September.[1]

The Rules of Court contain two separate parts or titles. Title I deals with the 'Organisation and Working of the Court'. It deals with such questions as the oath of office and incompatibility of function (mentioned above), the functions of the President and Vice-President, the election and duties of the Registrar and his staff,[2] publicity of hearings, secrecy of deliberations, and so on. The seat of the Court is to be at the seat of the Council of Europe in Strasbourg; the quorum is to be nine judges; decisions shall be taken by a majority of the judges present, and, if the voting is equal, the President will have a second and casting vote. Chapter V of Title I provides for the constitution of the Chambers of seven judges, and closely follows Article 43 of the Convention. There are appropriate provisions relating to the appointment of substitute judges (to serve in place of a judge chosen by lot who is unable to sit or has withdrawn) and *ad hoc* judges, who will sit in the Chamber if the Court does not include a judge having the nationality of one of the parties or if the judge called upon to sit in that capacity is unable to sit or withdraws. In such case the party concerned may appoint either another elected judge or some

---

[1] The full text of the Rules of Court is given in Appendix 5. See also M.-A. Eissen, 'La Cour Européenne des Droits de l'Homme—de la Convention au Règlement', *Annuaire Français*, 1959, p. 1 at pp. 21–39.

[2] The Court elected M. Polys Modinos as its Registrar on 16 September 1959. Mr. Heribert Golsong was elected Deputy Registrar on 11 April 1960.

other person of its choice who has the qualifications laid down in the Convention.

Title II of the Rules deals with the procedure of the Court. The official languages are English and French; there are appropriate provisions for interpretation and translation; judgments will be given in both languages and the Court will indicate which text is authoritative. The parties to a case will be represented by agents, who may be assisted by advocates or advisers, as in the International Court. These are the necessary rules about filing and notification of cases, exchange of written pleadings, hearing of oral pleadings, and the summoning and hearing of witnesses and experts. There are three rules of particular interest in this Title. The first of these (Rule 48) provides that a Chamber may refer a case to the plenary Court if it raises a serious question of interpretation of the Convention; indeed, it is obliged to do so in cases where the resolution of the question might have a result inconsistent with a judgment previously delivered by a Chamber or by the plenary Court. Once it is seised of such a case, the plenary Court may either continue to deal with the matter itself, or refer it back to the Chamber once it has decided the question of interpretation. Were it not for this provision, the plenary Court would have practically nothing to do, once it has adopted its Rules of Procedure and elected its President and Vice-President. The second point is that Rule 53 contains a provision, broadly comparable to that in Article 79 of the Rules of the Hague Court, authorising a party or the Commission to request the interpretation of a judgment already rendered, provided this is done within a period of three years. In such cases, the matter is to be dealt with so far as possible by the Chamber which pronounced the judgment in the first case, even if this means calling back judges who have retired.[1]

By far the most interesting provision, however, is that on relations between the Commission and the Court. Since a case can only come before the Court after it has been considered by

---

M. Modinos having resigned from the post of Registrar on his election as Deputy Secretary-General of the Council of Europe in May 1962, Mr. Golsong was elected Registrar on 21 May 1963.

[1] Rule 54 also contains provisions for the revision of judgments broadly comparable to Article 61 of the Statute of the Hague Court.

the Commission, it is obviously of importance to decide what the relations between the two organs will be. The Convention is silent on this point. It provides that the Court may only consider a case after the Commission has failed to bring about a friendly settlement, in which eventuality the Commission is required to draw up a Report which is to be sent to the Committee of Ministers and to the States concerned but is not to be published. Nothing is said about its communication to the Court. Is the Court to be allowed to see it? And is the Court to have the benefit of other knowledge of the proceedings before the Commission, for example by receiving a copy of the record?

The Court, being aware of this problem, adopted a Rule designed to meet it. Rule 29 reads as follows:

1. The Commission shall delegate one or more of its members to take part in the consideration of a case before the Court. The delegates may, if they so desire, have the assistance of any person of their choice.

2. The Court shall, whether a case is referred to it by a Contracting Party or by the Commission, take into consideration the report of the latter.

It will be observed that this text is in terms which are very general and leave plenty of room for manœuvre. In fact the procedural problems arising out of the relations between the Commission and the Court were discussed at length in the *Lawless Case*, which forms the subject of Chapter VII below.

From the purely formal point of view, the judgments of the Court are dealt with in Rule 50, which sets out what shall be their contents: they are to include statements of the proceedings and of the facts of the case, the reasons on points of law, the operative provisions of the judgment, and so on. What is more interesting to international lawyers, however, is the effect of the judgment.

In the first place, it must be remembered that the Court of Human Rights is not a *quatrième instance* to which appeal lies from the highest courts of the parties who have accepted its jurisdiction. It cannot therefore upset the judgment of a national court; it is in no sense a *Cour de Cassation*. Indeed, if this fact were more widely recognised, there might be less reluctance in certain countries to accept its jurisdiction as compulsory.

It is curious that the Convention does not anywhere state explicitly what the Court is supposed to decide. It is, however, clear from the whole tenor of the Convention and is stated indirectly (and in a conditional clause) in Article 50 that the function of the Court is to decide whether:

a decision or measure taken by a legal authority or any other authority of a High Contracting Party is completely or partially in conflict with the obligations arising from the present Convention. . . .

In other words, it is clearly the duty of the Court to decide whether there has been a violation of the Convention. One would expect that its judgment would go on to prescribe what measures should be taken to remedy this situation and to afford satisfaction to the injured party. But the Convention does not provide that it should do so. This is also surprising. What is even more surprising is that Article 50 (an extract from which has just been quoted) provides that if the Court decides that a violation has occurred and

if the internal law of the said Party allows only partial reparation to be made for the consequences of the decision or measure, the decision of the Court shall, if necessary, afford just satisfaction to the injured party.

What is so curious here is that the Convention specifically empowers the Court to 'afford just satisfaction to the injured party' (by the award of damages or otherwise) if the internal law only allows partial reparation but is silent as to the position if the internal law allows complete reparation—or none at all. It may be argued that in such cases the Court has *a fortiori* the power to 'afford satisfaction'. But the *argumentum e contrario* is also possible. And it is supported by the fact that Article 32, which relates to decisions by the Committee of Ministers when the case is not referred to the Court, provides that the Committee shall decide whether a violation has occurred and shall fix a period during which the Party concerned must take remedial measures—but leaves it to the Party concerned to decide what those measures shall be. It may thus be argued that any provisions of the Convention which appear to limit the sovereignty of States should be construed restrictively and that therefore the Court—like the Committee of Ministers—has power to decide whether a State has violated the Convention but that thereafter it is for the State concerned—and not for the Court—to decide what 'just satisfaction' should be awarded to the injured party, except in the specific case covered by Article 50.

This problem can only be decided in practice. It seems probable that the Court will take the wider view in interpreting the extent of its own powers and that, if it does so, the Contracting Parties will accept. But, once again, there is room for interesting argument.[1]

As regards the force of the judgment, the Convention is concise and clear. Article 53 provides:

The High Contracting Parties undertake to abide by the decisions of the Court in any case to which they are parties.

and Article 54:

The judgment of the Court shall be transmitted to the Committee of Ministers which shall supervise its execution.

It is therefore for the Party (or Parties) concerned to give effect to the judgment, and, should they fail to do so, it would be for the Committee of Ministers to decide what action should be taken. The Committee does not, of course, have power to force a State into compliance but it would undoubtedly, if the need arose, have strong persuasive authority backed, in the last resort, by the power of suspension from membership of the Council of Europe under Article 8 of the Statute.[2]

These provisions seem reasonable in the circumstances and all that could be expected in a treaty between States which are partners in an organisation like the Council of Europe which is based on the principle of intergovernmental co-operation. It is, however, interesting to contrast the provisions of the treaties setting up the three Six-Power Communities for Coal and Steel, the Common Market, and Euratom, which are based on the principles of 'integration' and 'supranational powers'. The

---

[1] See also on this subject Willem Vis, 'La Réparation des Violations de la Convention', in La Protection Internationale des Droits de l'Homme dans le cadre européen, 1961, p. 279.

[2] Article 8 reads as follows: 'Any member of the Council of Europe which has seriously violated Article 3 may be suspended from its rights of representation and requested by the Committee of Ministers to withdraw under Article 7. If such Member does not comply with this request, the Committee may decide that it has ceased to be a Member of the Council as from such date as the Committee may determine.' Article 3 provides for acceptance of the principles of the rule of law and of the enjoyment of human rights and fundamental freedoms.

Court of Justice which is the judicial organ of the three Communities renders judgments which are, in their own right, executory in the territory of the Member States; they may be put into forced execution under the legal procedure in effect in each State; a Minister of the national government is responsible for signing the necessary papers after satisfying himself as to the authenticity of the decision, but he may not question its substance.[1]

By the end of 1962 the Court had dealt with only two cases: *Lawless v. Ireland* and *De Becker v. Belgium*. The second of these is summarised in Chapter III, Section 4, while the Lawless case is dealt with more fully in Chapter VII below.

[1] See Articles 44 and 92 of the E.C.S.C. Treaty ; Articles 187 and 192 of the Economic Community Treaty ; and Articles 159 and 164 of the Euratom Treaty.

CHAPTER VI

THE GENERAL PROVISIONS OF THE CONVENTION

SECTION V of the Convention consists of Articles 57 to 66, which constitute the general provisions; some of them are of greater interest than is often the case in the concluding articles to a treaty.

Article 57 is of particular importance. It provides that 'on receipt of a request from the Secretary-General of the Council of Europe, any High Contracting Party shall furnish an explanation of the manner in which its internal law ensures the effective implementation of any of the provisions of this Convention'. This places in the hands of the Secretary-General a powerful instrument, namely the right to ask for explanations from a High Contracting Party as to the way it implements the Convention; not only does the Secretary-General have the right to enquire, but also the State concerned has the obligation to 'furnish an explanation'.

Under the Statute of the Council of Europe the powers of the Secretary-General are rather limited. The Charter of the United Nations confers on the Secretariat the status of one of the principal organs of the United Nations;[1] its European counterpart has a more humble position.[2] The Consultative Assembly has recommended that the Secretary-General should be recognised as an 'organ of the Council', but this the Committee of Ministers has refused.[3] In reply to the question which pinpoints the issue so nicely: 'Is the Secretary-General a Secretary or a General?'[4] it must be admitted that the powers conferred by the Statute

[1] Article 7 of the Charter.

[2] Under Articles 36 and 37 of the Statute the Secretary-General appoints the members of the Secretariat, furnishes such secretariat services as may be required and 'is responsible to the Committee of Ministers for the work of the Secretariat'.

[3] Opinion 13/14, para. 39, in *Texts Adopted by the Assembly*, July 1955; Communication of the Committee of Ministers of 3 April 1956, *Documents*, 1956, doc. 481.

[4] See S. M. Schwebel, *The Secretary-General of the United Nations*.

place him much nearer to the first category than the second.[1] It is therefore only the more surprising that the Convention on Human Rights should confer on him this power of calling on governments to furnish explanations as to the way in which they comply with their international obligations.

This power has not yet been exercised, but the time may come when it can be used with important effect. It could at least form the basis for a system of reporting by the Contracting Parties on the way in which their internal law ensures respect for the provisions of the Convention; if this were done, it would correspond broadly to the system instituted by the United Nations of triennial reports on 'general developments and progress achieved in the field of human rights and measures taken to safeguard human liberty in Member States'.[2]

Article 58 of the Convention provides that the expenses of the Commission and the Court shall be borne by the Council of Europe. This means in practice that they are determined by the Committee of Ministers, as explained in Chapter IV.

Article 59 deals with the privileges and immunities to which the members of the Commission and the Court shall be entitled for the unhampered discharge of their functions. Article 40 of the Statute of the Council of Europe already contains general provisions relating to the officials of the organisation; it was supplemented by the General Agreement on Privileges and Immunities of the Council of Europe, signed in Paris on 2 September 1949.[3] A separate Protocol to this Agreement was concluded on 15 December 1956 relating to the privileges and immunities of members of the Commission;[4] and another on 16 December 1961 for the Court.[5] A further Protocol relating to immunities of agents, counsel and witnesses was under discussion during 1962.[6]

[1] There have however been certain developments in recent years. See Robertson, *The Council of Europe, op. cit.*, pp. 71–3.

[2] See Resolution 624 (XXII) of the Economic and Social Council (1956). The action taken on this Resolution is summarised in successive reports of the United Nations Commission on Human Rights.

[3] European Treaty Series, No. 2. See Robertson, *The Council of Europe, op. cit.*, pp. 76–8.

[4] *European Treaty Series*, No. 22.

[5] *Ibid.*, No. 36.

[6] *Fourteenth Report of the Committee of Ministers to the Assembly*, April 1963.

Article 60 of the Convention then provides that its provisions shall not be construed as limiting in any way more favourable provisions in the law of the Contracting Parties or under other international agreements. Article 61 contains a similar provision in relation to the powers of the Committee of Ministers under the Statute of the Council of Europe. Article 62 then states that the Parties will not, except by special agreement, submit a dispute arising under the Convention to a means of settlement other than those provided for therein.

Article 63 is one of particular interest, sometimes known as 'the Colonial Clause'. One of the contentious issues which arose during the course of the negotiations was the question whether the Convention should apply to the overseas and colonial territories of the High Contracting Parties. One view held was that it should be so drafted as to apply automatically to such territories unless they were specifically excluded; the other view was that it should only apply in the first place to the metropolitan territories, but be capable of extension to overseas territories by express declaration. The protagonists of the first view were anxious to secure as extensive an application of the Convention as possible and felt that the governments were less likely to exclude the colonial territories if such exclusion involved a public declaration. The advocates of the second view maintained that certain countries, particularly the United Kingdom, could not constitutionally apply the Convention to their colonial territories without first consulting the colonial legislatures. Therefore, if extension to the colonies were automatic, it would not be possible for the governments of these countries to ratify the Convention before consulting a large number of separate legislatures to obtain their approval. Consequently, the practical result of the formula proposed would be to delay the ratification of the Convention by some of the principal signatories for such period as would be necessary for these consultations to take place—which might mean a very considerable delay. Belgium, France, the Netherlands, and the United Kingdom were all directly interested in this question, which, of course, had important political aspects.

The matter was referred for decision to the Committee of Ministers which, in August 1950, decided in favour of an article requiring express declarations by the High Contracting Parties before the Convention would extend to their colonial territories. This article provoked a lively discussion in the Assembly during the course of its examination of the draft Convention later in the same month, and a strong feeling was expressed by some members in favour of the principle of automatic extension. The Assembly inserted in its Recommendation[1] a paragraph calling on the Ministers to delete the 'colonial clause' which they had incorporated in their draft, which would mean that the Convention would apply automatically to overseas territories.[2] This Recommendation was considered by the Committee of Ministers in November, but was not found acceptable, with the result that Article 63 remained in the final text as approved by the Ministers in August; that is to say that any State may at the time of ratification or subsequently declare that the Convention shall extend to all or any of the territories for whose international relations it is responsible.

In accordance with this provision, the Danish Government, in April 1953, extended the application of the Convention to Greenland, the Netherlands Government in November 1955 to Surinam and the Netherlands West Indies, and the British Government in October 1953 to forty-one overseas territories.[3]

It was of course an excellent development that the Convention on Human Rights should apply in so many other parts of the world. This led to interesting developments when some of the territories concerned achieved independence, which will be considered in a later chapter.[4]

Article 64 then deals with reservations. They are permitted, but only 'in respect of any particular provision of the Convention, to the extent that any law in force . . . is not in conformity with the provision'. In that case the reservation must contain a brief statement of the law concerned. Reservations of a general character are not permitted.

---

[1] Recommendation 24, *Recommendations and Resolutions*, August 1950, p. 34.

[2] This paragraph was not the result of a proposal by the Legal Committee, whose Chairman opposed it during the debate. It was adopted by a narrow majority of 46 votes to 37. (Paragraph VII of Recommendation 24 of 25 August 1950.)

[3] The list is given in Appendix 3.

[4] See below, Ch. X, Sec. 2. Cf. K. Vasak : 'De la Convention Européenne à la Convention Africaine des Droits de l'Homme', *Revue Juridique et Politique d'Outre-Mer*, janvier–mars 1962, pp. 59–76.

A number of reservations have in fact been made and are set out in Appendix 3. Article 2 of the Protocol, on the right to education, is the provision which has given rise to the largest number.[1] The most interesting reservation is perhaps that of Norway in relation to Article 9 of the Convention on freedom of thought, conscience and religion. Article 2 of the Norwegian Constitution of 17 May 1814 contained a ban on Jesuits and Norway therefore only ratified the Convention subject to this limitation on its application of Article 9. A few years later the Norwegian Constitution was amended in this respect and on 4 December 1956 the reservation was withdrawn[2]—thus affording an interesting illustration of the way in which the European Convention can influence even the constitutions of the Member States.

Article 65 of the Convention then provides for the possibility of denunciation, which may only take place five years after a State has become a Party and after six months' notice. Denunciation will not affect the obligations of the denouncing State arising out of acts performed before the denunciation becomes effective. A State which ceases to be a Member of the Council of Europe will automatically cease to be a Party to the Convention.

Article 66 contains the arrangements about signature and ratification. Ten ratifications were necessary for the Convention to enter into force. It is to be noted that the Convention is only open to signature by Members of the Council of Europe; in this respect it differs from the usual practice established in the conventions and agreements subsequently concluded by the Members of the Council, which usually contain a clause providing that the Committee of Ministers may invite non-Member States to accede. In 1962 the Consultative Assembly proposed that the Convention on Human Rights should be amended so as to permit accession in this way;[3] but the Committee of Ministers had not taken a decision on this proposal by the end of the year.

[1] See above, Ch. II, Sec. 3, and Appendix 3.

[2] *Yearbook of the Convention*, Vol. 1, 1955–7, p. 42.

[3] Recommendation 316, *Texts Adopted by the Assembly*, May 1962.

CHAPTER VII

THE LAWLESS CASE

1. *The Facts of the Case*

GERARD RICHARD LAWLESS was arrested by agents of the Government of Ireland on 11 July 1957 and was detained without trial in a military detention camp (the Curragh) between 13 July and 11 December 1957 in pursuance of an Order made by the Minister of Justice under Section 4 of the Offences Against the State (Amendment) Act, 1940. This Act empowered the Government to arrest and detain persons without trial when it considered that the exercise of such powers was necessary to preserve peace and public order and after it had made a proclamation to that effect. Such a proclamation had been made on 5 July 1957 after a series of incidents disturbing the peace; and it was in accordance with the powers thus conferred on the Government that Lawless was arrested as being a suspected member of an illegal organisation, namely the Irish Republican Army.

On 8 September 1957 Lawless exercised the right conferred upon him by Section 8 of the 1940 Act to apply to have the continuation of his detention considered by the Detention Commission which had been set up by the Government in accordance with the Act; he appeared before the Commission on 17 September 1957 assisted by a solicitor and counsel. The following day, however, he also took *habeas corpus* proceedings in the High Court under Article 40 of the Irish Constitution to test the legality of his detention under the relevant provisions of the Constitution and of Irish law. The Detention Commission thereupon adjourned its consideration of the case pending the outcome of the *habeas corpus* proceedings in the ordinary courts.

In the High Court the Commandant of the military prison camp where Lawless was detained opposed the motion for a *habeas corpus* order, relying upon the order for his detention made by the Minister for Justice under the 1940 Act. The High Court delivered judgment on 11 October 1957, upholding the cause of detention shown by the Commandant and rejecting the application for *habeas corpus*.

On 14 October 1957, Lawless appealed to the Supreme Court, invoking not only the Constitution and laws of the Republic but also the provisions of the European Convention on Human Rights. The Supreme Court dismissed the appeal on 6 November 1957, and on 3 December 1957, delivered a reasoned judgment stating the grounds for dismissal, pointing out that (*a*) the constitutional validity of the Offences Against the State (Amendment) Act, 1940, was not open to question, and (*b*) the European Convention on Human Rights did not form part of the municipal law of the Irish Republic.[1]

Meanwhile, on 8 November 1957—that is two days after the announcement of the Supreme Court's rejection of his appeal—Lawless transmitted an application to the European Commission on Human Rights. In the application he alleged that his arrest and detention under the 1940 Act without charge or trial violated the Convention and claimed:

a. immediate release from detention;
b. payment of compensation and damages for his detention; and
c. payment of all the costs and expenses of the proceedings in the Irish courts and before the Commission to secure his release.

Shortly afterwards, the Detention Commission resumed its consideration of the case under Section 8 of the 1940 Act and held hearings for that purpose on 6 and 10 December 1957. On the latter date, at the invitation of the Attorney-General, Lawless in person before the Detention Commission gave a verbal undertaking that he would not 'engage in any illegal activities under the Offences Against the State Acts, 1939 and 1940', and on the following day an Order was made by the Minister for Justice, under Section 6 of the 1940 Act, releasing him from detention.

This was notified to the European Commission of Human Rights by his solicitor in a letter dated 16 December 1957. The letter at the same time stated that he intended to continue the proceedings before the Commission with regard to (*a*) the claim to compensation and damages for his detention, and (*b*) the claim to be reimbursed all costs and expenses in connection with the proceedings undertaken to obtain his release.

[1] The judgment of the Supreme Court of Ireland is given in *Yearbook of the Convention*, Vol. 2, 1958–9, pp. 608–26.

2. *The Proceedings before the Commission*

Under Article 33 of the Convention, the Commission meets *in camera*. Article 31 also provides that, in the event of failure of the attempts at friendly settlement (which occurred in this case) the Commission's report shall be transmitted to the Committee of Ministers, whose proceedings and documents are confidential; the report shall also be transmitted to the State concerned, which shall not be at liberty to publish it. The report of the Commission is not, therefore, a public document and has not been available for preparation of this chapter. The proceedings of the Court, on the other hand, are public and together with the communiqués issued to the Press by the Council of Europe are the source of the information contained herein.

The whole basis for the application to the Commission was that the arrest and detention of Lawless were in contravention of Article 5 of the Convention on Human Rights, which—as explained in Chapter II—provides that everyone has the right to liberty and security of person and that no one shall be deprived of his liberty save in certain circumstances which are specifically set out, such as lawful detention after conviction by a competent court. The Commission of Human Rights was unanimous in holding that arrest and detention without trial under the 1940 Act were not in accordance with Article 5 of the Convention.

Article 15 of the Convention, however, provides as follows:

In time of war or other public emergency threatening the life of the nation any High Contracting Party may take measures derogating from its obligations under this Convention to the extent strictly required by the exigencies of the situation, provided that such measures are not inconsistent with its other obligations under international law.

Moreover, any Party availing itself of this right of derogation is required to inform the Secretary-General of the Council of Europe of the measures taken and the reasons therefor. The Government had in fact informed the Secretary-General of the measures taken in a letter of 20 July 1957; the Commission, while of opinion that this letter did not indicate with sufficient clearness the reasons for the derogation, nevertheless accepted this letter as complying with the requirements of Article 15.

The crucial question, therefore, was whether or not at the relevant dates there existed 'a public emergency threatening the life of the nation' within the meaning of Article 15. Now it might be argued that this was a question of fact which could only be determined, in the light of all the circumstances, by the Government of the State concerned, to which alone all the facts would be known. This view, however, had already been rejected by the Commission when considering the *Cyprus* case, brought by Greece against the United Kingdom in 1956.[1] The Commission had then taken the view that:

a. The Commission always has the competence and the duty under Article 15 to examine and pronounce upon a Government's determination of the existence of a public emergency threatening the life of the nation for the purpose of that Article; but

b. some discretion and some margin of appreciation must be allowed to a Government in determining whether there exists a public emergency which threatens the life of the nation and which must be dealt with by exceptional measures derogating from its normal obligations under the Convention.

This position of principle was endorsed in the Lawless case. The Commission then concluded, by a majority of 9 votes to 5, that 'in making a determination on 5 July 1957 that there existed in the Republic of Ireland a public emergency threatening the life of the nation, the Respondent Government did not go beyond the proper margin of discretion allowed to it under Article 15, paragraph (1)'. This decision then led to consideration of the further question: whether the arrest and detention of persons without trial was a measure 'strictly required by the exigencies of the situation'. This question the Commission also answered in the affirmative, by a majority of 8 votes to 6, so that the conclusion of the Commission on the issue as a whole was that the facts found did not disclose a breach of the Convention by the Irish Government. The report of the Commission to this effect was transmitted to the Committee of Ministers of the Council of Europe on 1 February 1960.

Having reached this conclusion, the Commission then had to decide whether to limit itself to the transmission of its report to the Committee of Ministers, or whether to refer the matter to the Court of Human Rights. On 1 April 1960 it decided on the latter course, on the ground that the Lawless application raised

[1] See above, Ch. III, Sec. 4.

issues which were of fundamental importance in the application of the Convention. The Commission pointed out that it had been divided, with a substantial minority vote, on two questions arising under Article 15; it had therefore decided to refer the case to the Court for an authoritative decision. At the same time, the Commission pointed out that its decision to refer the case to the Court was not to be understood as qualifying in any way its opinion that the facts found did not disclose any breach by the Irish Government of its obligations under the Convention. On the contrary, the Commission asked the Court to confirm the opinions expressed by the Commission on the various matters dealt with in its Report and to find that no breach of the Convention by the Government had been established.

3. *The Preliminary Objections on Procedure*

The reference of the case by the Commission to the Court raised for the first time the problem of the role of the Commission in such circumstances. Was the Commission to appear as a party to the proceedings before the Court? If so, was the Commission to act as the advocate of the individual applicant, since he himself could not be heard, though justice required that his case should be stated? Was the Court to re-examine all the facts of the case or would it accept the findings of the Commission? Was the Commission authorised to transmit to the Court its report, which had been drawn up for the Committee of Ministers, when there was no provision to that effect in the Convention and this was bound to have the result of destroying, in whole or in part, its confidential character? If the Commission was not to act as the advocate of the applicant, how, if at all, was his point of view to be brought to the Court's attention?

To deal with the simpler problems first, that of transmission of the Commission's report to the Court was settled quite simply on a basis of common sense. It would obviously facilitate the proceedings that the report should be available to the Court and the latter clearly expected it, since paragraph 2 of Rule 29 of the Rules of Court reads as follows:

The Court shall, whether a case is referred to it by a Contracting Party or by the Commission, take into consideration the report of the latter.

The Commission thus transmitted its report to the Court and the correctness of this procedure has never been questioned.

As regards the right of the Commission to take part in the proceedings before the Court, the latter evidently considered this question when drawing up its rules. Paragraph 1 of Rule 29 reads as follows:

The Commission shall delegate one or more of its members to take part in the consideration of a case before the Court. The delegates may, if they so desire, have the assistance of any person of their choice.

Rule 21 of the Commission's Rules of Procedure contains a corresponding provision. In accordance with these texts then, the Commission, when referring the Lawless case to the Court on 1 April 1960, appointed Professor C. H. M. Waldock, its President, as its principal delegate and Mr. C. Th. Eustathiades and Mr. S. Petrén as assistant delegates. The nature of their rôle before the Court was thus described by Professor Waldock in his opening address:

The fact that in every case the Commission has to conduct an objective and impartial investigation into the facts and the law, and has confidentially to place itself at the disposal of the Parties for the purpose of seeking a friendly settlement of the case, makes it impossible for the Commission, when the case comes before the Court, to depart from its objectivity and impartiality, and impossible for it to identify itself either with the Government or with the individual.

This is not to say, Mr. President, that being objective and impartial is inconsistent with the Commission's having to express its opinion on the case. On the contrary, the Convention requires the Commission to state its opinion in its Report, and in the present case the Commission has given its opinion. But for the Commission to express its opinion on a case is one thing, and for it to take up the case of one side and to contend for the success of that case before the Court is quite another thing.

It is thus clearly established that the Commission does not consider that it should discharge the rôle of advocate for the individual applicant in the proceedings before the Court. The problem how the individual's case is to be presented to the Court thus still subsists.

It is clear, however, that the Commission has considered this problem. On 30 March 1960, the Commission adopted a new Rule 76 of its Rules of Procedure, reading as follows:

When a case brought before the Commission in pursuance of Article 25 of the Convention is subsequently referred to the Court, the Secretary of the Commission shall immediately notify the Applicant. Unless the Commission shall otherwise decide, the Secretary shall also in due course communicate to him the Commission's Report, informing him that he may, within a time limit fixed by the President, submit to the Commission his written observations on the said Report. The Commission shall decide what action, if any, shall be taken in respect of these observations.

In accordance with this provision, the Commission transmitted its report to the individual applicant on 13 April 1960—that is, after referring the case to the Court—and invited him to submit his observations to the Commission. At the same time, the Commission pointed out that the document must be kept secret and that the applicant was not entitled to publish it. The first objection made by the Government of Ireland to the procedure in the case related to this publication of the report.[1]

The publication of the report: The Government's argument may be summarised as follows: The Convention (as mentioned above) provides in its Article 31 that the Commission's report shall be transmitted to the Committee of Ministers and to the Governments concerned, which shall not be at liberty to publish it. It is therefore clearly the intention that the report shall be kept secret and not open to publication; and the absence of any provision in the Convention authorising its transmission to an individual is no mere accident. Furthermore, it was argued, the Government continued to be bound by the obligation of secrecy even after the case had been referred to the Court; it was inconceivable that a State should be in a position of inferiority to the Commission as regards the obligation of secrecy. In the course of the oral hearings, the Attorney-General of Ireland even disclosed

---

[1] The Irish Government also objected to the jurisdiction on the ground that the Commission had adopted its report on 19 December 1959 but only transmitted it to the Committee of Ministers and the Government on 1 February 1960. This meant that the decision to refer the case to the Court, taken on 1 April 1960, was within three months of the date of actual transmission of the report but not within three months of the date at which the report should, in the Government's view, have been transmitted. This objection was, however, withdrawn during the course of the oral hearings.

that the Government had asked the Committee of Ministers to publish the Commission's conclusion that no violation of the Convention had occurred, but this request was refused. Since the Commission had no means of compelling the applicant to respect the obligation of secrecy, this meant that the Government was even in a position of inferiority by comparison with him. The Government therefore asked the Court to hold that the publication of the report by the Commission was in contravention of the Convention and that Rule 76 was *ultra vires*.

The Commission's point of view on this preliminary objection was to recognise that Article 31 of the Convention imposed an obligation of secrecy as regards the publication of the report but to maintain that this was limited in two respects. First, it related to publication to the Press or to third parties but not to communication to a party to the proceedings; 'obvious considerations of equity militate in favour of a party to the proceedings before the Commission being informed of the Commission's conclusions concerning his own case'. Secondly, the obligation to secrecy, it was argued, related to the Commission's report once it had been transmitted to the Committee of Ministers and *while the case was pending before the Committee of Ministers*. The report should then be kept secret in order to make possible a last attempt at conciliation, in confidential discussions, before the Committee of Ministers was called on to decide whether a breach had occurred. The President of the Commission was able to quote from the *travaux préparatoires* to show that this was the intention of the authors of the Convention in inserting the stipulation of secrecy. However, once the matter was referred to the Court of Human Rights, the provisions of secrecy which relate to the proceedings before the Committee of Ministers would no longer apply and the problem should then be viewed in quite a new light, as the proceedings before the Court are public. It is to be observed, moreover, that the Commission's Rule 76 only provides for communication of the report to the individual applicant *after* the case has been referred to the Court. At that stage, the President of the Commission stated, the Commission considers that 'it is free, if it thinks fit, to publish or to communicate to any person the contents of its report in connection with proceedings before the Court'.

I

The rôle of the individual in the proceedings before the court: In accordance with its Rule 76, the Commission not only communicated the report to the individual applicant but also invited his written observations thereon. This was done with a view to transmitting them, if thought appropriate, in due course to the Court. This was the way in which the Commission sought to make it possible for the individual's point of view to be communicated to the Court even though he had no *locus standi* as a party to the proceedings. In its Memorial, the Commission specifically asked the Court:

1. to give leave for the Commission to submit to the Court the applicant's comments on the Commission's Report as one of Commission's documents in the case; and
2. in general, to give directions as to the right of the Commission to communicate to the Court the comments of the applicant in regard to matters arising in the proceedings.

The Irish Government took strong exception to this procedure. It pointed out that in the course of the *travaux préparatoires*, the Committee of Senior Officials which undertook the final drafting of the Convention had 'thought it necessary to point out clearly that only the High Contracting Parties and the Commission and not private individuals shall have the right to bring a case before the Court'. This, indeed, is stated *expressis verbis* in Article 44 of the Convention. The Government's Counter-Memorial continued:

The Commission in its present Memorial recognises this as being the position, but it attempts by a subterfuge to bestow on the individual the quality of a party before the Court, by enabling the individual to make submissions to the Court in the form of a document which the Commission wishes to annex to its Memorial, and further by seeking directions as to the communication to the Court of the comments of the applicant in regard to matters arising in the present proceedings. If this were permitted the Applicant would be enabled to play an active part in the proceedings before the Court in much the same way as if he were a party.

The Commission is in this way attempting to modify the Convention by an oblique procedure and without the approval of the High Contracting Parties who are the authors of the Convention.

The President of the Commission, however, adduced during the oral hearings some powerful arguments in support of the latter's position. He pointed out, in the first place, that the Convention was quite silent as to the position of the individual in the proceedings before the Court but that the Commission 'found it difficult to attribute to the authors of the Convention an intention to place an impenetrable curtain between the individual and an organ specifically set up as a judicial tribunal to make a judicial determination of his case'. The Commission agreed with the Government that Article 44 of the Convention clearly prevented an individual from appearing before the Court as a party to the proceedings, but it could not accept that this article was intended to prevent him from having any contact at all with the proceedings before the Court. The individual and the Government were on a footing of equality before the Commission; the Commission's report was a new factor in the case now before the Court; the Government would have every opportunity of challenging the contents of this report in the proceedings before the Court; the individual must be given, by some means or other, a similar opportunity.

In support of this view the President of the Commission cited the Opinion of the International Court of Justice in the case of the judgments of the Administrative Tribunal of the International Labour Organisation.[1] This concerned an appeal by UNESCO to the International Court against judgments of the Administrative Tribunal in favour of four individuals; under Article 66 of the Statute of the Court only States and international organisations have access to the Court; the latter nevertheless held that:

the judicial character of the Court requires that both sides directly affected by these proceedings should be in a position to submit their views and their argument to the Court.

and arrangements were made that UNESCO would transmit to the Court the observations in writing of the individuals concerned. In replying to this point, however, the Irish Attorney-General distinguished the UNESCO case on the ground that the procedure then followed was adopted after discussion, and by agreement with the organisation; in the present case he objected to the action of the Commission, which had been taken without consulting, and contrary to the wishes of, the Irish Government.

[1] *I.C.J. Reports*, 1956, p. 57 at p. 86.

He recognised that the acceptance of his view would place the individual in a certain position of inequality, but he thought this was 'more fanciful than real', and continued:

The inequality, such as it is, is in my submission, deliberate, not in the sense of States wishing to place individual citizens at a disadvantage, but because in agreeing to the limited, I concede very limited, jurisdiction of the Court created by the Convention, States went as far as it appeared to them that they would be warranted in doing at present in recognising, for individuals, a status of any kind in international law.

The Commission had also noticed that the Court itself had not apparently intended to shut itself off from any contact with the individual applicant. Rule 29 of the Rules of Court provides that the delegates of the Commission in the proceedings before the Court 'may, if they so desire, have the assistance of any person of their choice'; this certainly seemed to authorise the delegates to refer to the applicant himself, if they wished. The Commission therefore sought the directions of the Court as to the way in which the applicant's comments on the Commission's report or on any new points arising in the course of the proceedings should be brought to the Court's attention. In conclusion, the President of the Commission pointed out that, in raising this point, the Commission was thinking not only of the particular individual whose case was under examination but of all the individuals whose cases might come before the Court for final decision in the years to come.

The formulation of the issues submitted to the Court: The last of the preliminary objections of the Irish Government related to the manner in which the Commission had formulated the issues submitted to the Court. The Commission had, in its Memorial, asked the Court to confirm its view that no breach of the Convention had occurred; nevertheless, in its formal submission to the Court it had phrased the question in the interrogative form and had asked the Court to decide 'whether or not' the Government was guilty of a breach of its obligations under the Convention and, if so, what compensation, if any, was due to the applicant. Having already reached the conclusion, as stated in its own report, that the Government was not in breach of its obligations, the Commission was bound, in the Government's view, to stand by and defend its own conclusions. It was therefore not correct that it should pose a series of questions to the Court, as if the issues were quite open: the most it should have done was to seek the Court's confirmation of its own conclusions. The way in which the Commission had presented the case to the Court showed that 'its concern is to secure from the Court confirmation of its Opinions not in relation to the individual applicant named in this case, but in relation to the rights of all individuals. . . .' this in turn almost amounted to a request for an advisory opinion, for which no provision exists in the Convention.[1] In reply, the President of the Commission pointed out that the object of the Commission had been to present to the Court all possible material on which to base its judgment and that it was only by a majority of 8 votes to 6 that the Commission had reached a decision in favour of the Government. The most objective way of formulating the issue was thus in the simple interrogative form. But this did not amount to a request for an advisory opinion because the Court was now clearly called on to pronounce judgment under Articles 50 to 54 of the Convention.

In effect, the Attorney-General of Ireland did not press this objection during the course of the oral hearings and it was not included in the Government's final submissions to the Court (quoted below). The Court did not, therefore, pronounce on this point.

In conclusion of the oral hearings, the Government asked the Court:

1. to declare that any publication by the Commission of its report, other than that expressly authorised by the Convention, is a breach of the obligations imposed on the Commission by the Convention.

2. to rule that the comments of the applicant on the report of the Commission be not received by the Court.

3. to rule that no further comments of the applicant on matters arising in the proceedings may be received by the Court.

---

[1] The Consultative Assembly of the Council of Europe has proposed that a protocol should be concluded, conferring on the Court the competence to give advisory opinions—Recommendation 232 of 22 January 1960. See further below, Ch. IX.

4. to declare that a correct interpretation of the Convention does not permit of action of the nature contemplated by Rule 76 of the Rules of the Commission.

The Commission had asked the Court to reject the Government's objections as regards the publication of the report to the applicant and as regards the formulation of the issue for the decision of the Court; it then asked for leave to transmit to the Court the written comments of the applicant on the Commission's report and for directions as to the right of the Commission to communicate the applicant's comments on any further matters arising in the course of the proceedings.

The judgment on the preliminary objections: The oral hearings took place on 3 and 4 October 1960, and the Court delivered its judgment on the preliminary objections and questions of procedure on 14 November.[1]

After reciting the facts of the case and the history of the proceedings, it considered first of all the question: 'Is Rule 76 of the Rules of Procedure of the Commission in general contrary to the terms of the Convention?' The Court was here rather cautious as to its own competence in the matter. It pointed out that the Commission and the Court were independent organs set up by the Convention, each with its own functions and responsibilities; and that the Court had no general power to interpret the Convention in an abstract manner but only to decide particular cases referred to it in accordance with Articles 45 and 47. From these considerations it concluded that:

the Court is not competent to take decisions such as that to delete a rule from the Commission's Rules of Procedure—a step which would affect all Parties to the Convention—since this would amount to having power to make rulings on matters of procedure or to render advisory opinions; that accordingly the Court has no power to consider the point raised in a general manner by the Commission and the Irish Government.

[1] Publications of the Court : Series A. Lawless Case (Preliminary Objections and Questions of Procedure). The judges constituting the Chamber which heard this case were : MM. R. Cassin, President, and G. Maridakis, E. Rodenbourg, R. McGonigal (*ex officio* member), G. Balladore Pallieri, E. Arnalds, K. F. Arik. See also M.-A. Eissen, 'Le Premier Arrêt de la Cour Européenne des Droits de l'Homme', *Annuaire Français*, 1960, pp. 444–97.

The Court then turned from the general to the particular, namely to the communication of the Commission's report in this case to Mr. Lawless. It recognised the need for secrecy in the proceedings before the Commission and the Committee of Ministers; but it reaffirmed the public character of the hearings before the Court. After pointing out that this public character attached only to the oral proceedings and the judgment, but not to the documents in the case (except when authorised by the Court), it went on to distinguish between publication in general and communication to the person directly concerned subject to injunctions of secrecy. This distinction led to the conclusion that:

the Court is of the opinion that the Commission is enabled under the Convention to communicate to the Applicant, with the proviso that it must not be published, the whole or part of its Report or a summary thereof, whenever such communication seems appropriate; therefore, in the present case, the Commission, in communicating its Report to G. R. Lawless, the Applicant, did not exceed its powers. . . .

Finally, the Court considered the Commission's request for leave to communicate to the Court the applicant's observations on its own report and on other points which might arise during the proceedings. After reviewing the arguments on both sides, it drew attention to the fact that 'it is in the interests of the proper administration of justice that the Court should have knowledge of and, if need be, take into consideration, the applicant's point of view'. It went on to point out that there already existed three ways in which this could be done: in the Commission's report, in the statements of the delegates of the Commission before the Court and by hearing the applicant as a witness. Its conclusion, then, was that having been unable as yet to examine the merits of the case, it was not in a position to reach a decision on the Commission's request and reserved its right to do so at a later date.

The Court accordingly, by 6 votes to 1, rejected the first, third and fourth of the Government's objections in their final submissions, declared that 'at this stage there is no reason to authorise the Commission to transmit to it the applicant's written observations on the Commission's report', and decided unanimously to proceed to the examination of the merits of the case.

This decision was bound to have important consequences for the future, not only in relation to the Lawless case but also, as stated by the President of the Commission, as a precedent for all future cases brought before the Commission by individual applicants and subsequently referred to the Court.

While the Court considered that it was outside its competence to give a ruling on the general question whether Article 76 of the Commission's Rules of Procedure was in conformity with the Convention, it implicitly validated the rule, since the rule exists and is applied and the only body that could conceivably have invalidated it has declined to do so. Moreover, the Court held that, in this particular case, the communication of the report to Mr. Lawless, with the proviso that he should not publish it, was in order; this would therefore seem to be a clear precedent for the future.

The communication to the applicant, however, was only a first step. The main point of such communication is to permit the applicant to submit his observations on the report to the Commission and to enable the latter, if it considers appropriate, to forward them to the Court. It is the legality of this procedure which is the more important issue. On this point, the Court postponed its decision on the Commission's request for authorisation to submit a memorandum containing the applicant's observations, but it did state that 'it is in the interests of the proper administration of justice that the Court should have knowledge of and, if need be, take into consideration, the applicant's point of view'; moreover, the Court continued, it has at its disposal for this purpose '. . . the written and oral observations of the delegates and counsel of the Commission which, as the defender of the public interest, *is entitled of its own accord to make known the applicant's views to the Court*, even if it does not share them, as a means of throwing light on the points at issue'. This *dictum* was taken by the Commission as a guide for its future conduct and in due course formed the object of further interpretation by the Court at a later stage in the proceedings.

4. The Merits of the Case

A new procedural point came up at the opening of the hearings on the merits. Between the date of the judgment on the preliminary objections (14 November 1960) and the date of the hearings on the merits (7–11 April 1961), further written pleadings were exchanged in the form of a 'Statement' of the Commission (commenting on the Counter-Memorial of the Irish Government filed in August 1960) and 'Observations' of the Government in reply to this Statement. The Commission, in preparing the Statement, considered that it was entitled to submit to the Court the written observations of the applicant on its own earlier report— this evidently in reliance on the Court's decision that 'the Commission was entitled of its own accord . . . to make known the applicant's views to the Court . . . ' Accordingly, it included in the Statement a lengthy passage of nearly twenty pages of the applicant's views; its impartiality in doing so was shown by the fact that these views were in some respects sharply critical of the Commission's own findings and of the reasoning of some of its members. The Government again objected that this was improper. The Court, in a separate decision of 7 April,[1] ruled that the passage in the Commission's statement reproducing the applicant's views was not, at that stage, to be considered as part of the proceedings in the case; nevertheless the Commission could itself 'take account of' the applicant's views and, implicitly, make use of them in the oral hearings. The Court thus gave a rather restrictive interpretation of its own earlier judgment on the preliminary objections: it appears that the Commission may 'take account of' (in French, 'faire état') the applicant's views and summarise or quote them in the oral hearings, but not reproduce them in the written pleadings. This statement may perhaps be amplified as follows. The Court's decision would appear to mean that it is unwilling to allow the Commission simply to reproduce and submit to it extensive extracts from the applicant's own statement—in which case the rôle of the Commission is no more than that of a postbox; the Commission may, however, make use of the applicant's views (even though it does not agree with them) in presenting relevant arguments to the Court—in which case it plays an active rôle on its own responsibility, even though with the assistance of the individual applicant.[2]

[1] Publications of the Court: Series A. Lawless Case—Judgment of 7 April 1961.

[2] The apparent difference between the Court's more liberal attitude in November 1960 and the more restrictive interpretation in April 1961 appears to be due, at least in part, to a difficulty of translation. The earlier judgment,

In fact, during the oral hearings, the President of the Commission, in his capacity as principal delegate, informed the Court orally of the applicant's point of view on the main issues of the case and thus ensured that the Court was in possession of the information necessary to reach its conclusions in full knowledge of all relevant arguments.

On the merits of the case, there were three main issues for decision by the Court, which were the same as those considered by the Commission:

1. Were the arrest and detention of Lawless in contravention of Article 5 of the Convention?
2. If so, could the Government justify its action as a derogation permitted by Article 15? Was there in Ireland in the summer of 1957 'a public emergency threatening the life of the nation'?
3. If so, was the arrest and detention of persons without trial a means 'strictly required by the exigencies of the situation'?

Before coming to consider these questions, however, the Court still had another hurdle to jump, because the Irish Government raised a plea in bar based on Article 17 of the Convention. This article provides as follows:

Nothing in this Convention may be interpreted as implying for any State, group or person any right to engage in any activity or perform any act aimed at the destruction of any of the rights and freedoms set forth herein or at their limitation to a greater extent than is provided for in the Convention.

The Irish Government claimed that Lawless was a member of, or associated with, the Irish Republican Army, which had been banned precisely because it aimed at the destruction of the rights and freedoms set forth in the Convention within the meaning of Article 17; the Convention however must not be used as a pretext to permit him to carry on such activities; therefore it was

---

in French, said that 'la Commission a le droit . . . *de faire état* devant la Cour sous sa propre responsabilité des considérations du requérant . . .' This was translated, on the earlier occasion, as 'The Commission . . . is entitled of its own accord . . . *to make known* the applicant's views to the Court . . .' In the judgment of 7 April 1961, the Court still held that the Commission was entitled 'de faire état' of the applicant's views, but this was translated as 'to take (them) into account'. 'Faire état' is indeed a vague and nebulous expression. But the Court was careful to point out that only the French text was authentic.

claimed that he or any other person or persons in a similar situation could not be permitted to rely on the Convention at all. In support of this contention, the Government relied on the decision of the Commission on the application of the German Communist Party.[1]

The Commission in reply contended that the general purpose of Article 17 is to prevent totalitarian groups from exploiting in their own interest the principles enunciated by the Convention; but that to achieve that purpose it is not necessary to take away every one of the rights and freedoms guaranteed in the Convention from persons found to be engaged in activities aimed at the destruction of any of those rights and freedoms; that Article 17 therefore related essentially to the exercise of those rights (such as freedom of expression and freedom of assembly) which could themselves be used for political activities aimed at the destruction of human rights in general; and that the present case was thus not comparable to that of the German Communist Party and Article 17 therefore did not apply.

On this point, the Court rejected the submission of the Irish Government, holding that the purpose of Article 17 was to make it impossible for individuals to avail themselves of the rights set forth in the Convention in order to destroy human rights and freedoms, but that this could not be construed *a contrario* as depriving them of the fundamental individual rights guaranteed by Articles 5 and 6; Lawless, moreover, had not attempted to rely on the Convention in order to justify or perform improper acts but merely to avoid detention without trial. Article 17 therefore did not apply to his case.

Article 5: The relevant passages of Article 5 were as follows:

1. Everyone has the right to liberty and security of person. No one shall be deprived of his liberty save in the following cases and in accordance with a procedure prescribed by law:
   a. . . . .
   b. . . . .
   c. the lawful arrest or detention of a person effected for the purpose of bringing him before the competent legal authority on reasonable suspicion of having committed an offence or when it is reasonably considered necessary to prevent his committing an offence or fleeing after having done so;

[1] See above, Ch. II, p. 40.

2. . . . .

3. Everyone arrested or detained in accordance with the provisions of paragraph 1 (*c*) of this Article shall be brought promptly before a judge or other officer authorised by law to exercise judicial power and shall be entitled to trial within a reasonable time or to release pending trial. Release may be conditioned by guarantees to appear for trial.

As mentioned above, the Commission of Human Rights was unanimous in holding that arrest and detention without trial under the 1940 Act were not in accordance with Article 5. The Government nevertheless challenged this in the proceedings before the Court, on the ground that para. 1 (*c*) of Article 5 permits 'the lawful arrest or detention of a person . . . when it is reasonably considered necessary to prevent his committing an offence . . .' and that Lawless had in fact been detained precisely for this reason. The Commission in reply argued that it was necessary to look at the whole of para. 1 (*c*), which permits the arrest or detention of a person, in order to prevent his committing an offence, *when this is effected for the purpose of bringing him before the competent legal authority*. Paragraph 3 of Article 5, moreover, the Commission argued, made it perfectly clear that arrest or detention as authorised in paragraph 1 must only be a preliminary stage before the person detained is brought before a judge for trial. In reply to this argument, the Government claimed that the clear meaning of Article 5 could be found in the *travaux prépara-toires*. The original text of paragraph 1 (*c*) of Article 5 (which had been proposed by the United Kingdom) read:

the lawful arrest or detention of a person effected for the purpose of . . . etc. . . . *or which* is reasonably considered necessary to prevent his committing an offence. . . .

This showed, in the Government's submission, that the words 'effected for the purpose of bringing him before the competent legal authority' related only to cases of reasonable suspicion that an offence has been committed and *not* to cases of reasonable suspicion that an offence is about to be committed. Moreover, as regards paragraph 3 of Article 5, the earlier text limited this *expressis verbis* to cases of arrest or detention 'on a charge of having committed a crime'. Admittedly both texts had subsequently been altered but, the Government claimed, this was only done in the course of final comparison of the English and French texts and revision of the translation. No intention to change the sense of the earlier text could be traced in the *travaux préparatoires*. Therefore it was argued that the clear sense of the earlier text must be held to prevail over the Commission's interpretation of the final ambiguous text.

As the Commission pointed out, the *travaux préparatoires* of Article 5, when closely examined, do not appear to bear out the Government's deduction from them. The Court, however, did not find it necessary to examine the *travaux préparatoires*, for it upheld the Commission's interpretation of Article 5, on the ground that the plain and natural meaning of the words used was that which the Commission gave to them; and it further pointed out that the construction advocated by the Government would open the door wide to arrest and detention on suspicion without the requirement of bringing to trial. This meant that in the view of the Court the arrest and detention of Lawless were incompatible with Article 5,[1] and the Court then went on to examine whether the action of the Government could be justified by reason of its power to derogate under Article 15.

Article 15: The most interesting part of the case related to the validity of the Irish Government's derogation under the provisions of Article 15. If the derogation was valid, then the application would fail even though the applicant's arrest and detention were inconsistent with the provisions of Article 5.

The full text of Article 15 is as follows:

1. In time of war or other public emergency threatening the life of the nation any High Contracting Party may take measures derogating from its obligations under this Convention to the extent strictly required by the exigencies of the situation, provided that such measures are not inconsistent with its other obligations under international law.

2. No derogation from Article 2, except in respect of deaths resulting from lawful acts of war, or from Articles 3, 4 (paragraph 1) and 7 shall be made under this provision.

[1] The applicant had also claimed that his arrest and detention contravened Article 7 of the Convention, which prohibits the retroactive application of the law. The Commission having rejected this contention, the Irish Government naturally did not re-open it before the Court, and the latter upheld the view of the Commission.

3. Any High Contracting Party availing itself of this right of derogation shall keep the Secretary-General of the Council of Europe fully informed of the measures which it has taken and the reasons therefor. It shall also inform the Secretary-General of the Council of Europe when such measures have ceased to operate and the provisions of the Convention are again being fully executed.

'In time of war or other public emergency threatening the life of the nation' are strong words. Ireland was not at war in the summer of 1957; had there been a 'public emergency threatening the life of the nation'? The Commission had answered this question in the affirmative, but by a majority vote of 9 votes to 5. The Court now had to decide.

In the proceedings before the Commission, the Irish Government had cited a series of facts from which they deduced the existence of a public emergency threatening the life of the nation. The question of general principle which arose was whether the Court could now, so to speak, substitute itself for the Government and pass judgment on the conclusions that the latter had drawn.

This, the Government argued, was outside the competence of the Commission or the Court:

No machinery is provided under the Convention to enable a Government to take the opinion of the Commission or of the Court as to the existence of a state of emergency, or as to the measures which are necessary to deal with such an emergency, and it is inconceivable that a Government acting in good faith should be held to be in breach of their obligations under the Convention merely because their appreciation of the circumstances which constitute an emergency, or of the measures necessary to deal with the emergency, should differ from the views of the Commission or of the Court.

The Government recognised the danger that if a determination of this sort were left to the sole discretion of individual governments, then a government which wished to embark on a totalitarian policy might falsely claim the existence of a state of emergency and thus improperly suspend a number of guarantees. But this danger, it argued, was countered by Article 18 of the Convention, which reads:

The restrictions permitted under this Convention to the said rights and freedoms shall not be applied for any purpose other than those for which they have been prescribed. . . .

It would therefore be possible for the Court to determine, in the light of Article 18, whether or not a Government was acting in good faith. The Irish Government therefore asked the Court to declare that 'if, having regard to Article 18, the facts show that the Government acted in good faith, their appreciation of the situation or of the measures necessary to deal with it ought not to be set aside in favour of the appreciation of some other body, whether the Commission or the Court, not charged with the duty of maintaining law, order and good government in the territory of that Government'.

The point of view of the Commission was very different. It had indeed already come up against this problem in a different context, that is to say in the case brought by Greece against the United Kingdom relating to the emergency measures in Cyprus, with respect to which the British Government had made a similar derogation under Article 15 of the Convention. The Commission had then laid down the following rules:[1]

a. the Commission always has the competence and the duty under Article 15 to examine and pronounce upon a Government's determination of the existence of a public emergency threatening the life of the nation for the purpose of that Article; but

b. some discretion and some margin of appreciation must be allowed to a Government in determining whether there exists a public emergency which threatens the life of the nation and which must be dealt with by exceptional measures derogating from its normal obligations under the Convention.

This led to what came to be known as the doctrine of 'margin of appreciation'. The Commission could and must look behind the Government's own appraisal of the situation; nevertheless, the Government should be allowed a margin of discretion, having regard to its responsibilities for keeping law and order and to the fact that it was likely to have at its disposal sources of information which could not be available to the Commission. The President of the Commission explained this to the Court on 10 April 1961 as follows:

[1] Cf. *supra*, p. 115.

The concept behind this doctrine is that Article 15 has to be read in the context of the rather special subject matter with which it deals: the responsibilities of a Government for maintaining law and order in times of war or public emergency threatening the life of the nation. The concept of the margin of appreciation is that a Government's discharge of these responsibilities is essentially a delicate problem of appreciating complex factors and of balancing conflicting considerations of the public interest; and that, once the Commission or the Court is satisfied that the Government's appreciation is at least on the margin of the powers conferred by Article 15, then the interest which the public itself has in effective Government and in the maintenance of order justifies and requires a decision in favour of the legality of the Government's appreciation.

This view was reaffirmed by the Commission in the Lawless case but strongly attacked by the Irish Government, which asked the Court to declare that the Commission had 'erred in principle in its approach to the application of Article 15'.

The applicant of course took a wholly different view. He argued that before a Government is entitled to make a derogation under Article 15, it has the obligation of satisfying the Commission first as to the existence of the emergency, and secondly that neither the ordinary Courts nor any special criminal courts were able to function and deal with the threat to the life of the nation. The burden of proof, he argued, is on the government and it should produce evidence that can satisfy the Commission or the Court objectively—such as sworn evidence by a responsible Minister or other public official, which could be tested in cross-examination. The applicant in fact submitted a sworn affidavit by the Lord Mayor of Dublin in support of his view (that there was not an emergency threatening the life of the nation), which, he alleged, remained uncontroverted. He proposed four objective tests to determine whether such an emergency existed: whether (1) the government and parliament, (2) the Courts, and (3) the public administration were functioning normally; and (4) had there been any major upheaval or disaster in the country? He contended that the answers to these questions showed clearly that no emergency existed of the gravity that had been alleged.

The Commission's reply to this was that there was little difference of opinion as to the general facts of the situation; the dispute was as to the proper interpretation of the facts. In order

to interpret them, it maintained its doctrine of margin of appreciation and left it to the Court to decide which approach was the
right one.

On the general issue of principle, the Court decided against the
Government's view that once its good faith was established neither
the Commission nor the Court could look into the matter further.
It held that 'it is for the Court to decide whether the conditions
laid down in Article 15 for the exercise of the exceptional right
of derogation have been fulfilled in the present case' and again
'the Court must determine whether the facts and circumstances
which led the Irish Government to make their proclamation of
7 July 1957 come within this conception' (i.e. of an emergency
threatening the life of the nation). Nevertheless, on the facts of
the case, the Court held that the Government was justified in
the conclusion which it reached; the existence at the time of a
public emergency threatening the life of the nation was reasonably
deduced by the Irish Government from a combination of several
factors: the existence of a secret army engaged in unconstitutional
activities and using violence to attain its ends; secondly, the fact
that this illegal army also operated outside the territory of the
State, thus jeopardising relations between Ireland and its northern
neighbour; and thirdly, the steady and alarming increase in ter-
rorist activities during the autumn of 1956 and the first half of
1957. In this respect, therefore, the Court endorsed the findings
of the Commission in favour of the Irish Government; as regards
the 'margin of appreciation' theory, the Court did not endorse this
expressis verbis, but its whole approach to the matter was consistent with that of the Commission.

It then became material to enquire whether the arrest and
detention of persons without trial were measures 'strictly required by the exigencies of the situation'. The Commission had
answered this question in the affirmative, but only by the narrow
majority of 8 votes to 6. The eight members forming the majority,
taking into account the particular danger to be met, the alternative measures available to the Government, the safeguard provided
by the right of the applicant to have the continuation of his
detention considered by the Detention Commission and the
Government's practice of releasing any detained person willing
to give an undertaking in regard to his future conduct, had
concluded that in adopting the measure of detention without

K

trial in the special circumstances obtaining in Ireland, the Respondent Government did not go beyond its proper margin of appreciation under Article 15 of the Convention. Of the remaining six members of the Commission, five had already held that the facts did not disclose the existence of a public emergency threatening the life of the nation; the remaining member, while accepting the existence of such an emergency, thought that the Irish Government could have adopted less extreme measures than arrest and detention without trial.

The Government in its counter-memorial did not adduce any new arguments or evidence, because of its claim that, once the good faith of a government had been established, the Commission and the Court were not entitled to set aside its appreciation of the situation and of the measures necessary to deal with it.

The Court, after asserting its right to examine whether the Government's appreciation was justified, came to the conclusion that it was. It cited the facts that the ordinary processes of law had not been able to check the growing danger in the Republic; that the ordinary criminal courts, and even special and military courts, could not suffice to restore law and order; the great difficulty of collecting evidence against persons involved in the activities of the I.R.A.—partly due to fear of reprisals; and the fact that the sealing of the border (which might have been used to prevent raids into Northern Ireland) 'would have had extremely serious repercussions on the population as a whole, beyond the extent required by the exigencies of the emergency'. The Court also pointed out that the emergency measures applied were not used abusively, but were subject to a number of safeguards, including reports to Parliament, the existence of a Detention Commission and the release of persons who gave an undertaking to respect the law. Having thus admitted the justification of the emergency measures in general, the Court went on to enquire whether they were properly applied in the particular case of Lawless, and reached the conclusion that they were.

A final point arose under paragraph 3 of Article 15: The applicant claimed that the Irish Government's communication to the Secretary-General of the Council of Europe of 20 July 1957 was not an effective notice of derogation within the meaning of that paragraph, because it did not state that it was a notice of derogation and did not adduce the existence of a state of emergency threatening the life of the nation; moreover, he claimed that, even if it was effective, it had only been made public in Ireland on 23 October 1957, and could not be enforced with respect to events occurring before that date.[1]

On grounds of principle, this last argument was not without force. Everyone should be in a position to know whether the rights to which he is entitled under the Convention have been modified by a Government's recourse to its exceptional power to derogate from the Convention under Article 15. For more than three months after the emergency measures were in force, it was not known in Ireland that the Government had made a derogation under Article 15. If a derogation published in October was effective in July, could it not be argued that its application was retroactive? On the other hand, it could be said on behalf of the Government that its proclamation bringing into force the exceptional power to detain persons without trial under the 1940 Act had been brought to the attention of everyone in Ireland by being duly promulgated on 5 July 1957.

The Court held that the Government's communication, whatever its exact wording, had in fact given the Secretary-General sufficient information about the measures taken and the reasons therefor; and that the Convention did not require publication of the notice of derogation, but merely its communication to the Secretary-General of the Council of Europe.

It is curious that of all the many and complex arguments used in this case, the Irish Government—adopting perhaps the habits of one of their near neighbours—had lost practically every battle but the last. It had objected to the communication of the Commission's report to the applicant and to the Commission's proposal to inform the Court of the applicant's views thereon. Subsequently, on the merits of the case, it had claimed that Article 17 debarred the applicant from relying on the Convention at all; that Article 5 permitted detention without trial for the purpose of preventing the commission of an offence; and that, once a government's good faith is established, both the Commission and the Court must accept its appreciation of the existence of an emergency and of the measures necessary to deal with it. On all

---

[1] This last argument had not been used before the Commission. It was one of the additional observations made by the applicant to the Commission, after receiving its report, and was submitted by the Commission to the Court.

these points, the Court decided against the Irish Government. Yet on the crucial points of the existence of an emergency threatening the life of the nation and whether the measures taken were strictly required by the exigencies of the situation—points which, at least in the written pleadings, were not developed at all in the statement of its case—the Government's point of view prevailed and its action was upheld by the Court.

One of the most important aspects of this case is undoubtedly the precedent it will set for the future on relations between the Court, the Commission and the applicant. While respecting the provisions of the Convention to the effect that the applicant cannot be a party to its proceedings, the Court has nevertheless approved a procedure which permits his views to be made known to it, thus respecting the principle of *audi alteram partem*. This is an important innovation. Furthermore, the Court has upheld its own right and that of the Commission 'to examine and pronounce on a Government's determination of the existence of a public emergency threatening the life of the nation' and of the appropriateness of the measures taken; moreover, on the last point, the Court not only examined, in general terms, whether the measures taken were strictly necessary but also how they were applied in the particular case. In so doing, it has laid down important rules for the future which will undoubtedly reinforce the value of the Convention as an international guarantee for the protection of human rights and as a safeguard against the danger of authoritarian government.

In conclusion, when recounting this first case that has been through all the various stages of consideration by the two organs set up by the European Convention on Human Rights, one cannot help but notice the ponderous nature and protracted character of the proceedings. The application was filed on 8 November 1957. Written and oral pleadings were then submitted before the application was declared admissible on 30 August 1958. A Sub-Commission was then appointed, as required by the Convention, to ascertain the facts; it received and considered further written and oral pleadings and held no fewer than six sessions and meetings. On 20 April 1959 it proffered its good offices with a view to reaching a friendly settlement but, this having proved impossible, it remitted the matter to the full Commission. The latter drew up and, on 19 December 1959, adopted a report which was transmitted to the Committee of Ministers on 1 February 1960. Then, on 12 April 1960, the Commission referred the matter to the Court. After a further exchange of pleadings, hearings took place on the preliminary objections in October 1960 and judgment was given in November. More pleadings were exchanged before the hearings on the merits took place in the following April, after which judgment was pronounced on 1 July 1961, three years and eight months after the application was filed.

To put the matter in perspective it must, of course, be remembered that in the case of municipal courts recourse to the highest tribunal inevitably takes a long time and that proceedings before an international court can hardly be more rapid; moreover, in the Lawless case, the fact that the Irish Government raised preliminary objections on procedure added substantially to its duration. Nevertheless, it should not be impossible to find a way of accelerating the proceedings before the Commission and the Court. In fact, the Committee of Ministers of the Council of Europe in 1960 appointed a committee of governmental experts to consider various proposals for concluding a Second Protocol to the Convention on Human Rights and to study other matters relating to the Convention.[1] It is to be hoped that this committee will agree on, and that the governments will accept, measures which will not only give additional guarantees to the individual citizen but also improve and accelerate the procedure for the protection of his rights.

[1] See below, Ch. IX.

CHAPTER VIII

ECONOMIC AND SOCIAL RIGHTS: THE SOCIAL CHARTER

1. *History of the Charter*

ARTICLES 22 to 27 of the Universal Declaration proclaim a number of economic and social rights. These include the right to social security; the right to work, including free choice of employment, just and favourable conditions of work and protection against unemployment; equal pay for equal work; the right to leisure, including holidays with pay; the right to a reasonable standard of living, including special care and assistance for motherhood and childhood; the right to education, including free primary education; and the right freely to participate in the cultural life of the community, including the protection of scientific, literary or artistic works.

As is well known, the United Nations have been working for many years on the drafting of two Covenants, intended to give legal protection to the rights proclaimed in the Universal Declaration; one of these deals with civil and political rights, the other with economic, social and cultural rights.

At the regional level, the European Convention and its Protocol contain guarantees of the civil and political rights of the citizen. Once this had been concluded, the Council of Europe turned its attention to the conclusion of a further treaty for the protection of economic and social rights.

This task proved far more difficult. There were two principal reasons for this. The first was the wide difference in the economic and social development of the member States. It is sufficient to compare the economy and social services of Britain and the Scandinavian countries, on the one hand, with those of Greece and Turkey, on the other, in order to understand the problem of securing agreement on common standards. The second difficulty arose from the very nature of the rights to be protected. The civil and political rights of the citizen can be enforced by a court of law: if a man is wrongfully imprisoned, he can apply for a writ of *habeas corpus*; if he is not given a fair trial, he can appeal to a superior court; and so on. With economic and social rights, however, it is different. The realisation of the right to work depends on economic circumstances, and if the labour exchange is unable to find a man employment the writ of a court of law will be of no avail. A reasonable standard of living for everyone is an objective of social policy, but it depends much more on a flourishing export trade than on legislation. Consequently, the whole approach to the protection of economic and social rights had to be different from that of the European Convention dealing with civil and political rights.

The first step required was a political decision that a new legal instrument should be prepared. During the winter of 1953-4 the Committee of Ministers was engaged on preparing 'a well-defined programme of work for the Council of Europe to exploit more fully the potentialities of the Statute by extending the field of common action between members and by striving towards the adoption of a common policy with regard to particular matters'.[1] In transmitting this programme to the Assembly in May 1954, the Committee of Ministers recorded this decision as part of the social programme:[2]

Our Committee will endeavour to elaborate a European Social Charter which would define the social objectives aimed at by Members and would guide the policy of the Council in the social field, in which it would be complementary to the European Convention on Human Rights and Fundamental Freedoms.

The task of preparing this Social Charter was to be confided to the new Social Committee, whose constitution was decided at the same time, as a permanent organ of co-operation between the member States in social matters, under the authority of the Committee of Ministers.[3] The Assembly welcomed this new development[4] and instructed its Committee on Social Questions to prepare a draft setting

[1] Special Message of the Committee of Ministers transmitting to the Consultative Assembly the Programme of Work of the Council of Europe, *Documents of the Assembly*, 1954, doc. 238, para. 1.

[2] *Ibid.*, para. 45.

[3] *Ibid.*, paras. 42-4.

[4] Opinion No. 9. *Texts adopted by the Assembly*, May 1954.

out its views; by October 1955 the Committee had done so and submitted a complete draft Charter, containing far-reaching provisions for the protection of various economic and social rights;[1] this also proposed the creation of a European Economic and Social Council as an organ for its implementation, thus giving new form to an idea launched two years earlier, when the creation of such a Council was envisaged as one of the links to be established between the Council of Europe and the proposed European Political Community.[2]

A lively debate took place on these proposals, which met with certain criticisms from the Committee on Economic Questions, and the whole problem was then referred back to the two committees for further study and for report during the course of the Eighth Session of the Assembly in 1956.

A further draft was produced in the following April. This provided for rather less extensive rights for the workers than the earlier draft—it was therefore considered retrograde by some and more realistic by others; it also proposed the convocation of an Economic and Social Conference on an *ad hoc* basis (i.e. as and when required) instead of as a permanent institution established be treaty.[3] This draft was acceptable to the Economic Committee and the majority of the Social Committee, but the dissident minority then arranged to have the whole matter referred to the Political Committee for further study. This resulted in the preparation of a third draft which was discussed by the Assembly in the following October. This tried to strike a balance between the two earlier projects; its institutional provisions were more complicated, however, because it proposed the appointment of a 'European Commissioner for Social Affairs' to be assisted by a 'European Social Chamber' rather on the lines of the original Economic and Social Council.[4] Opinions, however, were still sharply divided, partly on the extent of the rights which governments could be expected to guarantee to their citizens in an international instrument; partly on the question of policy whether various social rights should be determined by governments in

[1] *Documents of the Assembly*, 1955, doc. 403.

[2] Resolution 26, *Texts adopted*, January 1953.

[3] *Documents*, 1956, doc. 488.

[4] *Documents*, 1956, doc. 536.

their legislation or left to negotiation between the two sides of industry; and also—and this was perhaps the most hotly disputed point—whether it was necessary to set up some new international machinery to supervise the implementation of the Charter. Faced with irreconcilable differences of opinion on these (and other) points, the Assembly refrained from endorsing the latest draft that had been submitted to it, but recommended that the Committee of Ministers should 'establish a European Convention on Social and Economic Rights, taking into consideration the present draft and the observations and suggestions during the debates in public session. . . .'[1]

It was now the turn of the governmental Social Committee to see what provisions were acceptable to the member Governments. In December 1958 the Committee of Ministers published a draft Charter which their experts had produced;[2] taking advantage of a provision in the agreement concluded between the Council of Europe and the I.L.O. in 1951, they invited the latter to convene a Tripartite Conference (with delegations representing governments, employers and workers) to examine this text. The Tripartite Conference was held in Strasbourg from 1 to 12 December 1958; it did not produce any formal conclusions, but published a Report which contained the record of its proceedings, including the views of the participants or of the various groups on the provisions contained in the draft Social Charter.[3]

When the Assembly convened for its eleventh session in April 1959, it received a formal request from the Committee of Ministers for its opinion on the draft Charter, taking account of the conclusions of the Tripartite Conference.[4] The Assembly's Social Committee worked on these documents for the rest of the year, and, as a result of its proposals, the Assembly adopted its *Opinion on the draft European Social Charter* in January 1960.[5] In this Opinion, the Assembly sought to strengthen the Charter by making more specific or more extensive the rights that would

[1] Recommendation 104, *Texts adopted*, October 1956.

[2] *Documents*, 1959, doc. 927.

[3] I.L.O., *Record of Proceedings of the Tripartite Conference convened by the I.L.O. at the request of the Council of Europe.*

[4] *Documents*, 1959, doc. 976.

[5] Opinion No. 32, *Texts adopted*, January 1960.

be guaranteed to the workers, for example by providing that the working week would be progressively reduced to a maximum of forty hours, that workers should receive a minimum of three weeks' annual holiday with pay, that its benefits should extend to agricultural as well as to industrial workers, and so on. As regards the institutional provisions, the idea of a separate Economic and Social Council (or something similar) had by now been abandoned; the Ministers proposed, and the Assembly accepted, that the governments should send in biennial reports on the implementation of the Charter; these reports would then be considered by a small committee of independent experts and transmitted, with their comments, to the governmental Social Committee, while the Assembly would be kept informed. It would then be for the Committee of Ministers, after receiving the views of these various bodies, to make recommendations to member Governments on the progressive implementation of the Charter.

By the spring of 1960, the Committee of Ministers was thus in possession of the draft worked out by their experts and the comments thereon of the Tripartite Conference and of the Consultative Assembly. The experts then worked out, in the light of all these discussions, the final draft of the Charter, which was duly signed at a ceremony held in Turin on 18 October 1961, in connection with the celebration of the centenary of the independence of Italy. In its final form the Charter has a character which is intended to correspond to the needs of contemporary free Europe and which might well be unacceptable both to Soviet planners and American liberals. Its ideal is security in freedom; by proposing a system of guarantees for what have been called 'the bread and butter rights of the working man', it is intended to bring him the practical benefits of the European idea.

2. *The main Principles of the Charter*

There are three basic characteristics of the Social Charter which it is necessary to observe *in limine*. The first is its approach to the problem that a number of the 'rights' which it seeks to assert are really objects of social policy rather than rights which are legally enforceable. The difficulty here was that if these 'rights' were merely proclaimed as objectives, the Charter would have little value as an effective guarantee of economic and social standards; on the other hand, if its provisions were limited to the legal obligations which member Governments could reasonably be expected to assume, its scope would be rather restricted and the results of so much work disappointing. At one stage, the Social Committee asked for instructions as to whether the Charter should include legally binding provisions and was told by the Committee of Ministers 'to determine whether and, if so, how far, definite and detailed provisions binding on the signatory States could be incorporated in the Charter',[1] with a clear implication that this should be done if possible. The solution adopted was to divide the Charter into several distinct parts. In the first part are set out nineteen separate rights, the realisation of which the Contracting Parties accept as the aim of their policy; this permits general affirmations of a far-reaching character, as statements of policy without precise legal commitments. Part II then contains the legal obligations which the Parties undertake with a view to ensuring the effective exercise of the rights proclaimed in Part I. With this double formulation it is thus possible to combine the general statement of long-term objectives with particular, more limited commitments of immediate application.[2]

The second basic characteristic of the Charter is its approach to the problem raised by the varying states of economic and social development in the different member States. It was clearly unrealistic to expect that the less developed countries could assume the same obligations as their more fortunate partners; equally it would have been contrary to the general policy of the Council of Europe to draft an instrument to which only the more developed countries could subscribe. It was therefore provided that a member State need not accept all the provisions of the Charter in order to be able to ratify, but that it could—at least initially—be bound only by a stated minimum, in the hope and expectation that it could accept additional obligations with the passage of time. In this way it was hoped to achieve the pro-

[1] Resolution (56) 25 of the Committee of Ministers in *Documents of the Assembly*, January 1957, doc. 595.

[2] The text of the Charter is given in Appendix 6. See also F. Tennfjord, 'The European Social Charter—an Instrument of Social Collaboration in Europe', *European Yearbook*, Vol. 9, pp. 71–83.

gressive implementation of a Charter which, when fully applied, would guarantee quite a high standard of economic and social rights.

The third basic feature of the Charter is the attention given to the question of supervision of its implementation. In the Convention on Human Rights, it was not considered enough that the Contracting Parties should undertake to ensure the rights set out in the Convention to all persons within their jurisdiction; the Commission and the Court were set up to provide an international guarantee to reinforce the national undertakings. Similarly, in the Social Charter it was thought necessary to have some international machinery to supervise its implementation. The Commission and Court of Human Rights were not suitable for this purpose, since the rights to be guaranteed did not have the same legal character. The Assembly had suggested an Economic and Social Council or Chamber, with representatives of employers, workers and consumers; the Governments did not favour this formula, but agreed to an elaborate system of control based on the sending of reports by Governments on the way in which they are implementing the Charter and the examination of these reports by the various committees and organs of the Council of Europe. This system will be described later in this chapter.

3. *The Rights guaranteed*

Part I of the Charter starts off by providing that 'the Contracting Parties accept as the aim of their policy, to be pursued by all appropriate means, both national and international in character, the attainment of conditions in which the following rights and principles may be effectively realised. . . .' These 'rights and principles' are then listed:

1. The right to work, which is thus formulated: 'Everyone shall have the opportunity to earn his living in an occupation freely entered upon'.
2. The right to just conditions of work.
3. The right to safe and healthy working conditions.
4. The right to a fair remuneration.
5. The right to organise.
6. The right to collective bargaining.
7. The right of children and young persons to protection.

8. The right of employed women to special protection, in case of maternity, when nursing their infants and so on.
9. The right to vocational guidance.
10. The right to vocational training.
11. The right to protection of health.
12. The right to social security.
13. The right to social and medical assistance.
14. The right to social welfare services.
15. The right of the disabled to special facilities.
16. The right of the family to social, legal and economic protection.
17. The right of mothers and children to social and economic protection.
18. The right to earn one's living in another country.
19. The right of migrant workers and their families to protection and assistance.

Part II of the Charter, as explained above, then contains more precise commitments which the Contracting Parties assume with a view to ensuring the effective exercise of these rights.[1] These provisions vary considerably, according to the nature of the right to be protected. The right to just conditions of work, for example, involves *inter alia* limitation of working hours, public holidays with pay, two weeks' annual holiday with pay and a weekly rest period; similarly, the right to a fair remuneration includes additional pay for overtime, equal pay for men and women and so on. The right of children and young persons to protection includes ten separate provisions for their benefit. The undertakings designed to secure the right to protection of the family and of mothers and children, on the other hand, are more general and imprecise.

A number of the rights dealt with in the Social Charter also form the subject of other conventions and agreements previously concluded by the member States of the Council of Europe. Though cross-references are, quite naturally, not given in the Charter, it is clear that its authors had these other instruments in mind. The right to organise, for example, is already guaranteed by Article 11 of the Convention on Human Rights. The right to social security in its international aspects forms the subject of the two Interim Agreements on Social Security signed in Paris on

[1] See below, Appendix 6.

11 December 1953,[1] while standards of social security will be dealt with in the European Code of Social Security on which negotiations are well advanced;[2] moreover, the right to social and medical assistance, also in its international aspects, forms the subject of the European Convention on Social and Medical Assistance of 11 December 1953.[3] Furthermore, the right to earn one's living in another country is one of the matters covered in the European Convention on Establishment of 13 December 1955.[4]

Part III of the Charter then contains the provisions which permit progressive implementation. They are rather complicated, but the essence of them is as follows. Seven rights were regarded as of particular importance. These are:

> the right to work
> the right to organise
> the right to collective bargaining
> the right to social security
> the right to social and medical assistance
> the right of the family to special protection
> the right of migrant workers and their families to protection and assistance.

Any Contracting Party must agree to be bound by the Articles in Part II of the Charter relating to at least five of these rights. In addition, it must agree to be bound by the provisions relating to at least five other rights as set out in Part II. It is possible, however, instead of accepting ten articles *in toto*, to accept a larger number in part.[5]

---

[1] *European Treaty Series*, Nos. 12 and 13. See also Robertson, *The Council of Europe, op. cit.*, pp. 140–1.

[2] *Ibid.*, p. 142.

[3] *European Treaty Series*, No. 14, *ibid.*, p. 141.

[4] *European Treaty Series*, No. 19, *ibid.*, pp. 185–8. This Convention, however, had not entered into force by January 1963, only three of the necessary five ratifications having been deposited.

[5] The 19 Articles in Part 2 of the Charter contain 68 numbered paragraphs. A State may ratify the Charter if it agrees to be bound by not fewer than 45 numbered paragraphs, provided that it accepts not fewer than 5 of Articles 1, 5, 6, 12, 13, 16 and 19.

4. *Implementation of the Charter*

Part IV of the Charter contains the provisions relating to the control of its implementation. The Committee of Ministers, while rejecting the idea of an Economic and Social Council—as proposed at one stage in the Assembly—did agree to the institution of an independent Committee of Experts 'of the highest integrity and of recognised competence in international social questions', who would be joined by a representative of the International Labour Organisation, participating in a consultative capacity.[1] This Committee of Experts is to receive and examine every two years reports by the Contracting Parties on the way in which they are applying the Charter. These reports, and the comments thereon of the Committee of Experts, are then to be examined by a Sub-Committee of the Social Committee, representing the Contracting Parties and assisted by organisations of employers and trade unions. The comments of the experts are also to be sent to the Consultative Assembly. Finally the Committee of Ministers is to examine the results of this consultation and may, by a two-thirds majority, make any necessary recommendations to each Contracting Party.[2]

This machinery is admittedly complicated, but it should institute a system of supervision whereby watch will be kept at regular intervals to ensure that the Charter is effectively applied and that any undue reticence by a particular government is exposed to the light of publicity and brought to the attention of a Committee of Foreign Ministers. The protracted negotiations for the Charter, both in the Assembly and in the various governmental committees, indicated clearly that it is not possible to secure the acceptance of any more stringent form of international guarantee of economic and social rights at this stage in the development of European co-operation.

The inclusion of a representative of the International Labour Organisation, in a consultative capacity, on the Committee of Experts which is to examine the reports of governments on the implementation of the Charter, is a recognition not only of the special competence of the I.L.O. in social matters but also of the great assistance which it afforded to the Council of Europe in

---

[1] Articles 25 and 26 of the Charter.

[2] Articles 27–9 of the Charter.

the preparation of the Charter. This was done in conformity with the agreement concluded between the two organisations on 23 November 1951.[1] The Consultative Assembly suggested that the Food and Agriculture Organisation of the United Nations should also be invited to appoint a representative to sit on the Committee of Experts,[2] in order to watch out for the interests of agricultural workers, but this proposal was not incorporated into the final text of the Charter.

Other points of interest in the final clauses (Part V) of the Charter are the inclusion of an article permitting derogations 'in time of war or other public emergency threatening the life of the nation' similar to Article 15 of the Convention on Human Rights; Article 32 of the Charter (similar to Article 60 of the Convention) which preserves any more favourable treatment that may already be provided for under domestic law or other international treaties; and Article 33 which preserves the principle of collective bargaining between the two sides of industry in relation to social rights for which it is appropriate.

The Charter was signed on 18 October 1961 on behalf of the following members of the Council of Europe: Belgium, Denmark, France, Germany, Greece, Ireland, Italy, Luxembourg, Netherlands, Norway, Sweden, Turkey and the United Kingdom. Article 35 provides for its entry into force after the deposit of the fifth instrument of ratification. By 31 December 1962 it had been ratified by Norway, Sweden and the United Kingdom.

[1] See *Second Supplementary Report of the Committee of Ministers*, September 1951, *Documents of the Assembly*, 1951, doc. 60, Appendix. Also Robertson, *The Council of Europe, op. cit.*, pp. 217, 227–30.

[2] Opinion 32 (Article 26), *Texts adopted by the Assembly*, January 1960.

CHAPTER IX

ADDITIONAL PROTOCOLS

1. *Protocols incorporating additional Rights*

THE Convention and the Protocol did not exhaust the list of rights and freedoms proclaimed in the Universal Declaration. In 1959 the Legal Committee of the Consultative Assembly therefore considered whether there were not additional rights and freedoms which should form the object of the system of guarantee laid down in the European Convention; having answered this question in the affirmative, the Committee proposed the conclusion of a Second Protocol to the Convention on Human Rights, and itself prepared a draft covering the following:

> freedom from imprisonment on the ground of inability to fulfil a contractual obligation;
> freedom of movement, including freedom to choose one's residence and to emigrate;
> freedom from exile;
> freedom of aliens from arbitrary expulsion;
> the right to recognition as a person before the law;
> the right to equality before the law.

The Consultative Assembly in January 1960 adopted a recommendation to the Committee of Ministers asking it to submit these proposals to a committee of governmental experts, with a view to the conclusion of a Second Protocol.[1] The Committee of Ministers agreed to this idea and appointed a Committee of Experts 'with instructions to study problems relating to the European Convention on Human Rights'.[2]

These wide terms of reference meant that the same Committee of Experts could also study another proposal made by the Assembly at the same time to extend the competence of the Court

---

[1] Recommendation 234, *Texts adopted*, January 1960.

[2] Resolution (60) 6 of the Committee of Ministers, *Documents of the Assembly*, 1960, doc. 1114, para. 79.

of Human Rights so as to enable it to give advisory opinions on the interpretation of the Convention.[1]

While the work on the Second Protocol proceeded, the Assembly made further proposals for the inclusion of additional rights therein. These were the rights of national minorities,[2] the right of asylum[3] and the principle of local autonomy.[4] The Committee of Ministers agreed that the experts should study the Assembly's proposals relating to minorities and asylum, but was opposed to the inclusion of the principle of local autonomy, on the ground that this was not a fundamental human right.

The basic idea behind these proposals, as explained in the Legal Committee's Report,[5] was that the Statute of the Council of Europe, as drafted in 1949, listed in its first article among the fields of activity of the organisation 'the maintenance *and further realisation* of human rights and fundamental freedoms'. Moreover, the Preamble to the Convention stated explicitly that it was designed 'to take the first steps for the collective enforcement of certain of the rights stated in the Universal Declaration'. The effect of the Convention and the first Protocol was only to maintain certain existing rights; the time had now come to take additional measures 'for the further realisation of human rights'. For this purpose the Legal Committee scrutinised the draft International Covenant of the United Nations on Civil and Political Rights[6] in order to see which of its provisions were not already included in the Convention or the first Protocol and might now form the subject of an international guarantee under the European system.

Freedom from imprisonment on the ground of inability to fulfil a contractual obligation formed the subject of Article 11 of the draft Covenant. The Consultative Assembly proposed to take over the United Nations text without change; this would

[1] Recommendation 232, *Texts adopted*, January 1960. See further below, p. 158.

[2] Recommendation 285, *Texts adopted*, April 1961.

[3] Recommendation 293, *Texts adopted*, September 1961.

[4] Recommendation 295, *ibid.*

[5] *Documents of the Assembly*, January 1960, doc. 1057.

[6] The draft Covenant was adopted by the U.N. Commission on Human Rights at its Tenth Session in 1954—see *Report of the Tenth Session*, April 1954, doc. E/2573–E/CN. 4/705 Annex 1.

strengthen the existing provision of Article 5 of the Convention on the right to liberty and security of person. It would apply to contractual obligations of any kind, including non-delivery and non-performance, and not only money debts; at the same time, it would not apply to public obligations (fiscal or military) nor to civil obligations imposed by statute or by the order of a court, such as maintenance obligations or a judgment debt for damages. It was thus designed to prevent imprisonment for the sole reason that the individual has not the material means to fulfil his contractual obligations.

The Article on freedom of movement was based on paragraph 1 of Article 12 of the draft Covenant. It provided that everyone legally within the territory of a State should enjoy freedom of movement within that territory and freedom to choose his residence; also 'that everyone shall be free to leave any State, including his own'. A third paragraph in the article would permit limitations on these rights provided they are prescribed by law and constitute measures which are necessary in a democratic society for national security, public safety and so forth—as found in a number of articles in the Convention itself.

Article 3 of the draft was based on paragraph 2 of Article 12 of the draft Covenant and provided for freedom from exile from the State of which one is a national and freedom to enter that State. It is to be observed that this relates to the exile of nationals, and not to the expulsion of aliens, which forms the subject of the next article. It is there provided that 'an alien lawfully residing in the territory of a High Contracting Party may be expelled only if he endangers national security or offends against *ordre public* or morality'; the following paragraphs are to the effect that an alien who has been two years in the country shall have an opportunity to be heard before being expelled, and that after ten years' residence he shall have additional guarantees. This corresponds rather generally to Article 13 of the United Nations draft Covenant, but more closely to the text of Article 3 of the European Convention on Establishment of 13 December 1955.[1] The Legal Committee considered that it was worth while reproducing here the provisions of the Establishment Convention because the benefits of the latter are only to be accorded to the nationals of the High

---

[1] *European Treaty Series*, No. 19.

Contracting Parties, whereas a Protocol to the Convention on Human Rights would secure those benefits to everyone within the jurisdiction, without regard to nationality.

Article 5 of the draft Second Protocol provided that 'every individual shall have the right to recognition everywhere as a person in the eyes of the law'—corresponding to Article 16 of the draft Covenant—while Article 6 provided for equality before the law. The Legal Committee recognised the difficulty of drafting a text on this subject (also dealt with in Article 24 of the draft Covenant) and actually submitted two alternative texts to the Committee of Ministers. It recognised that complete equality is impossible of achievement and that there are a number of matters which are outside the province of the law, such as the employment of workers in private enterprises, the lease of dwellings, the limitation by private associations or trade unions of their membership to certain categories of people, and so on. The Assembly text therefore sought to achieve *equality of protection* but not necessarily equality of rights.

As regards the right of asylum, the Legal Committee of the Assembly in its report[1] recognised that traditionally it has been considered a sovereign right of the State to accord or refuse admission to its territory to persons seeking asylum from persecution. 'Nevertheless, there is the other aspect of asylum: the right of the individual to seek, receive and enjoy asylum. Although, at the present stage of development of international law, this right cannot be considered as legally established, there are a number of factors which would seem to warrant its being dealt with in an international instrument. First, there is the undeniable fact of social necessity: at times of political upheavals, such as we know after two world wars, asylum takes on an urgent importance to which we cannot be blind. We are, therefore, in the first instance, confronted with a humanitarian duty. Secondly, a number of States have already, in their constitutions and municipal law, or by treaty, explicitly or implicitly recognised the individual's right of asylum,[2] which can thus be said to be an

---

[1] *Documents*, 1961, doc. 1329.

[2] Thus the Preamble to the French Constitution of 28 September 1958 provides *inter alia*: 'Anyone persecuted because of his activities in the cause of freedom has a right to asylum within the territories of the Republic'; the Basic Law of the Federal Republic of Germany (Article 16): 'The

incipient right.' Thirdly, there is 'the almost universal recognition in extradition treaties of the principle of non-extradition of political offenders, to such an extent that the late Judge Lauterpacht wondered whether it has not become one of those general principles of law recognised by civilised States to which Article 38 of the Statute of the Permanent Court of International Justice refers as one of the sources of international law'.[1] This same principle is, moreover, recognised in the Council of Europe's Convention on Extradition.[2] 'Thus, in a certain sense, a refusal to extradite may imply the granting of asylum, and vice versa'.

The Legal Committee pointed out that Article 14 of the Universal Declaration of Human Rights proclaimed that 'Everyone has the right to *seek* and *enjoy* in other countries asylum from persecution'; but that this text did not cover the third aspect of the matter, *the right to receive asylum*, which is really the kernel of the matter. It recognised that Member States could not be expected to accept an unlimited obligation to accord asylum, but thought that they should accept certain limited obligations when asylum is requested. The Commission of Human Rights of the United Nations had, at its Thirteenth Session in 1957, adopted a draft Declaration on the Right of Asylum which contained a general prohibition on rejection at the frontier, return or expulsion of a person seeking asylum 'which would result in compelling him to return to or remain in a territory, if there is well-founded fear of persecution endangering his life, physical integrity or liberty in that territory'.[3] There was also a somewhat similar provision in Article 33 of the Convention on the Status of Refugees, of 28 July 1951, which entered into force on 22 April 1954.

The Assembly, therefore, proposed a text by which Member States would recognise the right of persons to seek and enjoy asylum, agree not to reject or expel a person in circumstances

politically persecuted shall enjoy the right of asylum'; the Italian Constitution of 27 December 1947 (Article 10) : 'The foreigner who is denied in his own country the effective exercise of democratic freedoms . . . has a right to asylum in the territory of the Republic. . . .' There are similar provisions in the Danish law of 7 June 1952 and the Norwegian law of 27 June 1956.

[1] Lauterpacht, *B.Y.I.L.*, 1944, p. 88.

[2] *European Treaty Series*, No. 24, Article 3.

[3] Economic and Social Council, Thirtieth Session, Supplement No. 8 (E/3335), Ch. VI.

where there is a 'well-founded fear of persecution' 'except for overriding reasons of national security or safeguarding of the population', and undertake, if asylum is refused, to allow a reasonable period and the necessary facilities to obtain admission into another country.[1] It considered that this text should be the more readily acceptable to Member Governments if it was included in a Protocol to the Convention on Human Rights, because this would permit derogations under Article 15 'in time of war or other emergency threatening the life of the nation'.

The question of including a provision on the rights of national minorities had a long history. In its first report of 5 September 1949 proposing the conclusion of the Convention on Human Rights,[2] the Legal Committee had stressed the importance of 'the wider protection of the rights of national minorities'; it had repeated this a year later in commenting on the draft Convention prepared by the Committee of Ministers.[3] When proposing the conclusion of a Second Protocol in November 1959, the Committee had reserved its right to come back to this question[4] and finally did so in April 1961.[5]

A certain measure of protection is already given to national minorities[6] in the Convention and the first Protocol by Article 14 on non-discrimination, by Article 9 on freedom of thought, conscience and religion and by Article 2 of the Protocol on the right to education. These provisions ensure that persons belonging to a minority shall be treated on a basis of equality with other individuals or groups of individuals. The question was whether minorities should be given certain additional rights for the purpose of safeguarding their own individual character.

The Legal Committee answered this question in the affirmative.

[1] Recommendation 293, *Texts adopted*, September 1961.

[2] *Documents of the Assembly*, 1949, doc. 77.

[3] *Ibid.*, 1950, doc. 6.

[4] *Ibid.*, 1959, doc. 1057.

[5] *Ibid.*, 1961, doc. 1299, where the history of the matter is given more fully.

[6] The Legal Committee did not attempt to define the term 'national minority' though it explained what was meant by it ; among other things it quoted the Resolution adopted in January 1950 by the Sub-Commission on the Prevention of Discrimination and the Protection of Minorities of the United Nations—Document 1299, para. 10.

It noted that the Permanent Court of International Justice had once referred to two aspects inherent in the protection of minorities:[1]

i. the human rights and freedoms proper, that is to say the basic rights which, by reason of a guarantee against discrimination in respect of them, place the minority on an equal footing with other persons within the jurisdiction of a State; and

ii. those rights which give the minority, as it were, a kind of preferential treatment for the purpose of safeguarding its own character.

The Committee then took as its point of departure Article 25 of the United Nations draft Covenant on Civil and Political Rights, which provides for the right of minorities to enjoy their own culture, to profess and practise their own religion and to use their own language. It decided however to add a further right of minorities 'to establish their own schools and receive teaching in the language of their choice'. This led the Assembly to propose to the Committee of Ministers the inclusion in the Second Protocol of an article reading as follows:

Persons belonging to a national minority shall not be denied the right, in community with the other members of their group, and as far as compatible with public order, to enjoy their own culture, to use their own language, to establish their own schools and receive teaching in the language of their choice or to profess and practise their own religion.

The Committee of Experts on Human Rights appointed by the Committee of Ministers worked on these various proposals of the Assembly during the years 1961 and 1962. Early in 1963 the Committee of Ministers reported to the Assembly that the experts had completed their work on the draft Second Protocol. They had accepted with minor modifications the Assembly's proposals relating to three additional rights: freedom from imprisonment on the ground of inability to fulfil a contractual obligation; freedom of movement, including freedom to choose one's residence and to emigrate; and freedom from exile. As regards freedom of aliens from arbitrary expulsion, the experts had drafted a text prohibiting the collective expulsions of aliens but had considered it preferable to leave it to the Convention on

[1] Advisory Opinion of 6 April 1935 regarding Minority Schools in Albania, Series A/B, No. 64, p. 17.

Establishment to define the treatment to be accorded to individual aliens. As regards the right to recognition as a person before the law and the right to equality before the law, the Committee of Experts thought it better not to include these rights in the Second Protocol, since there was little need to do so and any text likely to be acceptable to the governments might be open to doubtful interpretation. As regards the right of asylum and the rights of minorities, the Committee of Experts had not yet completed their work.[1]

Though progress had been slow, it appeared that a Second Protocol to the Convention would at least guarantee certain additional rights and thus extend further the system of protection enshrined in the Convention itself, even though those rights might be less extensive than the Consultative Assembly had originally proposed.

2. *Advisory Opinions of the Court*

One of the most interesting lessons to be learnt from the Convention arises from the *lacunae* which can be detected in its provisions. A number of these were observed even before the Convention was signed; others have come to light subsequently.

As explained in Chapter I, the Committee of Ministers in August 1950 transmitted to the Assembly for its opinion the draft Convention that had then been prepared; the Assembly then proposed certain amendments to this draft in its Recommendation 24 of 25 August 1950. These amendments were considered by a Committee of Legal Experts which met in Rome immediately before the session of the Ministers on 3 November 1950. This Committee was a small one of reduced membership, since only about half a dozen of the foreign ministers had brought their legal advisers with them. It approved with considerable amendments the draft Preamble to the Convention proposed by the Legal Committee of the Assembly and agreed with the suggestion that the number of acceptances of the compulsory jurisdiction of the Court required by Article 56 should be reduced from nine to eight. As regards the Assembly's proposal to add

[1] Fourteenth Statutory Report of the Committee of Ministers to the Assembly, *Documents of the Assembly*, April, 1963. For the text prepared by the Committee of Experts, see Appendix 7.

to the Convention three additional articles on the right of property, the right to education and the right to free elections, the Committee of Legal Advisers 'ascertained that there was not a unanimous agreement' on accepting these proposals; the Ministers then decided to refer them to a further committee of experts, with a view to the preparation of a Protocol for signature at a later date, as was in fact done.

During the course of their work in Rome the Committee of Legal Advisers made a certain number of formal corrections to the text of the Convention and corrections of translation. While doing so, they discussed in detail many of the provisions of the Convention and detected a number of *lacunae*. One of these was the omission of any provision for filling casual vacancies in the Court or for the appointment of new judges in the event of the admission of new Members of the Council of Europe. The result was the addition of the present paragraph 2 of Article 39 and paragraph 3 of Article 40. But they also discussed a number of other points arising out of the Convention; here are three:

Effect of Declarations accepting the Compulsory Jurisdiction of the Court:
If a High Contracting Party makes a declaration under Article 46 accepting the compulsory jurisdiction of the Court on condition of reciprocity, can the Commission refer to the Court a case brought against that High Contracting Party by an individual applicant?

Article 48 provides that the Commission may bring a case before the Court provided that the High Contracting Party concerned is subject to the compulsory jurisdiction of the Court. From this it may be argued, as mentioned in Chapter V, that an acceptance of the jurisdiction of the Court subject to reciprocity does not mean an acceptance of the jurisdiction of the Court for cases referred to it by the Commission, because in such cases no reciprocity exists. On the other hand, the argument can also be made that the condition of reciprocity only relates to cases brought by other High Contracting Parties, and does not affect the ability of the Commission to refer a case to the Court, since the Commission is *sui generis*, and the right of the Commission to refer cases to the Court is an essential part of the procedure established by the Convention which cannot be excluded in default of a clear intention to do so.

It would appear that there is room for legitimate doubt and that the Court may one day have to give a ruling on this point.

Appointment of New Judges: As already mentioned, two new paragraphs on this subject were added to the Convention in Rome: paragraph 2 of Article 39 and paragraph 3 of Article 40.

Article 39(1) provides that the members of the Court shall be elected by the Assembly from a list of persons nominated by the Members of the Council of Europe. The new paragraph 2 of Article 39 provides that the same procedure shall be followed, as far as applicable, in the event of the admission of new Members of the Council of Europe and in filling casual vacancies. The question was asked whether this clause would mean:

1. that the new Member should nominate three candidates from which the Assembly should select the new judge; or
2. that all Members of the Council, including the new Member, should each nominate three candidates from among whom the Assembly would choose the new judge.

In favour of the first interpretation, it could be urged that the general intention of the Convention appears to be, as a general rule, that each member State should have one judge of its nationality (even though it is possible to have judges from non-member States). Consequently, if a new Member is elected, it should have the right to nominate three candidates in the same way as all the other Members, but there is no need for existing member States also to nominate candidates for the one new vacancy.

In favour of the second interpretation, the following argument was cited: the words used in Article 39(2) are 'as far as applicable the same procedure shall be followed. . . .' The words 'the same procedure' refer back to the procedure set out in the previous paragraph, which includes the phrase 'each Member shall nominate three candidates'. Therefore, if the words have been used with their normal meaning, it would seem to follow that 'in the event of the admission of new Members of the Council of Europe . . . each Member shall nominate three candidates'. The force of the argument is diminished by the inclusion of the words in paragraph 2 'as far as applicable'. However, one cannot give those words too wide a significance, because there would be no difficulty in applying the procedure set out in paragraph 1. The question is not so much whether this procedure is applicable as whether it is appropriate.[1]

This problem has now been settled in practice. When Cyprus became a Member of the Council of Europe in 1961, the Committee of Ministers transmitted to the Assembly only three candidates for the vacant post of judge, all proposed by the Government of Cyprus and all of Cypriot nationality.[2] It seems probable that this precedent will be followed without question in future.

Extension of the Jurisdiction of the Court to Colonial Territories: Another question discussed by the Committee of Legal Experts in Rome was the following: if a State declares that it accepts the jurisdiction of the Court in accordance with Article 46, and subsequently declares that the Convention shall extend to one or more of its colonial territories in accordance with Article 63, does the jurisdiction of the Court then automatically apply to the colonial territory in question?

On the one hand, it may be argued that as soon as the declaration has been made under Article 46 accepting the jurisdiction of the Court, then the jurisdiction applies 'in all matters concerning the interpretation and application of the present Convention'. Once a later declaration has been made under Article 63 extending the Convention to the colonial territories concerned, the meaning of the words 'all matters concerning the interpretation of the present Convention' is automatically extended to include those affecting the colonial territory.

On the other hand, the argument can be made that if the jurisdiction of the Court does not apply to the metropolitan territories without an express declaration, similarly it cannot apply to colonial territories without an express declaration, and that any declaration extending the Convention to colonial territories under Article 63(1) only refers to those provisions of the Convention which do not require an express declaration before they enter into force. This argument is strengthened by the fact that Article 63(4) makes provision for separate declarations extending to colonial territories the competence of the Commission to receive indivi-

---

[1] In January 1960 the Assembly suggested that the Committee of Ministers should, by special agreement, ask the opinion of the Court of Human Rights as to the procedure to be followed in such cases—Recommendation 235, *Texts adopted,* January 1960.

[2] Document 1361 in *Documents of the Assembly,* September 1961.

dual petitions. If separate declarations are required to extend to colonial territories the competence of the Commission, then it would seem to follow that separate declarations are also required to extend to colonial territories the competence of the Court.

From this line of argument certain legal experts in Rome concluded that an additional paragraph was required to the effect that express declarations might be made extending to colonial territories the jurisdiction of the Court; if such a paragraph were added, it would be clear that the jurisdiction of the Court would not apply to colonial territories in the absence of such an express declaration. Nevertheless, they did not press for its inclusion on that occasion, in order not to raise contentious issues at the last moment, having regard particularly to the contentious history of Article 63. At the same time, all the legal experts were agreed on the existence of an ambiguity which it was desirable to clarify if possible.

Other points of doubtful interpretation of the Convention have subsequently come to light. Three of them which have been mentioned in earlier chapters are: whether the Secretary-General should communicate to Contracting Parties the notices of derogation he receives under Article 15 of the Convention;[1] whether a simple or an absolute majority is required under Article 39 for election of the judges by the Consultative Assembly;[2] and the powers of the Court in pronouncing judgment under Article 50.[3]

Early in 1960, the Legal Committee of the Assembly studied the problem posed by the *lacunae* and obscure passages in the Convention and reached the conclusion that the best course to follow was to confer on the Court of Human Rights the power to give advisory opinions in order to settle doubtful points that might arise.

The court already has a limited power to interpret the Convention under Article 45, which reads as follows:

The jurisdiction of the Court shall extend to all cases concerning the interpretation and application of the present Convention which the High Contracting Parties or the Commission shall refer to it in accordance with Article 48.

[1] See Ch. IV, Sec. 1.
[2] See Ch. V, Sec. 2.
[3] See Ch. V, Sec. 4.

This power of interpretation, therefore, only comes into play when the Court is actually seised of a case of alleged violation; otherwise it has at present no competence to decide on such matters and, indeed, cannot even be seised of them. What is needed, therefore, is a competence to interpret the Convention by means of advisory opinions, even when no dispute has arisen, but when guidance is required by one of the bodies concerned with its application, that is to say the Committee of Ministers, the Consultative Assembly or the Secretary-General.

Discretion would be necessary in granting this additional competence to the Court. It would probably be better not to allow the Contracting Parties the right to request an advisory opinion on a matter which could form the subject of contentious proceedings. As stated by the Legal Committee in its Report:[1]

Those who are already empowered to institute contentious proceedings before either the Commission or the Court should perhaps not be empowered to apply to that Court for an advisory opinion. Indeed, experience has shown that if a natural or a legal person has the choice of instituting judicial proceedings or requesting an opinion, he will select the procedure that seems more likely to favour his own cause. Thus, requests for an opinion have been submitted to the German Constitutional Court on questions which, in substance, constituted a dispute between two organs of the Federal Republic. Such a procedure is not always conducive to the proper administration of justice, since an advisory opinion does not provide for a full hearing, which is the main feature of normal court procedure. For this reason, it might be preferable not to grant to States, or to natural or legal persons, the right to apply to the Court for an advisory opinion on a matter which could become the subject of contentious proceedings, lest the well-balanced system laid down by the Convention for the protection of Human Rights be upset.

These considerations led the Consultative Assembly to propose in its Recommendation 232 of 22 January 1960 that the Court should be empowered to give advisory opinions on the interpretation of the Convention at the request of the Committee of Ministers, the Consultative Assembly or the Secretary-General; and possibly also at the request of a Contracting Party, provided

[1] *Documents of the Assembly*, 1959, doc. 1061, p. 5.

that this would be limited to matters which might not subsequently form the subject of contentious proceedings before the Court.[1]

Such a competence would correspond to the competence of the International Court of Justice, under Article 65 of the Statute, to 'give an advisory opinion on any legal question at the request of whatever body may be authorised by, or in accordance with the Charter of the United Nations to make such a request'. Article 96 of the Charter authorises the General Assembly and the Security Council to request advisory opinions and empowers the General Assembly to authorise other organs of the United Nations and the Specialised Agencies to do so. Such authorisation has in fact been granted to the Economic and Social Council and most of the Specialised Agencies. There would therefore be nothing novel or exceptional in granting a similar competence to the European Court of Human Rights.

One other aspect of the matter which should be borne in mind is the following. If it is necessary for one of the organs of the Council of Europe to request an advisory opinion of the Court on some such matter as the procedure to be followed in the Committee of Ministers or the Assembly, it may well be that an answer is required rapidly. The normal procedure of the Court is inevitably slow and not geared to the speedy despatch of business. It may therefore be desirable to find some way of accelerating the normally slow-moving processes of the law.

Once again we are helped by reference to the Statute of the International Court of Justice. Article 29 of the Statute reads as follows:

With a view to the speedy despatch of business the Court shall form annually a chamber composed of five judges which, at the request of the Parties, may hear and determine cases by summary procedure. In addition, two judges shall be selected for the purpose of replacing judges who find it impossible to sit.

The present author is not aware of any cases in which use has been made of this possibility of 'the speedy despatch of business'.

---

[1] The Assembly adopted at the same time its Recommendation 231, in which it proposed that the Court should also be empowered to interpret conventions concluded under the auspices of the Council of Europe or other treaties concluded by two or more Members of the Council of Europe. This proposal is discussed in the first section of the following chapter.

But, while it may not be suitable for adoption by the European Court of Human Rights for the discharge of its present functions under the Convention of 1950, it might be very valuable if the Court is to be asked to give advisory opinions on matters of a certain urgency.

As related in the preceding section of this chapter, the Committee of Ministers of the Council of Europe decided early in 1960 to appoint a Committee of Experts 'with instructions to study problems relating to the European Convention on Human Rights'. One matter referred to it was the Assembly's Recommendation to confer on the Court the competence to give advisory opinions. The Committee of Experts worked on this problem in 1961 and 1962 and agreed with the general idea. They took a restrictive view, however, on the question as to who should be authorised to request advisory opinions; they proposed to limit this right to the Committee of Ministers and not confer it on the Consultative Assembly or the Secretary-General, as the former had proposed. The Commission of Human Rights then requested that it should be granted the right to request advisory opinions, but the Committee of Experts remained of the opinion that it should only be exercised by the Contracting Parties, as represented in the Committee of Ministers. They drafted a Protocol to the Convention in this sense, which was submitted to the Member Governments early in 1963.[1] This Protocol was signed on 6 May 1963. Another Protocol was signed at the same time, the object of which was to simplify the procedure of the Commission by abolishing the system of Sub-Commissions—see also Appendix 7.

[1] The text is given in Appendix 7.

CHAPTER X

WIDER HORIZONS

1. *A European Court of Justice?*

IT is going to be extremely interesting to watch the development of the European Court of Human Rights. The manner of its creation is the result of a compromise between those States which did not want a Court at all as part of the machinery set up by the European Convention and those States which responded to the appeal of the Hague Congress of 1948, strongly supported by the Consultative Assembly. The condition that eight Parties must accept its jurisdiction as compulsory before it could be set up appeared at one time equivalent to an indefinite postponement; in fact, it delayed the creation of the Court for five years. And while a bare majority of the Members of the Council of Europe have subscribed to what might be called the 'European Optional Clause' it is significant that of the four major powers in the Council (France, Western Germany, Italy, and the United Kingdom), only one of them—the Federal Republic—has done so. And it is to their credit that so many of the smaller States of Western Europe—Austria, Belgium, Denmark, Iceland, Ireland, Luxembourg and the Netherlands—should have been willing to give a lead and take the plunge when the larger countries hesitated on the brink.

The provisions of the Convention have been so drafted as to avoid any possibility of conflict of jurisdiction with the International Court at The Hague. The competence of the European Court is at present limited to matters arising out of the Convention on Human Rights, and the cases which come before it are likely for the most part to result from individual petitions. It is still quite uncertain whether the Court will have any appreciable volume of business, but this is probably inevitable at the start. It seems that the circumstances in which it will have jurisdiction are reasonably clear—which leads to the hope that it will not have the same difficulties as The Hague Court in this respect—but there are many uncertainties or gaps in the Convention which will no doubt require authoritative interpretation.

This led to the proposal, described in the preceding chapter, for conferring on the Court the competence to give advisory opinions.

Another way in which the competence of the Court might be extended is in the interpretation of other European treaties. The Member States of the Council of Europe have now concluded a whole series of treaties drafted by committees of the Council, which include *inter alia* conventions dealing with the following subjects: social security, social and medical assistance, the filing of patent applications, establishment, extradition, the compulsory insurance of motor vehicles and the liabilities of hotel-keepers. Other such conventions are in preparation.[1] Many of them are likely to come before the courts of Member States for interpretation. But if they are interpreted in different ways by the different national tribunals, their objective of securing the adoption by Member States of the same laws or the same practices will have been defeated. Another illustration will have been afforded of the proposition stated by Bartin more than sixty years ago that it is not possible to secure uniform decisions by the adoption of uniform rules; it is also necessary to secure uniform interpretation.[2]

Faced with this problem, Professor Wahl of Heidelberg, who was also a member of the Bundestag and of the Consultative Assembly, tabled a motion in October 1957 for the creation of a European Supreme Court to consider violations of European conventions at the request of individuals. While this motion was under consideration in the Assembly's Legal Committee, the Court of Human Rights was established. Professor Wahl then modified his original proposal to take account of this fact and suggested that the task of interpretation of European conventions should be vested in the new Court. The essence of his plan was that when the courts of a Member State are called on to interpret such a convention they should be able to refer the matter to the European Court for its opinion, and that they should be obliged to do so if they intend to depart from the interpretation already

---

[1] On the reduction of multiple nationality, on arbitration in private law, on the rights of corporate bodies incorporated in other Member States, on the payment of foreign money liabilities.

[2] Bartin, *De l'impossibilité d'arriver à la suppression définitive des conflits de lois*, Clunet, 1897, p. 225. See also Bartin in *Recueil des Cours* (1930), Vol. 1, 565.

given by the courts of another Member State. This proposal raised many problems, such as whether the opinion of the European Court would be binding or merely advisory; whether only courts of last resort should have the right of reference to the European Court; and whether the proposed procedure should apply to other treaties in addition to Council of Europe conventions, for example the conventions concluded by the Hague Conference on Private International Law. There are clearly implications of the plan which would require detailed negotiations between the Member States before it could become effective; but without doubt the proposal is an interesting attempt to find a solution to a real problem and, if adopted, would give the Court of Human Rights an important source of business and increased authority. The project was submitted by the Assembly to the Committee of Ministers of the Council of Europe in January 1960.[1]

In the following year, however, the Committee of Ministers informed the Assembly that it felt unable to act on these proposals. It had submitted them to Member Governments, which had examined them from the point of view of their compatibility with their existing constitutions and judicial practice. The Committee of Ministers reported that most governments saw serious difficulties in accepting the draft convention which the Assembly had proposed and gave the following reasons:[2]

Article 5, Alternative A, of the draft Convention appended to the Recommendation, pursuant to which an advisory opinion of the European Court should be binding on the national courts, is incompatible with the Constitutions of several member States. Alternative B, however, which provides that the advisory opinion shall have no binding force, would conflict less with those Constitutions but would in many cases entail fundamental alterations in the legal system at

---

[1] Recommendation 231 on the Uniform Interpretation of European Treaties, *Texts adopted*, January 1960. The idea had, of course, a good deal in common with the system set up by Article 177 of the Rome treaty, whereby national courts may, and in certain circumstances must, refer a question of interpretation of the treaty to the Court of Justice of the Community. For the history of the proposal and the reasons for it see the Report of the Legal Committee, *Documents of the Assembly*, 1959–60, doc. 1062.

[2] Twelfth Report of the Committee of Ministers, *Documents*, 1961, doc. 1257, para. 240.

present in force. In one country it would be contrary to constitutional practice for a court to seek an advisory opinion from a European court. In another country the interpretation of international treaties, except in cases involving private interests, is a matter for the Minister of Foreign Affairs, and a change in accordance with Recommendation 231 would not seem to be compatible with this principle.

In several States treaties are not normally applicable as such, but have to be incorporated into municipal law by an Act of Parliament. Thus, national courts apply only domestic laws and it appears that no action would be taken under the proposed Agreement which limits the competence of the European Court to interpret treaties 'insofar as the provisions of those . . . treaties are applicable by national courts'. Some Governments have expressed doubts as to the advisability of extending the competence of the European Court in view of the fact that the Court was set up to decide matters arising from the application of the Convention for the Protection of Human Rights and Fundamental Freedoms. Moreover since many European countries have recognised the competence of other international courts to render advisory opinions, there seems to be a danger that interpretations by the European Court might conflict with those of other international courts.

Several Governments pointed out that the application of the proposed Agreement might involve considerable practical difficulties, e.g. as regards ascertaining whether the decision envisaged would be at variance with an interpretation given by a Court in another contracting country. Thus, the proposed Agreement would also cause delay in the handling of a case.

In spite of this negative attitude, the Legal Committee of the Assembly decided in 1962 to give the matter further study. By that time the majority of the Member States of the Council of Europe were either members of the Economic Community or applicants for membership; they had therefore either accepted or indicated their willingness to accept the provisions of Article 177 of the Rome Treaty.[1] The Committee was also encouraged by the fact that several Ministers of Justice from the Member States had made important speeches to the Assembly,[2] in more than one of which the need was recognised for finding some means of securing the uniform interpretation of European

[1] See p. 168 n. 1.

[2] The Austrian Minister of Justice in May 1962 ; the Austrian and Netherlands Ministers in September ; and the Irish Minister in January 1963.

treaties. Further proposals on this subject were therefore to be expected and it was to be hoped that they might meet with greater success than the original Recommendation of January 1960.

This matter had a considerable history. As long ago as December 1951 the Consultative Assembly had adopted a Recommendation to the Committee of Ministers proposing the establishment of a single European Court of Justice to discharge the functions of the Court of Human Rights and the then still-projected Court of the Coal and Steel Community.[1] One of the reasons given for the creation of such a court was that:

it would be, in the nature of things, qualified to settle disputes between Members of the Council of Europe, regarding the interpretation and application of the Statute, and of all European Conventions, and could at the same time fulfil the same advisory functions in relation to the Committee of Ministers and to the Assembly, as the International Court of Justice does in relation to the United Nations Organisation.

These proposals were further developed in September 1952 when the Assembly adopted a *Recommendation for the establishment of a European Court of Justice and of a European Act for the Peaceful Settlement of Disputes*. This Recommendation stated categorically *inter alia*:

The European Court of Justice shall constitute the judicial organ of the Council of Europe.

It was intended that the jurisdiction of the Court should extend to disputes between Member States covered by the proposed European Act for the Peaceful Settlement of Disputes, matters referred to it by the restricted Communities such as the Coal and Steel Community, matters arising under the Convention on Human Rights, and questions submitted to it by the Consultative Assembly or the Committee of Ministers for an advisory opinion.[2]

When the Member Governments came to consider this proposal, they agreed to the idea of concluding an arrangement between themselves for the peaceful settlement of disputes and concluded

[1] Recommendation 22, *Texts adopted*, December 1951.

[2] Recommendation 36, *Texts adopted*, September 1952.

a convention for the purpose on 29 April 1957.[1] But they decided
to maintain the Hague Court as the judicial instrument for the
purpose, and the convention resembles fairly closely the General
Act of Geneva of 1926. It entered into force on 30 April 1958
and by December 1962 had been ratified by Austria, Denmark,
the Federal Republic, Italy, Luxembourg, the Netherlands,
Norway, Sweden and the United Kingdom. Nevertheless, having regard to the limited scope of this convention, it may be
that the idea of using a European Court for the interpretation of
European treaties may be revived.

However that may be, it seems clear that the European Court
of Human Rights will have an interesting future and that proposals
will not be lacking to extend its competence and increase its
authority. The quality of the judges is already sufficient guarantee
that confidence in the Court will not be misplaced. In the wider
context of the development of European institutions, the 'Greater
Europe' represented by the seventeen Member States of the
Council of Europe will need its judicial organ, in the same way as
the Six-Power Communities have their Court of Justice and the
United Nations have the International Court. We are at a stage in
the development of international institutions when the three
branches of government—executive, legislative, and judicial—
are beginning to take shape. They have already done so to a marked
degree in the Communities of the Six; and the Council of Europe
already has an active parliamentary organ and an executive in
embryo. It is reasonable to hope that the Court of Human Rights
will become the third partner in the institutions of Greater
Europe.

2. *The European Precedent followed in other Continents*

It may be objected very reasonably that the political aim of the
Council of Europe in securing the protection of human rights is
excellent in itself but that it would be better if it were realised on a
world-wide basis and not confined to a regional organisation in
Europe—and only a part of Europe at that. This is, of course,
perfectly true. There is no doubt that the universal recognition
of human rights must be the long-term objective of international

[1] *European Treaty Series*, No. 23. See Robertson, *The Council of Europe*,
op. cit., pp. 188–91.

lawyers; unfortunately the realisation of that objective is still remote.

The pioneer work in this field has, of course, been done by the United Nations in drawing up the *Universal Declaration of Human Rights* of 10 December 1948 and due tribute must be paid to the value of that declaration and to the ideals which inspired it. But when it came to drafting a convention or covenant that would make the rights proclaimed in the Universal Declaration legally enforceable in the Member States, this has not yet proved possible on a world-wide basis. The United Nations has been working for more than ten years on two draft International Covenants on Human Rights but the task is not yet completed.[1]

It is however a curious fact that while the work which started on a world-wide basis in the United Nations has made much greater progress over the last ten years in the more limited framework of Western Europe, nevertheless the pendulum now seems to be swinging back again and other continents are following, and profiting from, the European example.

As related above,[2] the European Convention contains an Article 63 which provides that any Contracting Party may at any time extend the application of the Convention 'to all or any of the territories for whose international relations it is responsible'. In accordance with this provision, the Danish Government, in April 1953, extended the application of the Convention to Greenland, the Netherlands Government in November 1955 to Surinam and the Netherlands Antilles and the British Government in October 1953 to forty-one overseas territories for whose international relations it was responsible.[3]

This was all to the good, but it raised the problem of what would happen as the various colonial territories become independent.

---

[1] At its Tenth Session in 1954 the Commission on Human Rights approved a draft Covenant on Economic, Social and Cultural Rights and a draft Covenant on Civil and Political Rights. Each draft contained both substantive articles on the rights to be protected and 'measures of implementation' laying down the procedure to be followed for this purpose (*Report of the Tenth Session of the Commission on Human Rights*, doc. E/CN.4/705 Appendix 1). By the end of 1962 the Third Committee of the General Assembly had revised and adopted all but two of the substantive articles of both Covenants (docs. A/C.3/L.978 of 25 September 1962 and A/5365 of 17 December 1962).

[2] See Ch. VI.

[3] See Appendix 3.

The metropolitan countries then cease to be responsible for their international relations and the provisions of the Convention will thus automatically cease to apply. It would, however, be highly regrettable if one of the results of independence was a diminution in the protection afforded to human rights in the newly-independent country. Some other means of ensuring their protection must therefore be found; and this is precisely what is happening.[1]

Nigeria affords an interesting example. It was one of the British colonies to which the Convention applied by virtue of the declaration made on 23 October 1953. When the decision was taken to grant Nigeria independence, it became necessary to ensure that human rights would continue to be protected, all the more so as one of the major problems that arose in determining its future political structure was that of the status of important minorities in the country. In 1957, the Government of the United Kingdom convened a Constitutional Conference for Nigeria which set up a Minorities Commission to 'ascertain the facts about the fears of minorities in any part of Nigeria and to propose means of allaying these fears whether well- or ill-founded'. The Minorities Commission recommended in its report that comprehensive provisions, based primarily on the European Convention, should be included in the Constitution for this purpose. The Conference accepted this recommendation and adopted a Chapter on Fundamental Rights which in many cases reproduced the exact text of the European Convention and which was included in the new Constitution which entered into force when Nigeria attained independence on 1 October 1960.[2]

Sierra Leone is another case. A Constitutional Conference for Sierra Leone was held in April and May 1960 and agreed that fundamental rights should be included in the Constitution to be adopted on independence and that the relevant provisions

[1] See on this subject Vasak, 'De la Convention Européenne à la Convention africaine des Droits de l'Homme', *Revue Juridique et Politique d'Outre-mer*, janvier-mars 1962, pp. 59–76.

[2] *Yearbook of the Convention*, Vol. 3, 1960, pp. 706–24. See also A. B. McNulty, 'Influences Directes exercées hors d'Europe par la Convention Européenne des Droits de l'Homme', *Strasbourg Recueil*, pp. 377–86. I am indebted to him and to Mr. K. Vasak for much of the information contained in this section. See T. O. Elias, 'The New Constitution of Nigeria and the Protection of Human Rights', *J.I.C.J.*, 1960, pp. 30–46.

should be based on those adopted by the Nigerian Conference. A list of human rights and freedoms was annexed to the Conference report and again followed closely the text of the corresponding provisions of the European Convention. It was finally incorporated in the new Constitution of Sierra Leone as Chapter II: Protection of the Fundamental Rights and Freedoms of the Individual.[1]

Cyprus: the independence of Cyprus gave rise to the same problem in a particularly acute form, since, as is well-known, one of the major difficulties in reaching a settlement on the political future of the island concerned the status of the different ethnic groups. The Constitution of Cyprus of 15 August 1960 contains provisions for the use of both Greek and Turkish as official languages and for the proportionate representation of the two Communities in the composition of the Government, of the House of Representatives, of the Communal Chambers and of the Courts. Part II of the Constitution then contains an extremely comprehensive list of 'Fundamental Rights and Liberties' for which the European Convention was clearly the source of inspiration.[2]

The Organisation of American States: something similar is happening in other parts of the world. The Organisation of American States, at a meeting held in Santiago in August 1959, adopted a Conclusion entitled 'Human Rights', containing the following statement:

That eleven years after the American Declaration of the Rights and Duties of Man was proclaimed, the climate in the hemisphere is ready for the conclusion of a Convention—there having been similar progress in the United Nations Organisation and in the union known as the Council of Europe in the setting of standards and in the orderly study of this field, until today a satisfactory and promising level has been reached.

The same Conclusion requested the Inter-American Council of Jurists to prepare a draft Convention on Human Rights and a draft Convention on the creation of an Inter-American Court

---

[1] *Yearbook of the Convention,* Vol. 4, 1961, p. 656. The same precedent was followed in the Constitution of Uganda of 1962 and the draft Constitution for Kenya elaborated at the Constitutional Conference held in London in the same year.

[2] *Yearbook of the Convention,* Vol. 3, 1960, pp. 678–704. See also McNulty, *op. cit.,* pp. 381–2.

for the Protection of Human Rights and of other appropriate organs. It also resolved to create an Inter-American Commission on human rights of seven members to be elected in their individual capacity by the Council of the Organisation from lists proposed by the Governments. The Inter-American Council of Jurists met in Santiago later in the year and prepared a draft Convention, of which Part I, containing the civil and political rights, is very similar to the corresponding provisions of the European Convention.[1] In addition, no fewer than fourteen articles relating to economic, social and cultural rights were included.

The procedural provisions (Parts II and III) of the draft Convention propose to set up a Commission and a Court. The Commission, however, is only intended to act in regard to an inter-State dispute if direct negotiations between the parties are unsuccessful; for individual applications, it would have an optional competence and the same dual rôle as the European Commission of fact-finding and achieving a friendly settlement. Moreover, as there is no equivalent in the organisation of American States to the Committee of Ministers of the Council of Europe, the Inter-American Commission would itself assume a judicial rôle in a case which is not referred to the Inter-American Court. The functions and procedure of the latter are also similar to those of the European Court of Human Rights.

Africa: the conclusion of an *African Convention on Human Rights* has also been proposed. The African Conference on the Rule of Law was organised by the International Commission of Jurists at Lagos, in Nigeria, in January 1961. It assembled together 194 judges, practising lawyers and teachers of law from twenty-three African and nine other countries. The conference adopted the '*Law of Lagos*' which declared *inter alia*:[2]

That in order to give full effect to the Universal Declaration of Human Rights of 1948, this Conference invites the African Governments to study the possibility of adopting an African Convention of Human Rights in such a manner that the Conclusions of this Conference will be safeguarded by the creation of a court of appropriate jurisdiction

[1] The Inter-American draft Convention may be found in the *Journal of the International Commission of Jurists*, Summer 1962, pp. 160–84. It was also influenced by the draft Covenants under preparation in the United Nations.

[2] International Commission of Jurists, 'African Conference on the Rule of Law—Report of the Conference at Lagos, Jan. 3–7, 1961'.

and that recourse thereto be made available for all persons under the jurisdiction of the signatory States.

This proposal was amplified in the Report of the Conference which stated:

While the objective of facilitating the economic and social development of African countries is certainly desirable and necessary, the lawyers assembled in Lagos felt that a matter of primary concern is the search for a unity of principles and effective international protection in the field of human rights. This viewpoint was expressed in a motion which was incorporated in the *Law of Lagos* inviting the African Governments to study the possibility of an African Convention on Human Rights and of a court of appropriate jurisdiction that would entertain petitions for redress from persons aggrieved by the violation of their fundamental rights. Governments interested in such a Convention could refer to the Universal Declaration of Human Rights of 1948, to the European Convention on Human Rights of 1950, to the practice of the European Court of Strasbourg and to the preliminary work of a special commission set up in Latin America to prepare an Inter-American Convention on Human Rights. It is possible that this Lagos proposal will take some time to materialize—the above-cited examples offer useful lessons in patience and perseverance— but the prospect of agreeing in Africa on an integrated system for the protection of human rights with an adequate judicial enforcing machinery is certainly worth a major effort.

The idea of an African Convention on Human Rights is thus in the air. It was discussed at the meeting of African Heads of State and of Government at Monrovia in May 1961 and was supported by the Governor-General of Nigeria, Dr. Azikiwé, in a speech in London in the following August. The existing provisions in the constitutions of a number of the former British colonies cannot but facilitate its realisation.

Canada: yet another development has recently taken place in Canada.[1] The Canadian Bill of Rights was passed by the Canadian House of Commons on 4 August 1960. Its first article recognises and declares:

that in Canada there have existed and shall continue to exist without discrimination by reason of race, national origin, colour, religion or sex, the following human rights and fundamental freedoms, namely:

[1] See M. Cohen, 'Bill C-60 and International Law', *Canadian Bar Review*, March 1959, pp. 228–33 ; B. Laskin, 'Canada's Bill of Rights—A Dilemma for the Courts?' *I.C.L.Q.*, 1962, pp. 519–36.

a. the right of the individual to life, security of the person and enjoyment of property, and the right not to be deprived thereof except by due process of law;

b. the right of the individual to equality before the law and the protection of the law;

c. freedom of religion;

d. freedom of speech;

e. freedom of assembly and association; and

f. freedom of the press.

Its second article provides that every law of Canada shall (unless it expressly provides to the contrary) be so construed as not to abrogate or infringe a further series of rights and freedoms, including freedom from arbitrary detention or imprisonment, the right to a fair trial and to the remedy of *habeas corpus*, and the right to be presumed innocent until proved guilty according to the law. There then follows an interesting and, it is believed, original provision, which requires the Minister of Justice to examine every bill introduced in the House of Commons and every draft regulation submitted to the Privy Council in order to determine whether they are consistent with this Bill of Rights; if they are not, he is required to report the fact to the House of Commons at the first convenient opportunity.

The cause of human rights is thus seen to be making significant headway in this troubled world. It has its roots, of course, far back in history: it is only necessary to think of the Declaration of the Rights of Man of 1793, the product of the French Revolution; the American Bill of Rights of 1789, subsequently incorporated into the first ten Amendments to the Constitution; the English Bill of Rights of 1689, which was a compact between Crown and Parliament for the rule of law after the excessive pretensions of the Executive which had led to the Civil War; and, further back, the *Magna Carta* of 1215, which we regard—perhaps erroneously—as the foundation of civil rights in England. It would be a fascinating subject for research to study the evolution of such measures for the protection of human rights through the centuries; no doubt it would be necessary to go back at least to the Digest, and perhaps even further. The theme would be the constant struggle to protect the common man against all forms of tyranny; in this unequal struggle between the individual and the power of the state, it is only the rule of law which can redress the balance.

It is precisely because the first half of the twentieth century has witnessed the rise (and, in some cases, the fall) of such powerful tyrannies, and because the modern state has acquired such extensive powers over its citizens, that we are today so acutely conscious of the need for the protection of human rights. Perhaps the second half of the twentieth century will be known to history as the age of human rights; at least, it is encouraging that positive action is being taken to secure them in so many countries and in several continents.

This development gives to Europe a unique opportunity and a special responsibility. At a time when large areas of the world are emerging from colonial status to independence, the former colonial powers will have justified their mission if they can leave behind them, when they go, the rule of law and respect for human rights. In order to do this, they have a mission and a duty of training and of education; and to the accomplishment of this mission the Council of Europe can make a significant contribution. It is this fact which has led to the launching of a proposal to set up in Strasbourg a centre of research and of teaching for students and officials not only from the Member States in Europe, but also from all other countries desirous of establishing the legislative and judicial protection of fundamental freedoms. As stated by the late Judge Lauterpacht, whose memory is particularly revered in this connection: 'The cause of human rights offers to the Council of Europe an opportunity which may raise it high above the level of a political expedient and invest it with a dignity and authority which may prove one of the main sources of its strength'.[1] Those words will apply with even greater force if the Council of Europe can not only secure human rights to all persons within the jurisdiction of its Members, but also help, by teaching and example, to achieve the same results in other countries.

[1] *International Law and Human Rights*, p. 456.

CONVENTION FOR THE
PROTECTION OF HUMAN RIGHTS
AND FUNDAMENTAL FREEDOMS

The Governments signatory hereto, being Members of the Council of Europe,

Considering the Universal Declaration of Human Rights proclaimed by the General Assembly of the United Nations on 10 December 1948;

Considering that this Declaration aims at securing the universal and effective recognition and observance of the Rights therein declared;

Considering that the aim of the Council of Europe is the achievement of greater unity between its Members and that one of the methods by which that aim is to be pursued is the maintenance and further realisation of Human Rights and Fundamental Freedoms;

Reaffirming their profound belief in those Fundamental Freedoms which are the foundation of justice and peace in the world and are best maintained on the one hand by an effective political democracy and on the other by a common understanding and observance of the Human Rights upon which they depend;

Being resolved, as the Governments of European countries which are like-minded and have a common heritage of political traditions, ideals, freedom and the rule of law, to take the first steps for the collective enforcement of certain of the Rights stated in the Universal Declaration;

Have agreed as follows:

ARTICLE 1

The High Contracting Parties shall secure to everyone within their jurisdiction the rights and freedoms defined in Section I of this Convention.

SECTION I

ARTICLE 2

1. Everyone's right to life shall be protected by law. No one shall be deprived of his life intentionally save in the execution of a sentence of a court following his conviction of a crime for which this penalty is provided by law.

2. Deprivation of life shall not be regarded as inflicted in contravention of this Article when it results from the use of force which is no more than absolutely necessary:

a. in defence of any person from unlawful violence;

b. in order to effect a lawful arrest or to prevent the escape of a person lawfully detained;

c. in action lawfully taken for the purpose of quelling a riot or insurrection.

ARTICLE 3

No one shall be subjected to torture or to inhuman or degrading treatment or punishment.

ARTICLE 4

1. No one shall be held in slavery or servitude.

2. No one shall be required to perform forced or compulsory labour.

3. For the purpose of this Article the term 'forced or compulsory labour' shall not include:

a. any work required to be done in the ordinary course of detention imposed according to the provisions of Article 5 of this Convention or during conditional release from such detention;

b. any service of a military character or, in case of conscientious objectors in countries where they are recognised, service exacted instead of compulsory military service;

c. any service exacted in case of an emergency or calamity threatening the life or well-being of the community;

d. any work or service which forms part of normal civic obligations.

ARTICLE 5

1. Everyone has the right to liberty and security of person.

No one shall be deprived of his liberty save in the following cases and in accordance with a procedure prescribed by law:

a. the lawful detention of a person after conviction by a competent court;

b. the lawful arrest or detention of a person for non-compliance with the lawful order of a court or in order to secure the fulfilment of any obligation prescribed by law;

c. the lawful arrest or detention of a person effected for the purpose of bringing him before the competent legal authority on reasonable suspicion of having committed an offence or when it is reasonably considered necessary to prevent his committing an offence or fleeing after having done so;

d. the detention of a minor by lawful order for the purpose of educational supervision or his lawful detention for the purpose of bringing him before the competent legal authority;

e. the lawful detention of persons for the prevention of the spreading of infectious diseases, of persons of unsound mind, alcoholics or drug addicts or vagrants;

f. the lawful arrest or detention of a person to prevent his effecting an unauthorised entry into the country or of a person against whom action is being taken with a view to deportation or extradition.

2. Everyone who is arrested shall be informed promptly, in a language which he understands, of the reasons for his arrest and of any charge against him.

3. Everyone arrested or detained in accordance with the provisions of paragraph 1 (*c*) of this Article shall be brought promptly before a judge or other officer authorised by law to exercise judicial power and shall be entitled to trial within a reasonable time or to release pending trial. Release may be conditioned by guarantees to appear for trial.

4. Everyone who is deprived of his liberty by arrest or detention shall be entitled to take proceedings by which the lawfulness of his detention shall be decided speedily by a court and his release ordered if the detention is not lawful.

5. Everyone who has been the victim of arrest or detention in contravention of the provisions of this Article shall have an enforceable right to compensation.

ARTICLE 6

1. In the determination of his civil rights and obligations or of any criminal charge against him, everyone is entitled to a fair and public hearing within a reasonable time by an independent and impartial tribunal established by law. Judgment shall be pronounced publicly but the press and public may be excluded from all or part of the trial in the interests of morals, public order or national security in a democratic society, where the interests of juveniles or the protection of the private life of the parties so require, or to the extent strictly necessary in the opinion of the court in special circumstances where publicity would prejudice the interests of justice.

2. Everyone charged with a criminal offence shall be presumed innocent until proved guilty according to law.

3. Everyone charged with a criminal offence has the following minimum rights:

a. to be informed promptly, in a language which he understands and in detail, of the nature and cause of the accusation against him;

b. to have adequate time and facilities for the preparation of his defence;

c. to defend himself in person or through legal assistance of his own choosing or, if he has not sufficient means to pay for legal assistance, to be given it free when the interests of justice so require;

d. to examine or have examined witnesses against him and to obtain the attendance and examination of witnesses on his behalf under the same conditions as witnesses against him;

e. to have the free assistance of an interpreter if he cannot understand or speak the language used in court.

ARTICLE 7

1. No one shall be held guilty of any criminal offence on account of any act or omission which did not constitute a criminal offence under national or international law at the time when it was committed. Nor shall a heavier penalty be imposed than the one that was applicable at the time the criminal offence was committed.

2. This Article shall not prejudice the trial and punishment of any person for any act or omission which, at the time when it was committed, was criminal according to the general principles of law recognised by civilised nations.

ARTICLE 8

1. Everyone has the right to respect for his private and family life, his home and his correspondence.

2. There shall be no interference by a public authority with the exercise of this right except such as is in accordance with the law and is necessary in a democratic society in the interests of national security, public safety or the economic well-being of the country, for the prevention of disorder or crime, for the protection of health or morals, or for the protection of the rights and freedoms of others.

ARTICLE 9

1. Everyone has the right to freedom of thought, conscience and religion; this right includes freedom to change his religion or belief and freedom, either alone or in community with others and in public or private, to manifest his religion or belief, in worship, teaching, practice and observance.

2. Freedom to manifest one's religion or beliefs shall be subject only to such limitations as are prescribed by law and are necessary

in a democratic society in the interests of public safety, for the protection of public order, health or morals, or for the protection of the rights and freedoms of others.

ARTICLE 10

1. Everyone has the right to freedom of expression. This right shall include freedom to hold opinions and to receive and impart information and ideas without interference by public authority and regardless of frontiers. This Article shall not prevent States from requiring the licensing of broadcasting, television or cinema enterprises.

2. The exercise of these freedoms, since it carries with it duties and responsibilities, may be subject to such formalities, conditions, restrictions or penalties as are prescribed by law and are necessary in a democratic society, in the interests of national security, territorial integrity or public safety, for the prevention of disorder or crime, for the protection of health or morals, for the protection of the reputation or rights of others, for preventing the disclosure of information received in confidence, or for maintaining the authority and impartiality of the judiciary.

ARTICLE 11

1. Everyone has the right to freedom of peaceful assembly and to freedom of association with others, including the right to form and to join trade unions for the protection of his interests.

2. No restrictions shall be placed on the exercise of these rights other than such as are prescribed by law and are necessary in a democratic society in the interests of national safety or public safety, for the prevention of disorder or crime, for the protection of health or morals or for the protection of the rights and freedoms of others. This Article shall not prevent the imposition of lawful restrictions on the exercise of these rights by members of the armed forces, of the police or of the administration of the State.

ARTICLE 12

Men and women of marriageable age have the right to marry and to found a family, according to the national laws governing the exercise of this right.

ARTICLE 13

Everyone whose rights and freedoms as set forth in this Convention are violated shall have an effective remedy before a national authority

N

notwithstanding that the violation has been committed by persons acting in an official capacity.

ARTICLE 14

The enjoyment of the rights and freedoms set forth in this Convention shall be secured without discrimination on any ground such as sex, race, colour, language, religion, political or other opinion, national or social origin, association with a national minority, property, birth or other status.

ARTICLE 15

1. In time of war or other public emergency threatening the life of the nation any High Contracting Party may take measures derogating from its obligations under this Convention to the extent strictly required by the exigencies of the situation, provided that such measures are not inconsistent with its other obligations under international law.

2. No derogation from Article 2, except in respect of deaths resulting from lawful acts of war, or from Articles 3, 4 (paragraph 1) and 7 shall be made under this provision.

3. Any High Contracting Party availing itself of this right of derogation shall keep the Secretary-General of the Council of Europe fully informed of the measures which it has taken and reasons therefor. It shall also inform the Secretary-General of the Council of Europe when such measures have ceased to operate and the provisions of the Convention are again being fully executed.

ARTICLE 16

Nothing in Articles 10, 11 and 14 shall be regarded as preventing the High Contracting Parties from imposing restrictions on the political activity of aliens.

ARTICLE 17

Nothing in this Convention may be interpreted as implying for any State, group or person any right to engage in any activity or perform any act aimed at the destruction of any of the rights and freedoms set forth herein or at their limitation to a greater extent than is provided for in the Convention.

ARTICLE 18

The restrictions permitted under this Convention to the said rights and freedoms shall not be applied for any purpose other than those for which they have been prescribed.

SECTION II

Article 19

To ensure the observance of the engagements undertaken by the High Contracting Parties in the present Convention, there shall be set up:

1. A European Commission of Human Rights, hereinafter referred to as 'the Commission';

2. A European Court of Human Rights, hereinafter referred to as 'the Court'.

SECTION III

Article 20

The Commission shall consist of a number of members equal to that of the High Contracting Parties. No two members of the Commission may be nationals of the same State.

Article 21

1. The members of the Commission shall be elected by the Committee of Ministers by an absolute majority of votes, from a list of names drawn up by the Bureau of the Consultative Assembly; each group of the Representatives of the High Contracting Parties in the Consultative Assembly shall put forward three candidates, of whom two at least shall be its nationals.

2. As far as applicable, the same procedure shall be followed to complete the Commission in the event of other States subsequently becoming Parties to this Convention, and in filling casual vacancies.

Article 22

1. The members of the Commission shall be elected for a period of six years. They may be re-elected. However, of the members elected at the first election, the terms of seven members shall expire at the end of three years.

2. The members whose terms are to expire at the end of the initial period of three years shall be chosen by lot by the Secretary-General of the Council of Europe immediately after the first election has been completed.

3. A member of the Commission elected to replace a member whose term of office has not expired shall hold office for the remainder of his predecessor's term.

4. The members of the Commission shall hold office until replaced. After having been replaced, they shall continue to deal with such cases as they already have under consideration.

ARTICLE 23

The members of the Commission shall sit on the Commission in their individual capacity.

ARTICLE 24

Any High Contracting Party may refer to the Commission, through the Secretary-General of the Council of Europe, any alleged breach of the provisions of the Convention by another High Contracting Party.

ARTICLE 25

1. The Commission may receive petitions addressed to the Secretary-General of the Council of Europe from any person, non-governmental organisation or group of individuals claiming to be the victim of a violation by one of the High Contracting Parties of the rights set forth in this Convention, provided that the High Contracting Party against which the complaint has been lodged has declared that it recognises the competence of the Commission to receive such petitions. Those of the High Contracting Parties who have made such a declaration undertake not to hinder in any way the effective exercise of this right.

2. Such declarations may be made for a specific period.

3. The declarations shall be deposited with the Secretary-General of the Council of Europe who shall transmit copies thereof to the High Contracting Parties and publish them.

4. The Commission shall only exercise the powers provided for in this Article when at least six High Contracting Parties are bound by declarations made in accordance with the preceding paragraphs.

ARTICLE 26

The Commission may only deal with the matter after all domestic remedies have been exhausted, according to the generally recognised rules of international law, and within a period of six months from the date on which the final decision was taken.

ARTICLE 27

1. The Commission shall not deal with any petition submitted under Article 25 which

a. is anonymous, or

b. is substantially the same as a matter which has already been examined by the Commission or has already been submitted to another procedure of international investigation or settlement and if it contains no relevant new information.

2. The Commission shall consider inadmissible any petition submitted under Article 25 which it considers incompatible with the provisions of the present Convention, manifestly ill-founded, or an abuse of the right of petition.

3. The Commission shall reject any petition to it which it considers inadmissible under Article 26.

ARTICLE 28

In the event of the Commission accepting a petition referred to it:

a. it shall, with a view to ascertaining the facts, undertake together with the representatives of the parties an examination of the petition and, if need be, an investigation, for the effective conduct of which the States concerned shall furnish all necessary facilities, after an exchange of views with the Commission;

b. it shall place itself at the disposal of the parties concerned with a view to securing a friendly settlement of the matter on the basis of respect for Human Rights as defined in this Convention.

ARTICLE 29

1. The Commission shall perform the functions set out in Article 28 by means of a Sub-Commission consisting of seven members of the Commission.

2. Each of the parties concerned may appoint as members of this Sub-Commission a person of its choice.

3. The remaining members shall be chosen by lot in accordance with arrangements prescribed in the Rules of Procedure of the Commission.

ARTICLE 30

If the Sub-Commission succeeds in effecting a friendly settlement in accordance with Article 28, it shall draw up a Report which shall be sent to the States concerned, to the Committee of Ministers and to the Secretary-General of the Council of Europe for publication. This Report shall be confined to a brief statement of the facts and of the solution reached.

ARTICLE 31

1. If a solution is not reached, the Commission shall draw up a Report on the facts and state its opinion as to whether the facts found disclose a breach by the State concerned of its obligations under the Convention. The opinions of all the members of the Commission on this point may be stated in the Report.

2. The Report shall be transmitted to the Committee of Ministers. It shall also be transmitted to the States concerned, who shall not be at liberty to publish it.

3. In transmitting the Report to the Committee of Ministers the Commission may make such proposals as it thinks fit.

ARTICLE 32

1. If the question is not referred to the Court in accordance with Article 48 of this Convention within a period of three months from the date of the transmission of the Report to the Committee of Ministers, the Committee of Ministers shall decide by a majority of two-thirds of the members entitled to sit on the Committee whether there has been a violation of the Convention.

2. In the affirmative case the Committee of Ministers shall prescribe a period during which the High Contracting Party concerned must take the measures required by the decision of the Committee of Ministers.

3. If the High Contracting Party concerned has not taken satisfactory measures within the prescribed period, the Committee of Ministers shall decide by the majority provided for in paragraph (1) above what effect shall be given to its original decision and shall publish the Report.

4. The High Contracting Parties undertake to regard as binding on them any decision which the Committee of Ministers may take in application of the preceding paragraphs.

ARTICLE 33

The Commission shall meet in camera.

ARTICLE 34

The Commission shall take its decisions by a majority of the Members present and voting; the Sub-Commission shall take its decisions by a majority of its members.

ARTICLE 35

The Commission shall meet as the circumstances require. The meetings shall be convened by the Secretary-General of the Council of Europe.

ARTICLE 36

The Commission shall draw up its own rules of procedure.

ARTICLE 37

The secretariat of the Commission shall be provided by the Secretary-General of the Council of Europe.

SECTION IV

ARTICLE 38

The European Court of Human Rights shall consist of a number of judges equal to that of the Members of the Council of Europe. No two judges may be nationals of the same State.

ARTICLE 39

1. The members of the Court shall be elected by the Consultative Assembly by a majority of the votes cast from a list of persons nominated by the Members of the Council of Europe; each Member shall nominate three candidates, of whom two at least shall be its nationals.

2. As far as applicable, the same procedure shall be followed to complete the Court in the event of the admission of new Members of the Council of Europe, and in filling casual vacancies.

3. The candidates shall be of high moral character and must either possess the qualifications required for appointment to high judicial office or be jurisconsults of recognised competence.

ARTICLE 40

1. The members of the Court shall be elected for a period of nine years. They may be re-elected. However, of the members elected at the first election the terms of four members shall expire at the end of three years, and the terms of four more members shall expire at the end of six years.

2. The members whose terms are to expire at the end of the initial periods of three and six years shall be chosen by lot by the Secretary-General immediately after the first election has been completed.

3. A member of the Court elected to replace a member whose term of office has not expired shall hold office for the remainder of his predecessor's term.

4. The members of the Court shall hold office until replaced. After having been replaced, they shall continue to deal with such cases as they already have under consideration.

ARTICLE 41

The Court shall elect its President and Vice-President for a period of three years. They may be re-elected.

ARTICLE 42

The members of the Court shall receive for each day of duty a compensation to be determined by the Committee of Ministers.

ARTICLE 43

For the consideration of each case brought before it the Court shall consist of a Chamber composed of seven judges. There shall sit as an ex officio member of the Chamber the judge who is a national of any State party concerned, or, if there is none, a person of its choice who shall sit in the capacity of judge; the names of the other judges shall be chosen by lot by the President before the opening of the case.

ARTICLE 44

Only the High Contracting Parties and the Commission shall have the right to bring a case before the Court.

ARTICLE 45

The jurisdiction of the Court shall extend to all cases concerning the interpretation and application of the present Convention which the High Contracting Parties or the Commission shall refer to it in accordance with Article 48.

ARTICLE 46

1. Any of the High Contracting Parties may at any time declare that it recognises as compulsory *ipso facto* and without special agreement the jurisdiction of the Court in all matters concerning the interpretation and application of the present Convention.

2. The declarations referred to above may be made unconditionally or on condition of reciprocity on the part of several or certain other High Contracting Parties or for a specified period.

3. These declarations shall be deposited with the Secretary-General of the Council of Europe who shall transmit copies thereof to the High Contracting Parties.

ARTICLE 47

The Court may only deal with a case after the Commission has acknowledged the failure of efforts for a friendly settlement and within the period of three months provided for in Article 42.

ARTICLE 48

The following may bring a case before the Court, provided that the High Contracting Party concerned, if there is only one, or the High Contracting Parties concerned, if there is more than one, are subject to the compulsory jurisdiction of the Court, or, failing that, with the consent of the High Contracting Party concerned, if there is only one, or of the High Contracting Parties concerned, if there is more than one:

a. the Commission;

b. a High Contracting Party whose national is alleged to be a victim;

c. a High Contracting Party which referred the case to the Commission;

d. a High Contracting Party against which the complaint has been lodged.

ARTICLE 49

In the event of dispute as to whether the Court has jurisdiction, the matter shall be settled by the decision of the Court.

ARTICLE 50

If the Court finds that a decision or a measure taken by a legal authority or any other authority of a High Contracting Party is completely or partially in conflict with the obligations arising from the present Convention, and if the internal law of the said Party allows only partial reparation to be made for the consequences of this decision or measure, the decision of the Court shall, if necessary, afford just satisfaction to the injured party.

ARTICLE 51

1. Reasons shall be given for the judgment of the Court.
2. If the judgment does not represent in whole or in part the unanimous opinion of the judges, any judge shall be entitled to deliver a separate opinion.

ARTICLE 52

The judgment of the Court shall be final.

ARTICLE 53

The High Contracting Parties undertake to abide by the decision of the Court in any case to which they are parties.

ARTICLE 54

The judgment of the Court shall be transmitted to the Committee of Ministers which shall supervise its execution.

ARTICLE 55

The Court shall draw up its own rules and shall determine its own procedure.

ARTICLE 56

1. The first election of the members of the Court shall take place after the declarations by the High Contracting Parties mentioned in Article 46 have reached a total of eight.
2. No case can be brought before the Court before this election.

SECTION V

ARTICLE 57

On receipt of a request from the Secretary-General of the Council of Europe any High Contracting Party shall furnish an explanation of the manner in which its internal law ensures the effective implementation of any of the provisions of this Convention.

ARTICLE 58

The expenses of the Commission and the Court shall be borne by the Council of Europe.

ARTICLE 59

The members of the Commission and of the Court shall be entitled, during the discharge of their functions, to the privileges and immunities provided for in Article 40 of the Statute of the Council of Europe and in the agreements made thereunder.

ARTICLE 60

Nothing in this Convention shall be construed as limiting or derogating from any of the human rights and fundamental freedoms which may be ensured under the laws of any High Contracting Party or under any other agreement to which it is a Party.

ARTICLE 61

Nothing in this Convention shall prejudice the powers conferred on the Committee of Ministers by the Statute of the Council of Europe.

ARTICLE 62

The High Contracting Parties agree that, except by special agreement, they will not avail themselves of treaties, conventions or declarations in force between them for the purpose of submitting, by way of petition, a dispute arising out of the interpretation or application of this Convention to a means of settlement other than those provided for in this Convention.

ARTICLE 63

1. Any State may at the time of its ratification or at any time thereafter declare by notification addressed to the Secretary-General of the Council of Europe that the present Convention shall extend to all or any of the territories for whose international relations it is responsible.

2. The Convention shall extend to the territory or territories named in the notification as from the thirtieth day after the receipt of this notification by the Secretary-General of the Council of Europe.

3. The provisions of this Convention shall be applied in such territories with due regard, however, to local requirements.

4. Any State which has made a declaration in accordance with paragraph 1 of this Article may at any time thereafter declare on behalf of one or more of the territories to which the declaration relates that it accepts the competence of the Commission to receive petitions from individuals, non-governmental organisations or groups of individuals in accordance with Article 25 of the present Convention.

ARTICLE 64

1. Any State may, when signing this Convention or when depositing its instrument of ratification, make a reservation in respect of any particular provision of the Convention to the extent that any law then in force in its territory is not in conformity with the provision. Reservations of a general character shall not be permitted under this Article.

2. Any reservation made under this Article shall contain a brief statement of the law concerned.

ARTICLE 65

1. A High Contracting Party may denounce the present Convention only after the expiry of five years from the date on which it became a Party to it and after six months' notice contained in a notification addressed to the Secretary-General of the Council of Europe, who shall inform the other High Contracting Parties.

2. Such a denunciation shall not have the effect of releasing the High Contracting Party concerned from its obligations under this Convention in respect of any act which, being capable of constituting a violation of such obligations, may have been performed by it before the date at which the denunciation became effective.

3. Any High Contracting Party which shall cease to be a Member of the Council of Europe shall cease to be a Party to this Convention under the same conditions.

4. The Convention may be denounced in accordance with the provisions of the preceding paragraphs in respect of any territory to which it has been declared to extend under the terms of Article 63.

ARTICLE 66

1. This Convention shall be open to the signature of the Members of the Council of Europe. It shall be ratified. Ratifications shall be deposited with the Secretary-General of the Council of Europe.

2. The present Convention shall come into force after the deposit of ten instruments of ratification.

3. As regards any signatory ratifying subsequently, the Convention shall come into force at the date of the deposit of its instrument of ratification.

4. The Secretary-General of the Council of Europe shall notify all the Members of the Council of Europe of the entry into force of the Convention, the names of the High Contracting Parties who have ratified it, and the deposit of all instruments of ratification which may be effected subsequently.

Done at Rome this 4th day of November 1950 in English and French, both texts being equally authentic, in a single copy which shall remain deposited in the archives of the Council of Europe. The Secretary-General shall transmit certified copies to each of the signatories.

Ratifications

Austria	3 September 1958
Belgium	14 June 1955
Cyprus	6 October 1962
Denmark	13 April 1953
Federal Republic of Germany	5 December 1952
Greece	28 March 1953
Iceland	29 June 1953
Ireland	25 February 1953
Italy	26 October 1955
Luxembourg	3 September 1953
Netherlands	31 August 1954
Norway	15 January 1952
Saar[1]	14 January 1953
Sweden	4 February 1952
Turkey	18 May 1954
United Kingdom	8 March 1951

Entry into Force

3 September 1953

[1] The Saar ceased to be a Contracting Party on 1 January 1957.

PROTOCOL TO THE CONVENTION

The Governments signatory hereto, being Members of the Council of Europe,

Being resolved to take steps to ensure the collective enforcement of certain rights and freedoms other than those already included in Section I of the Convention for the Protection of Human Rights and Fundamental Freedoms signed at Rome on 4 November 1950 (hereinafter referred to as 'the Convention'),

Have agreed as follows:

ARTICLE 1

Every natural or legal person is entitled to the peaceful enjoyment of his possessions. No one shall be deprived of his possessions except in the public interest and subject to the conditions provided for by law and by the general principles of international law.

The preceding provisions shall not, however, in any way impair the right of a State to enforce such laws as it deems necessary to control the use of property in accordance with the general interest or to secure the payment of taxes or other contributions or penalties.

ARTICLE 2

No person shall be denied the right to education. In the exercise of any functions which it assumes in relation to education and to teaching, the State shall respect the right of parents to ensure such education and teaching in conformity with their own religious and philosophical convictions.

ARTICLE 3

The High Contracting Parties undertake to hold free elections at reasonable intervals by secret ballot, under conditions which will ensure the free expression of the opinion of the people in the choice of the legislature.

ARTICLE 4

Any High Contracting Party may at the time of signature or ratification or at any time thereafter communicate to the Secretary-General of the Council of Europe a declaration stating the extent to which it undertakes that the provisions of the present Protocol shall apply to such of the territories for the international relations of which it is responsible as are named therein.

Any High Contracting Party which has communicated a declaration in virtue of the preceding paragraph may from time to time communicate a further declaration modifying the terms of any former declaration or terminating the application of the provisions of this Protocol in respect of any territory.

A declaration made in accordance with this Article shall be deemed to have been made in accordance with Paragraph (1) of Article 63 of the Convention.

ARTICLE 5

As between the High Contracting Parties the provisions of Articles 1, 2, 3 and 4 of this Protocol shall be regarded as additional Articles to the Convention and all the provisions of the Convention shall apply accordingly.

ARTICLE 6

This Protocol shall be open for signature by the Members of the Council of Europe, who are the signatories of the Convention; it shall be ratified at the same time as or after the ratification of the Convention. It shall enter into force after the deposit of ten instruments of ratification. As regards any signatory ratifying subsequently, the Protocol shall enter into force at the date of the deposit of its instrument of ratification.

The instruments of ratification shall be deposited with the Secretary-General of the Council of Europe, who will notify all Members of the names of those who have ratified.

Done at Paris on the 20th day of March 1952, in English and French, both texts being equally authentic, in a single copy which shall remain deposited in the archives of the Council of Europe. The Secretary-General shall transmit certified copies to each of the signatory Governments.

Ratifications

Austria	3 September 1958
Belgium	14 June 1955
Cyprus	6 October 1962
Denmark	13 April 1953

Federal Republic of Germany	13 February 1957
Greece	28 March 1953
Iceland	29 June 1953
Ireland	25 February 1953
Italy	26 October 1955
Luxembourg	3 September 1953
Netherlands	31 August 1954
Norway	18 December 1952
Saar[1]	14 January 1953
Sweden	22 June 1953
Turkey	18 May 1954
United Kingdom	3 November 1952

Entry into Force

18 May 1954

[1] The Saar ceased to be a Contracting Party on 1 January 1957.

APPENDIX 3

OPTIONAL DECLARATIONS AND RESERVATIONS

ARTICLE 25

The following have made declarations recognising the competence of the Commission to receive individual petitions:

Austria	Ireland
Belgium	Luxembourg
Denmark	Netherlands
Federal Republic of Germany	Norway
Iceland	Sweden

ARTICLE 46

The following have made declarations recognising as compulsory the jurisdiction of the Court:

Austria	Iceland
Belgium	Ireland
Denmark	Luxembourg
Federal Republic of Germany	Netherlands

ARTICLE 63

The following have made declarations extending the application of the Convention to the territories indicated:

Denmark — Greenland
(Greenland however became part of metropolitan Denmark on 5 June 1953)

Netherlands — Surinam
Netherlands Antilles
(except as regards the provision of free legal assistance under Article 6 (3) (c))

United Kingdom

Aden Colony	Channel Islands:
The Bahamas	The Bailiwick of
Barbados	Jersey
Basutoland	The Bailiwick of
Bechuanaland	Guernsey
Bermuda	Cyprus
British Guiana	Falkland Islands
British Honduras	Fiji
British Solomon Islands	Gambia

Gibraltar	Sarawak
Gilbert and Ellice Islands	Seychelles
Gold Coast	Sierra Leone
Jamaica	Singapore
Kenya	Somaliland
Leeward Islands	Swaziland
Federation of Malaya	Tanganjika
Malta	Trinidad
Isle of Man	Uganda
Mauritius	Windward Islands:
Nigeria	Dominica
Northern Rhodesia	Grenada
North Borneo	St. Lucia
Nyasaland	St. Vincent
St. Helena	Zanzibar,

and at the request of the Government of that Kingdom, for whose international relations Her Majesty's Government in the United Kingdom is responsible, Kingdom of Tonga

Reservations under Article 64 and other Declarations

1. AUSTRIA

'The Federal President declares this Convention ratified with the reservation:

1. The provisions of Article 5 of the Convention shall be so applied that there shall be no interference with the measures for the deprivation of liberty prescribed in the laws on administrative procedure, BGB1 No. 172/1950, subject to review by the Administrative Court or the Constitutional Court as provided for in the Austrian Federal Constitution;

2. The provisions of Article 6 of the Convention shall be so applied that there shall be no prejudice to the principles governing public court hearings laid down in Article 90 of the 1929 version of the Federal Constitution Law;

and being desirous of avoiding any uncertainty concerning the application of Article 1 of the Protocol in connection with the State Treaty of 15 May 1955 for the Restoration of an Independent and Democratic Austria, declares the Protocol ratified with the reservations that there shall be no interference with the provisions of Part IV "Claims arising out of the War" and Part V "Property, Rights and Interests" of the above-mentioned State Treaty".

2. FEDERAL REPUBLIC OF GERMANY

a. 'The Federal Republic of Germany remains of the opinion that the second sentence of Article 2 of the Protocol does not create for the State any obligation to finance in whole or in part schools of a religious or philosophical character, since this question is not, according to the unanimous declaration of the Committee on Legal Questions of the Consultative Assembly and of the Secretary-General of the Council of Europe, within the framework of the Convention of Human Rights and Fundamental Freedoms or of the Protocol thereto'.

b. 'The territory to which the Convention applies shall also extend to Berlin (West)'.

c. 'In accordance with Article 64 of the Convention the Federal Republic of Germany makes the reservation that it will only apply the provisions of Article 7 paragraph 2 of the Convention within the limits of Article 103 paragraph 2 of the Basic Law of the Federal Republic of Germany. The latter provides "no act shall be punished unless the Law provided that it was punishable before it was committed"'.

d. '. . . the Protocol to the Convention on Human Rights and Fundamental Freedoms signed at Paris on 20 March 1952, will also apply to Land Berlin, with effect from 13 February 1957, the date on which the Protocol entered into force for the Federal Republic of Germany'.

3. GREECE

'At the time of signature of this Protocol, the Greek Government, pursuant to Article 64 of the Convention, makes the following reservation relating to Article 2 of the Protocol: The application of the word "philosophical", which is the penultimate word of the second sentence of Article 2, will, in Greece, conform with the relevant provisions of internal legislation'.

4. IRELAND

'. . . the Government of Ireland do hereby confirm and ratify the aforesaid Convention and undertake faithfully to perform and carry out all the stipulations therein contained, subject to the reservation that they do not interpret Article 6 (3) (c) of the Convention as requiring the provision of free legal assistance to any wider extent than is now provided in Ireland'.

5. LUXEMBOURG

'The Government of the Grand Duchy of Luxembourg, having regard to Article 64 of the Convention and desiring to avoid any uncertainty as regards the application of Article 1 of the Protocol in relation to the Luxembourg Law of 26 April 1951 concerning the liquidation of certain ex-enemy property, rights and interests which have been subjected to measures of sequestration, makes a reservation relating to the provisions of the above-mentioned Law of 26 April 1951'.

6. Norway

'Since Article 2 of the Norwegian Constitution of 17 May 1814 contains a provision according to which Jesuits are banned, a corresponding reservation is made as regards the application of Article 9 of the Convention'.

(This reservation was withdrawn on 4 December 1956).

7. Sweden

'. . . We wish to ratify, approve and accept the said Protocol with all its articles, points and clauses, subject however to a reservation relating to Article 2 of the Protocol, which reservation is to the effect that Sweden cannot grant to parents the right to obtain, on the grounds of their philosophical convictions, dispensation for their children from the obligation to participate in certain parts of the teaching in the public schools; and also to the effect that the dispensation from the obligation to participate in the teaching of Christianity in these schools can only be accorded to children of a religion other than the Swedish Church for which satisfactory religious instruction has been organised—this reservation being based on the provisions of the new regulations of 17 March 1933 for establishments of secondary education in the Kingdom and the comparable provisions relating to other teaching establishments'.

8. Turkey

'Having seen and examined the Convention and Protocol, we have approved them subject to a reservation formulated as to the Second Article of the Protocol, by reason of the provisions of Law No. 6366, which was adopted by the Turkish Grand National Assembly on 10 March 1954'.

(The Law of 10 March 1954 approved the provisions of the Convention and Protocol, with the reservation that Article 2 of the Protocol should not prejudice the provisions of Law No. 430 of 3 March 1924 on the unification of teaching).

9. United Kingdom

'At the time of signing the present Protocol, I declare that, in view of certain provisions of the Education Acts in force in the United Kingdom, the principle affirmed in the second sentence of Article 2 is accepted by the United Kingdom only so far as it is compatible with the provision of efficient instruction and training, and the avoidance of unreasonable public expenditure'.

APPENDIX 4

RULES OF PROCEDURE OF THE
EUROPEAN COMMISSION OF HUMAN RIGHTS

*(as amended by the Commission during its 24th Plenary Session,
1–5 August 1960)*

Title I
ORGANISATION AND WORKING OF THE COMMISSION

Title II
PROCEDURE

Title III
RELATIONS OF THE COMMISSION WITH THE COURT

TITLE I
ORGANISATION AND WORKING OF THE COMMISSION

CHAPTER I
Members of the Commission

RULE 1

1. The duration of the term of office of members of the Commission elected on 18 May 1954 shall be calculated as from this date. Similarly, the duration of the term of office of any member elected as a consequence of a State becoming a Party to the Convention after 18 May 1954 shall be calculated as from his election.

2. However, when a member is re-elected on the expiry of his term of office or is elected to replace a member whose term of office has expired or is about to expire, the duration of his term of office shall, in either case, be calculated as from the date of such expiry.

3. In accordance with Article 22, paragraph (3), of the Convention, a member elected to replace a member whose term of office has not expired shall hold office for the remainder of his predecessor's term.

4. In accordance with Article 22, paragraph (4), of the Convention, members shall hold office until replaced. After having been replaced, they shall continue to deal with such cases as they already have under consideration.

RULE 2

Before taking up his duties, each member of the Commission shall, at the first meeting of the Commission at which he is present after his election, make the following oath or solemn declaration:

'I swear', or 'I solemnly declare'—'that I will exercise all my powers and duties honourably and faithfully, impartially and conscientiously and that I will keep secret all deliberations'.

RULE 3

1. Members of the Commission shall take precedence after the President and Vice-President according to the length of time they have been in office.

2. Members having the same length of time in office shall take precedence according to age.

3. Re-elected members shall take precedence having regard to the duration of their previous terms of office.

RULE 4

Resignation of a member shall be notified to the President who shall transmit it to the Secretary-General of the Council of Europe. Subject to the provisions of Rule 1, paragraph (4), it shall constitute vacation of office.

CHAPTER II

Presidency of the Commission

RULE 5

1. The Commission shall elect the President and Vice-President during the month following the date of the entry into office of members

elected at periodical elections of part of the Commission in accordance with paragraph (1) of Article 22 of the Convention.

2. If the President or Vice-President, before the normal expiry of his term of office as President or Vice-President, ceases to be a member of the Commission or resigns his office, the Commission shall elect a successor to hold office for the remainder of the said term.

3. The elections referred to in this Rule shall be by secret ballot; only the members present shall take part. Election shall be by an absolute majority of votes.

If no member receives an absolute majority, a second ballot shall take place. The member receiving the most votes shall then be elected. In the case of equal voting the member having precedence under Rule 3 shall be elected.

RULE 6

The President shall direct the work and preside at the meetings of the Commission.

RULE 7

The Vice-President shall take the place of the President if the latter is unable to carry out his duties or if the office of President is vacant.

RULE 8

If the President and Vice-President are at the same time unable to carry out their duties or if their offices are at the same time vacant, the duties of President shall be carried out by another member according to the order of precedence laid down in Rule 3.

RULE 9

1. If the President is a national of a High Contracting Party which is party to a case brought before the Commission, he shall relinquish the office of President in respect of that case.

2. The President shall also relinquish the office of President in respect of any case in which he has acted in a Sub-commission as member appointed by a party pursuant to Article 29, paragraph (2), of the Convention.

RULE 10

If the President of the Commission for some special reason considers that he should relinquish the office of President in a particular case, he shall so inform the Vice-President or the member acting in his place.

CHAPTER III

Secretariat of the Commission

RULE 11

1. Pursuant to Article 37 of the Convention, the Secretariat of the Commission shall be provided by the Secretary-General of the Council of Europe.

2. The Secretary-General shall appoint the Secretary of the Commission.

RULE 12

The Secretary of the Commission

a. shall assist the Commission, Sub-commissions and the members of the Commission in the fulfilment of their duties;

b. shall be the channel for all communications concerning the Commission;

c. shall have custody of the seals, stamps and archives of the Commission.

RULE 13

1. A special register shall be kept at the Secretariat in which all cases, relevant pleadings and exhibits shall be entered in the order of their submission and without intervening spaces or deletions. Nothing shall be written in the register in abbreviated form.

2. A note of the entry in the register shall be endorsed by the Secretary of the Commission on the original documents and, at the request of the parties, on copies presented by them for that purpose.

3. Entries in the register and the notes of entries provided for in paragraph (2) of this Rule shall have effect as certified matters of record.

4. The manner of keeping the register shall be laid down by the President in agreement with the Secretary of the Commission.

RULE 14

The duties of the Secretariat shall be laid down by the President in agreement with the Secretary-General of the Council of Europe.

CHAPTER IV

Sub-commissions

RULE 15

1. Any party wishing to exercise the right, provided for in paragraph (2) of Article 29 of the Convention, to appoint a member of its

choice as a member of a Sub-commission shall give notice of the name of such member within an appropriate time-limit to be laid down by the President.

2. If, before the Sub-commission has been constituted, a member so appointed is unable to accept the appointment, the President shall notify the party concerned and shall lay down a new and appropriate time-limit within which such party shall, if it so desires, appoint another member.

RULE 16

If the Commission considers that several parties have the same interest, it shall lay down a time-limit within which such parties shall, acting in agreement, appoint a single member of their choice. In the event of a dispute that the same interest exists, the Commission shall decide, if necessary, after receiving the observations of the parties.

RULE 17

In the event of the non-appointment of a member within the time-limit laid down by the President or the Commission, as the case may be, under Rule 15 or 16, the procedure in Rule 18 shall immediately be applied.

RULE 18

1. On the expiry of the time-limits referred to in Rules 15 and 16, the prescribed number of members of the Sub-commission shall be achieved by a drawing of lots which the President shall carry out with the assistance of the Secretary of the Commission.

2. The remaining members of the Commission shall, if necessary, be called upon to sit as substitute members in the order in which they have been chosen by lot in the same manner as provided for in paragraph (1).

3. As soon as a Sub-commission has been constituted the Secretary of the Commission shall communicate its composition to all members of the Commission and to the parties.

RULE 19

If, after the Sub-commission has been constituted, a member appointed by a party is prevented from carrying out his duties, the President shall notify the party concerned and shall lay down a new and appropriate time-limit within which such party shall, if it so desires, appoint another member. In the event of the non-appointment of a member within the time-limit laid down by the President, one of the substitute members provided for in Rule 18, paragraph (2), shall be called upon in accordance with the order in which these members have been chosen by lot.

RULE 20

1. Of those members chosen by lot according to paragraph (1) of Rule 18, the member having precedence under Rule 3 shall preside at the Sub-commission.

2. If the President of the Sub-commission for some special reason considers that he should relinquish the office of President, he shall so inform the Sub-commission. He shall relinquish the office of President in the circumstances set out in paragraph (1) of Rule 9.

RULE 21

If the President of the Sub-commission relinquishes the office of President, that office shall be assumed by another member of the Sub-commission in accordance with the order of precedence laid down in Rule 3.

CHAPTER V

The working of the Commission and Sub-commissions

RULE 22

The seat of the Commission shall be at the seat of the Council of Europe at Strasbourg. The Commission or any of its organs may, however, if they think fit, carry out their duties elsewhere.

RULE 23

1. The Commission shall meet at the decision of the President when the latter considers that circumstances so require. It shall also meet if at least one-third of its members so request.

2. Pursuant to Article 35 of the Convention, the Commission shall be convened by the Secretary-General of the Council of Europe.

RULE 24

1. The date and time of meetings shall be laid down by the President of the Commission.

2. The date and time of meetings of a Sub-commission shall be laid down by its President.

Rule 25

A quorum of the Commission shall be nine members. However, seven members shall constitute a quorum when the Commission considers the admissibility of an application submitted under Article 25 of the Convention and provided that the group of three members referred to in Rule 34 has unanimously reported that the application appears to be inadmissible.

Rule 26

Sessions of the Commission and Sub-commissions shall be held in camera.

Rule 27

1. The Commission and Sub-commissions shall deliberate in private. Their deliberations shall be and shall remain secret.

2. Only the members of the Commission shall take part in the deliberations of the Commission. Only the members of a Sub-commission shall take part in the deliberations of such Sub-commission.

3. The Secretary of the Commission shall as a rule be present at the deliberations. No other person may be admitted except by decision of the Commission or Sub-commission.

Rule 28

Every member present at the deliberations shall state his opinion and the reasons therefor. The junior member according to the order of precedence laid down in Rule 3 shall speak first.

Rule 29

1. Pursuant to Article 34 of the Convention, decisions of the Commission shall be taken by a majority of members present and voting and decisions of a Sub-commission shall be taken by a majority of its members.

2. The votes shall be cast in the inverse order to the order of precedence laid down in Rule 3.

3. If the voting is equal, the President shall have a casting vote.

Rule 30

The minutes of deliberations shall be secret; they shall be limited to a record of the subject of the discussions, the votes taken, the names of those voting for and against a motion and any statements expressly made for insertion in the minutes.

Rule 31

Members who are prevented by illness or other serious reason from taking part in the meetings shall as soon as possible give notice thereof to the Secretary of the Commission who shall inform the President.

Rule 32

1. If a member for some special reason considers that he should not take part in the examination of a particular case, the President and the member concerned shall consult together. In the event of disagreement, the Commission or Sub-commission, as the case may be, shall decide.

2. If the President considers that a member should not, for some special reason, take part in the examination of a particular case, he shall so notify the member concerned and refer the question for a decision by the Commission or Sub-commission as the case may be.

Rule 33

Members of the Commission may not take part in the examination of any case in which they have previously acted as the agents, advisers or legal representatives of one of the parties or concerning which they have been required to state an opinion as members of a tribunal, commission of enquiry, or in any other capacity. In the event of doubt or dispute, the Commission or Sub-commission, as the case may be, shall decide.

Rule 34

1. The Commission shall, as circumstances require, constitute one or more groups, each consisting of three of its members, to carry out the duties laid down in Rule 45. It shall also appoint two substitute members for each group.

2. During the interval between sessions of the Commission, the President may, if necessary, either constitute a group or replace any member who is unable to take part in the work of a group already constituted.

3. The President of each group shall be the member of that group who has precedence under Rule 3.

TITLE II
PROCEDURE
CHAPTER I
General Rules

Rule 35

1. The official languages of the Commission shall be French and English.

2. The President may authorise a member to speak in another language.

RULE 36

1. The High Contracting Parties shall be represented before the Commission by their agents who may have the assistance of counsel or advocates.

2. The persons, non-governmental organisations and groups of individuals referred to in Article 25 of the Convention may represent their case in person before the Commission. They may be assisted or represented by a member of the Bar, by a solicitor or by a professor of law, or by any other lawyer approved by the Commission.

RULE 37

The Commission or a Sub-commission may, at the request of a party or of a person representing or assisting that party, permit the use by such party or person of a language other than French or English.

RULE 38

1. The Commission shall deal with cases in the order in which they become ready for hearing. It may, however, decide to give precedence to a particular case.

2. The Commission or a Sub-commission or, if it is not in session, its President may at the request of a party or *ex officio* order a case to be adjourned.

RULE 39

The Commission may, if it considers necessary, order the joinder of two or more cases.

CHAPTER II

Institution of proceedings

RULE 40

1. Any claims submitted under Article 24 or 25 of the Convention shall be submitted in the form of an application in writing and shall be signed by the applicant or his representative.

2. Where an application is submitted by a non-governmental organisation or by a group of individuals, it shall be signed by those persons competent to represent such organisation or group, if such organisation or group is properly constituted according to the laws of

the State to which it is subject. The application shall in all other cases be signed by the persons composing the group submitting the application.

RULE 41

1. The application shall mention:
   a. the name of the applicant;
   b. the name of the High Contracting Party against which the claim is made;
   c. the object of the claim;
   d. as far as possible the provision of the Convention alleged to have been violated;
   e. a statement of the facts and arguments;
   f. any attached documents.

2. The applicant shall provide information enabling it to be shown that the conditions laid down in Article 26 of the Convention have been satisfied.

RULE 42

Where the applicant intends to claim damages for an alleged injury, the amount of damages claimed may be stated in the application.

RULE 43

The Secretary-General of the Council of Europe shall transmit the application and any relevant documents to the President of the Commission.

RULE 44

Where, pursuant to Article 24 of the Convention, an application is brought before the Commission by a High Contracting Party, the President of the Commission shall through the Secretary-General of the Council of Europe give notice of such application to the High Contracting Party against which the claim is made and shall invite it to submit to the Commission its observations in writing on the admissibility of such application.

RULE 45

1. Any application submitted pursuant to Article 25 of the Convention shall be referred by the President of the Commission to the group of three members mentioned in Rule 34, which shall make a preliminary examination as to its admissibility. The group of three members shall then submit to the Commission a Report on such preliminary examination.

2. If the group of three members unanimously reports that the application appears to be admissible, the President of the Commission shall through the Secretary-General of the Council of Europe give notice of such application to the High Contracting Party against which the claim is made and shall invite it to submit to the Commission its observations in writing on the admissibility of such application.

3. If the group of three members does not unanimously report that the application appears to be admissible, the Commission shall consider the application and may

    a. either, declare at once that the application is inadmissible,

    b. or, through the Secretary-General of the Council of Europe give notice of such application to the High Contracting Party against which the claim is made and invite it to submit to the Commission its observations in writing on the admissibility of such application.

Rule 46

1. Except for the case provided for in Rule 45, paragraph (3) (a), the Commission, before it decides as to the admissibility of an application, may, if it thinks fit, invite the parties to submit to it their further comments in writing. It may also invite the parties to make oral explanations.

2. During the interval between sessions of the Commission, the President may, if he thinks fit, exercise the powers mentioned in paragraph (1) of this Rule.

3. The decision of the Commission in regard to the admissibility of the application shall be accompanied by reasons. The Secretary of the Commission shall communicate such decision to the applicant and, except for the case provided for in Rule 45, paragraph (3) (a), to the respondent party.

Rule 47

1. The Commission shall, if it accepts an application, set up a Sub-commission according to the provisions of Chapter IV of Title I of the present Rules.

2. If the Commission accepts an application, the facts of which are connected with those of a case between the same parties for which a Sub-commission has already been set up it may refer the new case to the said Sub-commission with the agreement of the parties.

3. The President shall lay down the time-limits within which the parties shall submit their arguments, evidence and submissions.

RULE 48

1. Each pleading shall be signed in the original by the party or its representative.

2. Each pleading shall be dated. For the purpose of determining any time-limits, the date of the filing of the pleading with the Secretariat-General of the Council of Europe shall alone be taken into consideration.

3. Any document submitted as an appendix and written in a language other than the official languages shall, unless the President otherwise decides, be accompanied by translation into one of the official languages. Translations of extracts may be submitted, however, in the case of lengthy documents. The Commission may at any time require a more complete translation or a certified translation to be submitted.

RULE 49

As soon as a Sub-commission has been set up the file shall be sent to it to enable it to carry out the duties laid down in Article 28 of the Convention.

CHAPTER III

Procedure before Sub-commissions

RULE 50

1. A Sub-commission may take any measure which it considers expedient in order to carry out the duties laid down in Article 28 of the Convention.

2. A Sub-commission shall take formal note of the refusal of a party to comply with such measures.

RULE 51

A Sub-commission may instruct one or more of its members to undertake an enquiry or any other form of investigation. It may also appoint one of its members as rapporteur.

RULE 52

The President of a Sub-commission shall direct the proceedings.

RULE 53

1. A Sub-commission may put questions to the parties and request them to give explanations.

2. Each member of a Sub-commission shall have the same right and shall give notice to the President if he wishes to exercise it.

Rule 54

1. A Sub-commission may, at the request of a party or *proprio motu*, decide to hear as witness or expert or in any other capacity any person whose evidence or statements seem likely to assist it in the carrying out of its task.

2. Any witness, expert or other person whom a Sub-commission decides to hear shall be summoned by the Secretary of the Commission. The summons shall indicate:

the names, first names, occupation and domicile of the parties in the case;

the facts or points regarding which the person concerned will be heard;

the arrangements made, in accordance with paragraph (3), paragraph (4) or paragraph (5) of this Rule, to reimburse the person concerned for any expenses incurred by him.

3. The expenses incurred by any witness, expert or other person whom a Sub-commission decides to hear at the request of a High Contracting Party shall be borne by that Party.

4. The expenses incurred by any witness, expert or other person whom a Sub-commission decides to hear at the request of a person, non-governmental organisation or group of individuals, which has referred a matter to the Commission under Article 25 of the Convention, shall be borne either by the applicant or by the Council of Europe as the Sub-commission may decide. In the latter case they shall be fixed by the President of the Sub-commission.

5. The expenses incurred by any witness, expert or other person whom a Sub-commission *proprio motu* decides to hear shall be fixed by the President of the Sub-commission and be borne by the Council of Europe.

6. Any witness, expert or other person whom a Sub-commission decides to hear may, if he has not sufficient knowledge of French or English, be authorised by the President to speak in another language.

Rule 55

1. After establishing the identity of the witnesses or experts, the President of a Sub-commission or the member or members mentioned in Rule 51 shall request them to take the following oath:

a. for witnesses: 'I swear that I will speak the truth, the whole truth and nothing but the truth'.

b. for experts: 'I swear that my statement will be in accordance with my sincere belief'.

2. Instead of taking the oath in the terms set out in paragraph (1) of this Rule, the witnesses or experts may make the following declaration:

P

a. for witnesses: 'I solemnly declare upon my honour and conscience that I will speak the truth, the whole truth and nothing
but the truth'.

b. for experts: 'I solemnly declare upon my honour and conscience that my statement will be in accordance with my sincere
belief'.

RULE 56

Questions may be put to the witnesses, experts or other persons
mentioned in Rule 54, paragraph (1):

a. by the President or any member of a Sub-commission;

b. by a party, with the permission of the President of the Sub-
commission or of the member or members mentioned in Rule
51.

RULE 57

Where, without good reason, a witness, expert or other person who
has been duly required to appear, fails to appear or refuses to give
evidence, the Secretary-General of the Council of Europe shall, at the
request of the President, so inform that High Contracting Party to
whose jurisdiction the person concerned is subject. The same provisions
shall apply where a witness or expert has, in the opinion of a Sub-
commission, violated the oath or solemn declaration mentioned in
Rule 55.

RULE 58

If a Sub-commission considers that it is expedient to examine a case
in a place other than the seat of the Council of Europe, it shall, through
the Secretary-General of the Council of Europe, request any High
Contracting Party concerned to grant it all necessary facilities, as
mentioned in paragraph (a) of Article 28 of the Convention, in order
that it may carry out its task.

RULE 59

The secretariat of the Commission shall draw up the minutes of the
hearings. The minutes shall be signed by the President and by the
Secretary of the Commission. The minutes shall constitute certified
matters of record.

RULE 60

The Report provided for in Article 30 of the Convention shall
contain:

the date on which it was drawn up;

the names of the President and members of a Sub-commission;
a description of the parties;
the names of the representatives and counsel of the parties;
a statement of the facts;
the terms of the solution reached.

RULE 61

The Report referred to in the preceding Rule shall be signed by the President of a Sub-commission and by the Secretary of the Commission. The Report shall be sent to the High Contracting Parties concerned, to the Committee of Ministers and to the Secretary-General of the Council of Europe for publication.

RULE 62

If a Sub-commission fails to effect a friendly settlement, it shall make a Report for the sole use of the Commission. That Report shall, in particular, include:

a. the facts established, including an account of the proceedings;
b. the result of the attempt to reach a friendly settlement.

CHAPTER IV

Procedure before the Commission

RULE 63

The provisions of Chapter III of the present Title shall apply, *mutatis mutandis*, to proceedings before the Commission.

CHAPTER V

The Report of the Commission

RULE 64

If, with a view to the preparation of the Report provided for in Article 31 of the Convention, the Commission considers it necessary to obtain additional information, it shall in each case determine the manner in which this shall be done.

RULE 65

The Report provided for in Article 31 of the Convention shall be drawn up after deliberation by the Commission in plenary session.

Rule 66

The Report shall contain:
the date on which it was drawn up;
the names of the President and members who took part in the deliberation mentioned in Rule 65;
a description of the parties;
the names of the representatives and counsel of the parties;
a statement of the proceedings;
a statement of the facts;
the opinion of the Commission as to whether the facts found disclose a breach by the High Contracting Party concerned of its obligations under the Convention;
the reasons on which that opinion is based;
a statement of the number of members forming the majority;
any proposal which the Commission may consider appropriate.

Rule 67

Each member may, in accordance with paragraph (1) of Article 31 of the Convention, include in the Report a statement of his opinion.

Rule 68

Where the Commission decides to make proposals concerning damages as envisaged in Rule 42, it shall make them in pursuance of paragraph (3) of Article 31 of the Convention.

Rule 69

The Report and any proposals shall be signed by the President and by the Secretary of the Commission. They shall be sent through the Secretary-General of the Council of Europe to the Committee of Ministers and only to those High Contracting Parties which are concerned.

Rule 70

During the period of three months following the transmission of the Report to the Committee of Ministers, the Commission shall consider at a plenary session whether or not to bring the case before the European Court to Human Rights in pursuance of Article 48, paragraph (a), of the Convention.

TITLE III

RELATIONS OF THE COMMISSION WITH THE COURT

RULE 71

The Commission shall assist the European Court of Human Rights in any case brought before the Court. For this purpose and in accordance with Rule 29, paragraph (1) of the Rules of Court, the Commission shall as soon as possible appoint, at a plenary session, one or more of its members to take part, as a delegate, in the consideration of the case before the Court. These delegates may be assisted by any person appointed by the Commission. In discharging their functions they shall act in accordance with such directives as they may receive from the Commission.

RULE 72

1. When, in pursuance of Article 48, paragraph (a) of the Convention, the Commission decides to bring a case before the Court, it shall, in accordance with Rule 31, paragraph (2) of the Rules of Court, draw up a request indicating in particular:

    a. the parties to the proceedings before the Commission;

    b. the date on which the Commission adopted its Report;

    c. the date on which, as certified by the Secretary of the Commission in a document attached to the request, the Report was transmitted to the Committee of Ministers;

    d. the names and addresses of its delegates.

2. The Secretary of the Commission shall transmit to the Registry of the Court thirty copies of the request referred to in paragraph (1) of this Rule.

RULE 73

When, in pursuance of Article 48, paragraph (b), (c) or (d) of the Convention, a High Contracting Party brings a case before the Court, the Secretary of the Commission shall communicate to the Registry of the Court as soon as possible:

    a. the names and addresses of the Commission's delegates;

    b. any other information which the Commission may consider appropriate.

RULE 74

The Secretary of the Commission shall, as soon as he has transmitted the request referred to in Rule 72, paragraph (2) above, or has received the communication mentioned in Rule 32, paragraph (1) (c) of the Rules of Court, file with the Registry of the Court an adequate number of copies of the Commission's Report.

RULE 75

The Commission shall communicate to the Court, at its request, any memorial, evidence, document or information concerning the case, with the exception of documents relating to the attempt to secure a friendly settlement in accordance with Article 28, paragraph (b) of the Convention. The communication of those documents shall be subject in each case to a decision of the Commission.

RULE 76

When a case brought before the Commission in pursuance of Article 25 of the Convention is subsequently referred to the Court, the Secretary of the Commission shall immediately notify the applicant. Unless the Commission shall otherwise decide, the Secretary shall also in due course communicate to him the Commission's Report, informing him that he may, within a time-limit fixed by the President, submit to the Commission his written observations on the said Report. The Commission shall decide what action, if any, shall be taken in respect of those observations.

APPENDIX 5

RULES OF COURT OF THE EUROPEAN COURT OF HUMAN RIGHTS

Rule 1 Definitions

TITLE I

ORGANISATION AND WORKING OF THE COURT

TITLE II

PROCEDURE

RULE 1

(*Definitions*)

For the purposes of these Rules:

a. the term 'Convention' means the Convention for the Protection of Human Rights and Fundamental Freedoms, and Protocol;

b. the expression 'plenary Court' means the European Court of Human Rights sitting in plenary session;

c. the term 'Chamber' means any Chamber constituted in pursuance of Article 43 of the Convention;

d. the term 'Court' means either the plenary Court or the Chambers;

e. the expression '*ad hoc* judge' means any person, other than an elected judge, chosen by a Contracting Party in pursuance of Article 43 of the Convention to sit as a member of a Chamber;

f. the term 'judge' or 'judges' means the judges elected by the Consultative Assembly of the Council of Europe or *ad hoc* judges;

g. the term 'Parties' means those Contracting Parties which are the Applicant and Respondent Parties;

h. the term 'Commission' means the European Commission of Human Rights;

i. the expression 'delegates of the Commission' means the member or members of the Commission delegated by it to take part in the consideration of a case before the Court;

j. the expression 'report of the Commission' means the report provided for in Article 31 of the Convention;

k. the expression 'Committee of Ministers' means the Committee of Ministers of the Council of Europe.

TITLE I

ORGANISATION AND WORKING OF THE COURT

CHAPTER I

Judges

RULE 2

(*Calculation of term of office*)

1. The duration of the term of office of an elected judge shall be calculated as from his election. However, when a judge is re-elected on the expiry of his term of office or is elected to replace a judge whose term of office has expired or is about to expire, the duration of his term of office shall, in either case, be calculated as from the date of such expiry.

2. In accordance with Article 40, § 3, of the Convention, a judge elected to replace a judge whose term of office has not expired shall hold office for the remainder of his predecessor's term.

3. In accordance with Article 40, § 4, of the Convention, elected judges shall hold office until replaced. After having been replaced, they shall continue to deal with any case, or any part of a case, or any particular point, in connection with which hearings have begun before them.

Rule 3

(*Oath or solemn declaration*)

1. Before taking up his duties, each elected judge shall, at the first sitting of the Court at which he is present after his election, take the following oath or make the following solemn declaration:

'I swear', or 'I solemnly declare'—'that I will exercise my functions as a judge honourably, independently and impartially and that I will keep secret all deliberations'.

2. This act shall be recorded in minutes.

Rule 4

(*Obstacle to the exercise of the functions of judge*)

A judge may not exercise his functions while he is a member of a Government or while he holds a post or exercises a profession which is likely to affect confidence in his independence. In case of need the Court shall decide.

Rule 5

(*Precedence*)

1. Elected judges shall take precedence after the President and the Vice-President according to their seniority in office; in the event of re-election, even if it is not an immediate re-election, the length of time during which they previously exercised their functions shall be taken into account.

2. Elected judges having the same seniority in office shall take precedence according to age.

3. *Ad hoc* judges shall take precedence after the elected judges according to age.

Rule 6

(*Resignation*)

Resignation of a judge shall be notified to the President who shall transmit it to the Secretary-General of the Council of Europe. Subject to the provisions of Rule 2, § 3, resignation shall constitute vacation of office.

CHAPTER II

Presidency of the Plenary Court

Rule 7

(*Election of the President and Vice-President*)

1. The President and Vice-President of the Court shall, in accordance with Article 41 of the Convention, be elected for a period of three years, provided that such period shall not exceed the duration of their term of office as judges. They may be re-elected.

2. The plenary Court shall elect the President and Vice-President following the entry into office of the judges elected at periodical elections of part of the Court in accordance with Article 40, § 1, of the Convention. The President and Vice-President shall continue to exercise their functions until the election of their respective successors.

3. If the President or Vice-President ceases to be a member of the Court or resigns his office before its normal expiry, the plenary Court shall elect a successor for the remainder of the term of that office.

4. The elections referred to in this Rule shall be by secret ballot; only the elected judges who are present shall take part. If no judge receives an absolute majority, a ballot shall take place between the two judges who have received most votes. In the case of equal voting, preference shall be given to the judge having precedence in accordance with Rule 5.

Rule 8

(*Functions of the President*)

The President shall direct the work and administration of the Court; he shall preside at plenary sessions.

Rule 9

(*Functions of the Vice-President*)

The Vice-President shall take the place of the President if the latter is unable to carry out his functions or if the office of President is vacant.

RULE 10

(*Replacement of the President and Vice-President*)

If the President and Vice-President are at the same time unable to carry out their functions or if their offices are at the same time vacant, the office of President shall be assumed by another elected judge in accordance with the order of precedence provided for in Rule 5.

CHAPTER III

The Registry

RULE 11

(*Election of the Registrar*)

1. The Court shall elect its Registrar after the President has in this respect obtained the opinion of the Secretary-General of the Council of Europe. The candidates must possess the legal knowledge and the experience necessary to carry out the duties of the post and must have an adequate working knowledge of the two official languages of the Court.

2. The Registrar shall be elected for a term of seven years. He may be re-elected.

3. The elections referred to in this Rule shall be by secret ballot; only the elected judges who are present shall take part. If no candidate receives an absolute majority, a ballot shall take place between the two candidates who have received most votes. In the case of equal voting, preference shall be given to the oldest candidate.

4. Before taking up his duties, the Registrar shall take the following oath or make the following solemn declaration before the Court or, if the Court is not in session, before the President:

'I swear', or 'I solemnly declare'—'that I will exercise loyally, discreetly and conscientiously the functions conferred upon me as Registrar of the European Court of Human Rights'.

RULE 12

(*Election of the Deputy Registrar*)

1. The Court shall also elect a Deputy Registrar according to the conditions and in the manner and for the term prescribed in Rule 11.

2. Before taking up his duties, the Deputy Registrar shall take an oath or make a solemn declaration before the Court, or, if the Court is not in session, before the President, in similar terms to that prescribed in respect of the Registrar.

RULE 13

(*Other officials of the Registry*)

The President shall request the Secretary-General of the Council of Europe to provide the Court with the necessary staff, equipment and facilities.

RULE 14

(*Duties of the Registrar*)

1. The Registrar shall be the channel for all communications and notifications made by, or addressed to, the Court.

2. The Registrar shall ensure that the dates of despatch and receipt of any communication or notification may be easily verified. Communications or notifications addressed to the agents of the Parties or to the delegates of the Commission shall be considered as having been addressed to the Parties themselves or the Commission itself. The date of receipt shall be noted on each document received by the Registrar who shall transmit to the sender a receipt bearing this date and the number under which the document has been registered.

3. The Registrar shall, subject to the discretion attaching to his duties, reply to all requests for information concerning the work of the Court, in particular, from the Press. He shall announce the date and time fixed for the hearings in open Court.

4. General instructions drawn up by the Registrar and sanctioned by the President shall provide for the working of the Registry.

CHAPTER IV

The Working of the Court

RULE 15

(*Seat of the Court*)

The seat of the European Court of Human Rights shall be at the seat of the Council of Europe at Strasbourg. The Court may, however, if it considers it expedient, exercise its functions in any territories to which the Convention applies.

RULE 16

(*Sessions of the plenary Court*)

The plenary sessions of the Court shall be convened by the President and the Court shall be so convened at least once annually.

RULE 17

(*Quorum*)

1. The quorum of the plenary Court shall be nine of the elected judges.

2. If there is no quorum, the President shall adjourn the sitting.

RULE 18

(*Public character of the hearings*)

The hearings shall be public, unless the Court shall in exceptional circumstances decide otherwise.

RULE 19

(*Deliberations*)

1. The Court shall deliberate in private. Its deliberations shall be and shall remain secret.

2. Only the judges shall take part in the deliberations. The Registrar or his substitute shall be present. No other person may be admitted except by special decision of the Court.

3. Each judge present at such deliberations shall state his opinion and the reasons therefor.

4. Any question which is to be voted upon shall be formulated in precise terms in the two official languages and the text shall, if a judge so requests, be distributed before the vote is taken.

5. The minutes of the private sittings of the Court for deliberations shall be secret; they shall be limited to a record of the subject of the discussions, the votes taken, the names of those voting for and against a motion and any statements expressly made for insertion in the minutes.

RULE 20

(*Majority required*)

1. The decisions of the Court shall be taken by the majority of judges present.

2. The votes shall be cast in the inverse order to the order of precedence provided for in Rule 5.

3. If the voting is equal, the President shall have a second and casting vote.

CHAPTER V

The Chambers

RULE 21

(Composition of the Court when constituted in a Chamber)

1. When a case is brought before the Court either by the Commission or by a Contracting Party having the right to do so under Article 48 of the Convention, the Court shall be constituted in a Chamber of seven judges. The judge or judges who have the nationality of the State or States which are Parties to the case shall, in accordance with Article 43 of the Convention, sit as *ex officio* members of this Chamber. The names of the other judges shall be chosen by lot.

2. The Registrar shall invite any Contracting Party which appears to have the right, under Article 48 of the Convention, to bring a case before the Court and which has not availed itself of that right, to inform him within thirty days whether it wishes to appear as a Party to the case of which the Court has been seized and, if so, to supply him with the name and address of its agent.

3. As soon as the above-mentioned information has been obtained or the said period has expired, the President of the Court shall, in the presence of the Registrar, choose by lot the names of the judges called upon to complete the Chamber.

4. In the case of doubt or dispute as to whether a Contracting Party has the right under Article 48 of the Convention to bring a case before the Court, the President shall submit that question to the plenary Court for decision.

5. If the President of the Court finds that a new case concerns the same Party or Parties as another case already before a Chamber and that it relates, wholly or in part, to the same Article or Articles of the Convention, he may refer the new case to the same Chamber.

6. The office of President of the Chamber shall be held *ex officio* by the President of the Court if he has been chosen by lot as member of the Chamber; if he has not been so chosen, the Vice-President, if chosen by lot, shall preside. In the absence of both the President and Vice-President, the office of President shall be held by the senior judge of the judges chosen by lot according to the order of precedence provided for in Rule 5. The same rule shall apply where the person called upon to act as President is unable to attend or withdraws.

RULE 22

(Substitute judges)

1. Where it is necessary to constitute the Court in a Chamber, the President shall also draw by lot the names of three substitute judges

from among the remaining judges other than the President and Vice-President of the Court. The susbtitute judges shall be called upon to sit according to the order determined by the drawing of lots, in place of any judges chosen by lot who are unable to sit or have withdrawn. After being replaced, a judge chosen by lot shall cease to be a member of the Chamber.

2. The substitute judges shall be supplied with the documents relating to the proceedings. The President may convoke one of them, according to the above order of precedence, to attend the hearings.

RULE 23

(*Ad hoc judges*)

1. If the Court does not include an elected judge having the nationality of a Party or if the judge called upon to sit in that capacity is unable to sit or withdraws, the President of the Court shall invite the agent of the Party concerned to inform him within thirty days whether his Government wishes to appoint to sit as judge either another elected judge or, as an *ad hoc* judge, any other person possessing the qualifications required under Article 39, § 3, of the Convention and, if so, to state the name of the person so appointed. The same rule shall apply if an *ad hoc* judge is unable to sit or withdraws.

2. If a reply has not been received within thirty days, the Government concerned shall be presumed to have waived such right of appointment and, if the seat falls vacant during the proceedings, a substitute judge shall be called upon to fill that vacancy, according to the order in which such judges have been chosen by lot.

3. An *ad hoc* judge shall, at the opening of the first sitting fixed for the consideration of the case for which he has been appointed, take the oath or make the solemn declaration provided for in Rule 3.

RULE 24

(*Inability to attend and withdrawal*)

1. Any judge who is prevented by illness or other serious reasons from taking part in sittings for which he has been convoked shall, as soon as possible, give notice thereof to the President of the Chamber.

2. A judge may not take part in the consideration of any case in which he has a personal interest or in which he has previously acted either as the agent, advocate or adviser of a Party or of a person having an interest in the case, or as member of a tribunal or commission of enquiry, or in any other capacity.

3. If a judge considers that he should withdraw from consideration

of a particular case or if the President considers such withdrawal to be desirable, the President and the judge shall consult together. In case of disagreement, the Chamber shall decide.

RULE 25

(*Common interest*)

1. If several Parties have a common interest, they shall for the purposes of the provisions of this Chapter, be deemed to be one Party. The President of the Court shall invite them to agree to appoint a single elected judge or *ad hoc* judge in accordance with Article 43 of the Convention. If the Parties are unable to agree, the President shall choose by lot, from among the persons proposed as judges by these Parties, the judge called upon to sit *ex officio*. The names of the other judges and substitute judges shall then be chosen by lot by the President of the Court from among the elected judges who are not nationals of any of these Parties.

2. In the case of dispute as to the existence of a common interest, the plenary Court shall decide.

TITLE II

PROCEDURE

CHAPTER I

General Rules

RULE 26

(*Possibility of particular derogations*)

The provisions of this Title shall not prevent the Court from derogating from them for the consideration of a particular case with the agreement of the Party or Parties and after having obtained the opinion of the delegates of the Commission.

RULE 27

(*Official languages*)

1. The official languages of the Court shall be French and English.

2. The Court may authorise any Party to use a language other than French or English. The Party concerned shall, in that event, attach to the original of each document submitted by it a translation into French or English and shall be responsible for the interpretation into French

Q

or English of the oral arguments or statements made by its agents, advocates or advisers.

3. Any witness, expert or other person appearing before the Court may use his own language if he does not have sufficient knowledge of either of the two official languages. The Court shall, in that event, make the necessary arrangements for the interpretation into French or English of the statements of the witness, expert or other person concerned.

4. All decisions of the Court shall be given in French and English and the Court shall state which of the two texts shall be authentic.

RULE 28

(*Representation of the Parties*)

The Parties shall be represented by agents who may have the assistance of advocates or advisers.

RULE 29

(*Relations between the Court and the Commission*)

1. The Commission shall delegate one or more of its members to take part in the consideration of a case before the Court. The delegates may, if they so desire, have the assistance of any person of their choice.

2. The Court shall, whether a case is referred to it by a Contracting Party or by the Commission, take into consideration the report of the latter.

RULE 30

(*Communications, notifications and summonses addressed to persons other than the agents of the Parties or the delegates of the Commission*)

1. If, for any communication, notification or summons addressed to persons other than the agents of the Parties or the delegates of the Commission, the Court considers it necessary to have the assistance of the Government of the State on whose territory such communication, notification or summons is to have effect, the President shall apply directly to that Government in order to obtain the necessary facilities.

2. The same rule shall apply when the Court desires to make or arrange for the making of an investigation on the spot in order to establish the facts or to procure evidence or when it orders the appearance of a person resident in, or having to cross, that territory.

CHAPTER II

Institution of Proceedings

RULE 31

(Filing of the application or request)

1. Any Contracting Party which intends to bring a case before the Court in accordance with the provisions of Article 48 of the Convention shall file with the Registry an application, in thirty copies, indicating:
   a. the parties to the proceedings before the Commission;
   b. the date on which the Commission adopted its report;
   c. the date on which, as certified by the Secretariat of the Commission in a document attached to the application, the report was transmitted to the Committee of Ministers;
   d. the object of the application, including any objections made to the opinion of the Commission;
   e. the name and address of the person appointed as agent.

2. If the Commission intends to bring a case before the Court in accordance with the provisions of Article 48 of the Convention, it shall file with the Registry a request, in thirty copies, signed by its President and containing the particulars set out in sub-paragraphs (a), (b) and (c) of paragraph 1 of this Rule together with the names and addresses of the delegates of the Commission.

RULE 32

(Communication of the application or request)

1. On receipt of an application or request, the Registrar shall immediately transmit a copy thereof:
   a. to the President, Vice-President and judges;
   b. to any Contracting Party mentioned in Article 48 of the Convention which has not brought the application before the Court;
   c. to the President and members of the Commission if the Commission has not brought the case before the Court.

He shall also inform the Committee of Ministers, through the Secretary-General of the Council of Europe, of the filing of the application or request.

2. The communications mentioned in sub-paragraphs (a) and (b) of paragraph 1 of this Rule shall include a copy of the report of the Commission.

RULE 33

(*Notice of composition of the Chamber*)

As soon as a Chamber has been constituted for the consideration of a case, the Registrar shall communicate its composition to the judges, to the agents of the Parties and to the President of the Commission.

RULE 34

(*Interim measures*)

1. Before the constitution of a Chamber, the President of the plenary Court may, at the request of a Party, of the Commission, of any person concerned or *proprio motu*, bring to the attention of the Parties any interim measure the adoption of which seems desirable. The Chamber when constituted, or, if the Chamber is not in session, its President, shall have the same right.

2. Notice of these measures shall be immediately given to the Committee of Ministers.

CHAPTER III

Examination of Cases

RULE 35

(*Written Procedure*)

1. After the Chamber has been constituted and before its first sitting, the President of the Chamber shall convoke the agents of the Parties and the delegates of the Commission. He shall, after ascertaining their views upon the procedure to be followed, lay down the order and time-limits for the filing of the memorial, counter-memorial and other documents.

2. If a Chamber already constituted for the consideration of a case is seized, in pursuance of Rule 21, § 5, of a new case and if, at that time, the written procedure in the first case has not been completed, the President of that Chamber may, in the interest of the proper administration of justice and after having obtained the opinion of the agents of the Parties and the delegates of the Commission, order that the proceedings in both cases be conducted simultaneously, without prejudice to the decision of the Chamber on the joinder of the cases.

3. The memorials, counter-memorials and documents annexed thereto shall be filed with the Registry in thirty copies. The Registrar shall transmit copies of all these documents to the judges, to the agents of the Parties and to the delegates of the Commission.

RULE 36

(*Fixing of the date of the opening of the oral proceedings*)

When the case is ready for hearing, the President of the Chamber shall, after consulting the agents of the Parties and the delegates of the Commission, fix the date of the opening of the oral proceedings.

RULE 37

(*Conduct of the hearings*)

The President of the Chamber shall direct the hearings. He shall prescribe the order in which the agents, the advocates or advisers of the Parties and the delegates of the Commission, as well as any other person appointed by them in accordance with Rule 29, § 1, shall be called upon to speak.

RULE 38

(*Enquiry, expert opinion and other measures for obtaining information*)

1. The Chamber may, at the request of a Party or of delegates of the Commission or *proprio motu*, decide to hear as a witness or expert or in any other capacity any person whose evidence or statements seem likely to assist it in the carrying out of its task.

2. The Chamber may, at any time during the proceedings, depute one or more of its members to conduct an enquiry, to carry out an investigation on the spot or to obtain information in any other manner.

3. The Chamber may entrust any body, office, commission or authority of its choice with the task of obtaining information, expressing an opinion, or making a report, upon any specific point.

4. Any report prepared in accordance with the preceding paragraphs shall be addressed to the Registrar.

RULE 39

(*Convocation of witnesses, experts and other persons; expenses of their appearance*)

1. Witnesses, experts or other persons whom the Chamber decides to hear shall be summoned by the Registrar. If they are called by a Party, the expenses of their appearance shall be taxed by the President and, unless the Chamber shall otherwise decide in pursuance of Rule 50, paragraph 1(k), shall be borne by that Party. In other cases, such expenses shall be fixed by the President and borne by the Council of Europe.

2. The summons shall indicate:

the names of the Party or Parties;

the object of the enquiry, expert opinion or any other measure for obtaining information as ordered by the Chamber;

any provisions for the payment of the sum due to the person summoned.

RULE 40

(Oath or solemn declaration by witnesses and experts)

1. After the establishment of his identity and before giving evidence, every witness shall take the following oath or make the following solemn declaration:

'I swear'—or 'I solemnly declare upon my honour and conscience'— 'that I will speak the truth, the whole truth and nothing but the truth'.

2. After the establishment of his identity and before carrying out his task, every expert shall take the following oath or make the following solemn declaration:

'I swear'—or 'I solemnly declare upon my honour and conscience'— 'that I will discharge my duty as expert honourably and conscientiously'.

This oath may be taken or this declaration made before the President of the Chamber or before a judge or local authority nominated by the President.

RULE 41

(Objection to a witness or expert; hearing of a person for purpose of information)

The Chamber shall decide in the case of any dispute arising from an objection to a witness or expert. Nevertheless, it may, if it considers it necessary, hear for the purpose of information a person who cannot be heard as a witness.

RULE 42

(Questions put during the hearings)

1. The President of the Chamber or any judge may put questions to the agents, advocates or advisers of the Parties, to the witnesses and experts, to the delegates of the Commission, and to any other persons appearing before the Chamber.

2. The witnesses, experts and other persons referred to in Rule 38,

§ 1, may, subject to the control of the President who has power to decide as to the relevance of the questions put, be examined by the agents, advocates or advisers of the Parties, by the delegates of the Commission, and by any person appointed by them in accordance with Rule 29, § 1.

RULE 43

(*Failure to appear or false evidence*)

When, without good reason, a witness or any other person who has been duly summoned fails to appear or refuses to give evidence, the Registrar shall, on being so required by the President, inform that Contracting Party to whose jurisdiction such witness or other person is subject. The same provisions shall apply when a witness or expert has, in the opinion of the Chamber, violated the oath or solemn declaration mentioned in Rule 40.

RULE 44

(*Minutes of hearings*)

1. Minutes shall be made of each hearing and shall be signed by the President and the Registrar.
2. These minutes shall include:
the names of the judges present;
the names of the agents, advocates and advisers and of the delegates of the Commission present;
the surname, first names, description and residence of the witnesses, experts or other persons heard;
the declarations expressly made for insertion in the minutes on behalf of the Parties or of the Commission;
a summary record of the questions put by the President or other judges and of the replies made thereto;
any decision by the Chamber delivered during the hearing.
3. Copies of the minutes shall be given to the agents of the Parties and to the delegates of the Commission.
4. The minutes shall constitute certified matters of record.

RULE 45

(*Shorthand note of hearings*)

1. The Registrar shall be responsible for the making of a shorthand note of each hearing.
2. The agents, advocates and advisers of the Parties, the delegates

of the Commission and the witnesses, experts and other persons mentioned in Rules 29, § 1, and 38, § 1, shall receive the shorthand note of their arguments, statements or evidence, in order that they may, subject to the control of the Registrar or of the Chamber, make corrections within the time-limits laid down by the President.

RULE 46

(*Preliminary objections*)

1. A preliminary objection must be filed by a Party at the latest before the expiry of the time-limit fixed for the delivery of its first pleading.

2. If a Party raises a preliminary objection, the Chamber shall, after having received the replies or comments of every other Party and of the delegates of the Commission, give its decision on the objection or join the objection to the merits.

RULE 47

(*Discontinuance*)

1. When the Party which has brought the case before the Court notifies the Registrar of its intention not to proceed with the case and when the other Parties agree to such discontinuance, the Chamber shall, after having obtained the opinion of the Commission, decide whether or not it is appropriate to approve the discontinuance and accordingly to strike the case out of its list. In the affirmative, the Chamber shall give a reasoned decision which shall be communicated to the Committee of Ministers in order to allow them to supervise, in accordance with Article 54 of the Convention, the execution of any undertakings which may have been attached to the discontinuance by the order or with the approval of the Chamber.

2. The Chamber may, having regard to the responsibilities of the Court in pursuance of Article 19 of the Convention, decide that, notwithstanding the notice of discontinuance, it should proceed with the consideration of the case.

3. When the Commission, after having brought a case before the Court, informs the Court that a friendly settlement which satisfies the conditions of Article 28 of the Convention has subsequently been reached, the Chamber may, after having obtained the opinion, if necessary, of the delegates of the Commission, strike the case out of its list.

RULE 48

(Relinquishment of jurisdiction by the Chamber in favour of the plenary Court)

1. Where a case pending before a Chamber raises a serious question affecting the interpretation of the Convention, the Chamber may, at any time, relinquish jurisdiction in favour of the plenary Court. The relinquishment of jurisdiction shall be obligatory where the resolution of such question might have a result inconsistent with a judgment previously delivered by a Chamber or by the plenary Court. Reasons need not be given for the decision to relinquish jurisdiction.

2. The plenary Court, having been seized of the case, may either retain jurisdiction over the whole case or may, after deciding on the question of interpretation, order that the case be referred back to the Chamber which shall, in regard to the remaining part of the case, recover its original jurisdiction.

3. Any provisions governing the Chambers shall apply, *mutatis mutandis*, to the proceedings before the plenary Court.

4. When the Court has been seized, in accordance with paragraph 1 above, of a case pending before a Chamber, any *ad hoc* judge who is a member of that Chamber shall sit as a judge of the plenary Court.

CHAPTER IV

Judgments

RULE 49

(Procedure by default)

Where a Party fails to appear or to present its case, the Chamber shall, subject to the provisions of Rule 47, give a decision in the case.

RULE 50

(Contents of the judgment)

1. The judgment shall contain:
   a. the names of the President and the judges constituting the Chamber and the name of the Registrar;
   b. the date on which it was delivered at a hearing in public;
   c. a description of the Party or Parties;
   d. the names of the agents, advocates or advisers of the Party or Parties;
   e. the names of the delegates of the Commission;
   f. a statement of the proceedings;

g. the submissions of the Party or Parties and, if any, of the delegates of the Commission;

h. the facts of the case;

i. the reasons in point of law;

j. the operative provisions of the judgment;

k. the decision, if any, in regard to costs;

l. the number of judges constituting the majority;

m. a statement as to which of the two texts, French or English, is authentic.

2. Any judge who has taken part in the consideration of the case shall be entitled to annex to the judgment either a separate opinion, concurring or dissenting with that judgment, or a bare statement of dissent.

RULE 51

(Signature, delivery and communication of the judgment)

1. The judgment shall be signed by the President and by the Registrar.

2. The judgment shall be read by the President at a public hearing in one of the two official languages. It shall not be necessary for all the other judges to be present. The agents of the Parties and the delegates of the Commission shall be informed in due time of the date of delivery of judgment.

3. The judgment shall be sent by the President to the Committee of Ministers for the purposes of the application of Article 54 of the Convention.

4. The original copy, duly signed and sealed, shall be placed in the archives of the Court. The Registrar shall send certified copies to the Party or Parties, to the Commission, to the Secretary-General of the Council of Europe and to any other person directly concerned.

RULE 52

(Publication of judgments and other decisions)

The Registrar shall be responsible for the publication of judgments and of such other decisions and documents whose publication may have been authorised by the Court.

RULE 53

(Request for interpretation of a judgment)

1. A Party or the Commission may request the interpretation of a judgment within a period of three years following the delivery of that judgment.

2. The request shall state precisely the point or points in the operative provisions of the judgment on which interpretation is required.

3. The Registrar shall communicate the request to any other Party and, where appropriate, to the Commission, and shall invite them to submit any written comments within a period fixed by the President of the Chamber.

4. The request for interpretation shall be considered by the Chamber which gave the judgment and which shall, as far as possible, be composed of the same judges. Those judges who have ceased to be members of the Court shall be recalled in order to deal with the case in accordance with Article 40, § 4, of the Convention. In case of death or inability to attend, they shall be replaced in the same manner as was applied for their appointment to the Chamber.

5. The Chamber shall decide by means of a judgment.

RULE 54

(*Request for revision of a judgment*)

1. A Party or the Commission may, in the event of the discovery of a fact which might by its nature have a decisive influence and which, when a judgment was delivered, was unknown both to the Court and to that Party or the Commission, request the Court, within a period of six months after that Party or the Commission, as the case may be, acquired knowledge of such fact, to revise that judgment.

2. The request shall mention the judgment of which the revision is requested and shall contain the information necessary to show that the conditions laid down in paragraph 1 of this Rule have been complied with. It shall be accompanied by the original or a copy of all supporting documents.

3. The Registrar shall communicate the request to any other Party and, where appropriate, to the Commission, and shall invite them to submit any written comments within a period fixed by the President.

4. The request for revision shall be considered by a Chamber constituted in accordance with Article 43 of the Convention, which shall decide in a first judgment whether the request is admissible or not under paragraph 1 of this Rule. In the affirmative, the Chamber shall refer the request to the Chamber which gave the original judgment or, if in the circumstances that is not reasonably possible, it shall retain the request and give a judgment upon the merits of the case.

5. The Chamber shall decide by means of a judgment.

APPENDIX 6

THE EUROPEAN SOCIAL CHARTER

The Governments signatory hereto, being Members of the Council of Europe,

Considering that the aim of the Council of Europe is the achievement of greater unity between its Members for the purpose of safe-guarding and realising the ideals and principles which are their common heritage and of facilitating their economic and social progress, in particular by the maintenance and further realisation of human rights and fundamental freedoms;

Considering that in the European Convention for the Protection of Human Rights and Fundamental Freedoms signed at Rome on 4 November 1950, and the Protocol thereto signed at Paris on 20 March 1952, the member States of the Council of Europe agreed to secure to their populations the civil and political rights and freedoms therein specified;

Considering that the enjoyment of social rights should be secured without discrimination on grounds of race, colour, sex, religion, political opinion, national extraction or social origin;

Being resolved to make every effort in common to improve the standard of living and to promote the social well-being of both their urban and rural populations by means of appropriate institutions and actions,

Have agreed as follows:

PART I

The Contracting Parties accept as the aim of their policy, to be pursued by all appropriate means, both national and international in character, the attainment of conditions in which the following rights and principles may be effectively realised:

1. Everyone shall have the opportunity to earn his living in an occupation freely entered upon.

2. All workers have the right to just conditions of work.

3. All workers have the right to safe and healthy working conditions.

4. All workers have the right to a fair remuneration sufficient for a decent standard of living for themselves and their families.

5. All workers and employers have the right to freedom of association in national or international organisations for the protection of their economic and social interests.

6. All workers and employers have the right to bargain collectively.

7. Children and young persons have the right to a special protection against the physical and moral hazards to which they are exposed.

8. Employed women, in case of maternity, and other employed women as appropriate, have the right to a special protection in their work.

9. Everyone has the right to appropriate facilities for vocational guidance with a view to helping him choose an occupation suited to his personal aptitude and interests.

10. Everyone has the right to appropriate facilities for vocational training.

11. Everyone has the right to benefit from any measures enabling him to enjoy the highest possible standard of health attainable.

12. All workers and their dependents have the right to social security.

13. Anyone without adequate resources has the right to social and medical assistance.

14. Everyone has the right to benefit from social welfare services.

15. Disabled persons have the right to vocational training, rehabilitation and resettlement, whatever the origin and nature of their disability.

16. The family as a fundamental unit of society has the right to appropriate social, legal and economic protection to ensure its full development.

17. Mothers and children, irrespective of marital status and family relations, have the right to appropriate social and economic protection.

18. The nationals of any one of the Contracting Parties have the right to engage in any gainful occupation in the territory of any one of the others on a footing of equality with the nationals of the latter, subject to restrictions based on cogent economic or social reasons.

19. Migrant workers who are nationals of a Contracting Party and their families have the right to protection and assistance in the territory of any other Contracting Party.

PART II

The Contracting Parties undertake, as provided for in Part III, to consider themselves bound by the obligations laid down in the following Articles and paragraphs.

Article 1

The right to work

With a view to ensuring the effective exercise of the right to work, the Contracting Parties undertake:

1. to accept as one of their primary aims and responsibilities the achievement and maintenance of as high and stable a level of employment as possible, with a view to the attainment of full employment;

2. to protect effectively the right of the worker to earn his living in an occupation freely entered upon;

3. to establish or maintain free employment services for all workers;

4. to provide or promote appropriate vocational guidance, training and rehabilitation.

Article 2

The right to just conditions of work

With a view to ensuring the effective exercise of the right to just conditions of work, the Contracting Parties undertake:

1. to provide for reasonable daily and weekly working hours, the working week to be progressively reduced to the extent that the increase of productivity and other relevant factors permit;

2. to provide for public holidays with pay;

3. to provide for a mimimum of two weeks' annual holiday with pay;

4. to provide for additional paid holidays or reduced working hours for workers engaged in dangerous or unhealthy occupations as prescribed;

5. to ensure a weekly rest period which shall, as far as possible, coincide with the day recognised by tradition or custom in the country or region concerned as a day of rest.

Article 3

The right to safe and healthy working conditions

With a view to ensuring the effective exercise of the right to safe and healthy working conditions, the Contracting Parties undertake:

1. to issue safety and health regulations;

2. to provide for the enforcement of such regulations by measures of supervision;

3. to consult, as appropriate, employers' and workers' organisations on measures intended to improve industrial safety and health.

ARTICLE 4

The right to a fair remuneration

With a view to ensuring the effective exercise of the right to a fair remuneration, the Contracting Parties undertake:

1. to recognise the right of workers to a remuneration such as will give them and their families a decent standard of living;

2. to recognise the right of workers to an increased rate of remuneration for overtime work, subject to exceptions in particular cases;

3. to recognise the right of men and women workers to equal pay for work of equal value;

4. to recognise the right of all workers to a reasonable period of notice for termination of employment;

5. to permit deductions from wages only under conditions and to the extent prescribed by national laws or regulations or fixed by collective agreements or arbitration awards.

The exercise of these rights shall be achieved by freely concluded collective agreements, by statutory wage-fixing machinery, or by other means appropriate to national conditions.

ARTICLE 5

The right to organise

With a view to ensuring or promoting the freedom of workers and employers to form local, national or international organisations for the protection of their economic and social interests and to join those organisations, the Contracting Parties undertake that national law shall not be such as to impair, nor shall it be so applied as to impair, this freedom. The extent to which the guarantees provided for in this Article shall apply to the police shall be determined by national laws or regulations. The principle governing the application to the members of the armed forces of these guarantees and the extent to which they shall apply to persons in this category shall equally be determined by national laws or regulations.

ARTICLE 6

The right to bargain collectively

With a view to ensuring the effective exercise of the right to bargain collectively, the Contracting Parties undertake:

1. to promote joint consultation between workers and employers;

2. to promote, where necessary, and appropriate, machinery for voluntary negotiations between employers or employers' organisations

and workers' organisations, with a view to the regulation of terms and conditions of employment by means of collective agreements;

3. to promote the establishment and use of appropriate machinery for conciliation and voluntary arbitration for the settlement of labour disputes;

and recognise:

4. the right of workers and employers to collective action in cases of conflicts of interest, including the right to strike, subject to obligations that might arise out of collective agreements previously entered into.

ARTICLE 7

The right of children and young persons to protection

With a view to ensuring the effective exercise of the right of children and young persons to protection, the Contracting Parties undertake:

1. to provide that the minimum age of admission to employment shall be 15 years, subject to exceptions for children employed in prescribed light work without harm to their health, morals or education;

2. to provide that a higher minimum age of admission to employment shall be fixed with respect to prescribed occupations regarded as dangerous or unhealthy;

3. to provide that persons who are still subject to compulsory education shall not be employed in such work as would deprive them of the full benefit of their education;

4. to provide that the working hours of persons under 16 years of age shall be limited in accordance with the needs of their development, and particularly with their need for vocational training;

5. to recognise the right of young workers and apprentices to a fair wage or other appropriate allowances;

6. to provide that the time spent by young persons in vocational training during the normal working hours with the consent of the employer shall be treated as forming part of the working day;

7. to provide that employed persons of under 18 years of age shall be entitled to not less than three weeks' annual holiday with pay;

8. to provide that persons under 18 years of age shall not be employed in night work with the exception of certain occupations provided for by national laws or regulations;

9. to provide that persons under 18 years of age employed in occupations prescribed by national laws or regulations shall be subject to regular medical control;

10. to ensure special protection against physical and moral dangers to which children and young persons are exposed, and particularly against those resulting directly or indirectly from their work.

ARTICLE 8

The right of employed women to protection

With a view to ensuring the effective exercise of the right of employed women to protection, the Contracting Parties undertake:

1. to provide either by paid leave, by adequate social security benefits or by benefits from public funds for women to take leave before and after childbirth up to a total of at least 12 weeks;

2. to consider it as unlawful for an employer to give a woman notice of dismissal during her absence on maternity leave or to give her notice of dismissal at such a time that the notice would expire during such absence;

3. to provide that mothers who are nursing their infants shall be entitled to sufficient time off for this purpose;

4. *a.* to regulate the employment of women workers on night work in industrial employment;

   b. to prohibit the employment of women workers in underground mining, and, as appropriate, on all other work which is unsuitable for them by reason of its dangerous, unhealthy, or arduous nature.

ARTICLE 9

The right to vocational guidance

With a view to ensuring the effective exercise of the right to vocational guidance, the Contracting Parties undertake to provide or promote, as necessary, a service which will assist all persons, including the handicapped, to solve problems related to occupational choice and progress, with due regard to the individual's characteristics and their relation to occupational opportunity: this assistance should be available free of charge, both to young persons, including school children, and to adults.

ARTICLE 10

The right to vocational training

With a view to ensuring the effective exercise of the right to vocational training, the Contracting Parties undertake:

1. to provide or promote, as necessary, the technical and vocational training of all persons, including the handicapped, in consultation with

R

employers' and workers' organisations, and to grant facilities for access to higher technical and university education, based solely on individual aptitude;

2. to provide or promote a system of apprenticeship and other systematic arrangements for training young boys and girls in their various employments;

3. to provide or promote, as necessary:

    a. adequate and readily available training facilities for adult workers;

    b. special facilities for the re-training of adult workers needed as a result of technological development or new trends in employment;

4. to encourage the full utilisation of the facilities provided by appropriate measures such as:

    a. reducing or abolishing any fees or charges;

    b. granting financial assistance in appropriate cases;

    c. including in the normal working hours time spent on supplementary training taken by the worker, at the request of his employer, during employment;

    d. ensuring, through adequate supervision, in consultation with the employers' and workers' organisations, the efficiency of apprenticeship and other training arrangements for young workers, and the adequate protection of young workers generally.

ARTICLE 11

The right to protection of health

With a view to ensuring the effective exercise of the right to protection of health, the Contracting Parties undertake, either directly or in co-operation with public or private organisations, to take appropriate measures designed *inter alia*:

1. to remove as far as possible the causes of ill-health;

2. to provide advisory and educational facilities for the promotion of health and the encouragement of individual responsibility in matters of health;

3. to prevent as far as possible epidemic, endemic and other diseases.

ARTICLE 12

The right to social security

With a view to ensuring the effective exercise of the right to social security, the Contracting Parties undertake:

1. to establish or maintain a system of social security;

2. to maintain the social security system at a satisfactory level at least equal to that required for ratification of International Labour Convention (No. 102) Concerning Minimum Standards of Social Security;

3. to endeavour to raise progressively the system of social security to a higher level;

4. to take steps, by the conclusion of appropriate bilateral and multilateral agreements, or by other means, and subject to the conditions laid down in such agreements, in order to ensure:

    a. equal treatment with their own nationals of the nationals of other Contracting Parties in respect of social security rights, including the retention of benefits arising out of social security legislation, whatever movements the persons protected may undertake between the territories of the Contracting Parties;

    b. the granting, maintenance and resumption of social security rights by such means as the accumulation of insurance of employment periods completed under the legislation of each of the Contracting Parties.

ARTICLE 13

The right to social and medical assistance

With a view to ensuring the effective exercise of the right to social and medical assistance, the Contracting Parties undertake:

1. to ensure that any person who is without adequate resources and who is unable to secure such resources either by his own efforts or from other sources, in particular by benefits under a social security scheme, be granted adequate assistance, and, in case of sickness the care necessitated by this condition;

2. to ensure that persons receiving such assistance shall not, for that reason, suffer from a diminution of their political or social rights;

3. to provide that everyone may receive by appropriate public or private services such advice and personal help as may be required to prevent, to remove, or to alleviate personal or family want;

4. to apply the provisions referred to in paragraphs 1, 2 and 3 of this Article on an equal footing with their nationals to nationals of other Contracting Parties lawfully within their territories, in accordance with their obligations under the European Convention on Social and Medical Assistance, signed at Paris on 11 December 1953.

ARTICLE 14

The right to benefit from social welfare services

With a view to ensuring the effective exercise of the right to benefit from social welfare services, the Contracting Parties undertake:

1. to promote or provide services which, by using methods of social work, would contribute to the welfare and development of both individuals and groups in the community, and to their adjustment to the social environment;

2. to encourage the participation of individuals and voluntary or other organisations in the establishment and maintenance of such services.

ARTICLE 15

The right of physically or mentally disabled persons to vocational training, rehabilitation and social resettlement

With a view to ensuring the effective exercise of the right of the physically or mentally disabled to vocational training, rehabilitation and resettlement, the Contracting Parties undertake:

1. to take adequate measures for the provision of training facilities, including, where necessary, specialised institutions, public or private;

2. to take adequate measures for the placing of disabled persons in employment, such as specialised placing services, facilities for sheltered employment and measures to encourage employers to admit disabled persons to employment.

ARTICLE 16

The right of the family to social, legal and economic protection

With a view to ensuring the necessary conditions for the full development of the family, which is a fundamental unit of society, the Contracting Parties undertake to promote the economic, legal and social protection of family life by such means as social and family benefits, fiscal arrangements, provision of family housing, benefits for the newly married, and other appropriate means.

ARTICLE 17

The right of mothers and children to social and economic protection

With a view to ensuring the effective exercise of the right of mothers and children to social and economic protection, the Contracting Parties will take all appropriate and necessary measures to that end, including the establishment or maintenance of appropriate institutions or services.

ARTICLE 18

*The right to engage in a gainful occupation
in the territory of other Contracting Parties*

With a view to ensuring the effective exercise of the right to engage
in a gainful occupation in the territory of any other Contracting
Party, the Contracting Parties undertake:

1. to apply existing regulations in a spirit of liberality;
2. to simplify existing formalities and to reduce or abolish chancery
dues and other charges payable by foreign workers or their employers;
3. to liberalise, individually or collectively, regulations governing
the employment of foreign workers;
and recognise:
4. the right of their nationals to leave the country to engage in a
gainful occupation in the territories of the other Contracting Parties.

ARTICLE 19

*The right of migrant workers and their families
to protection and assistance*

With a view to ensuring the effective exercise of the right of migrant
workers and their families to protection and assistance in the territory
of any other Contracting Party, the Contracting Parties undertake:

1. to maintain or to satisfy themselves that there are maintained
adequate and free services to assist such workers, particularly in
obtaining accurate information, and to take all appropriate steps, so
far as national laws and regulations permit, against misleading propaganda relating to emigration and immigration;
2. to adopt appropriate measures within their own jurisdiction to
facilitate the departure, journey and reception of such workers and
their families, and to provide, within their own jurisdiction, appropriate
services for health, medical attention and good hygienic conditions
during the journey;
3. to promote co-operation, as appropriate, between social services,
public and private, in emigration and immigration countries;
4. to secure for such workers lawfully within their territories,
insofar as such matters are regulated by law or regulations or are
subject to the control of administrative authorities, treatment not less
favourable than that of their own nationals in respect of the following
matters:
    a. remuneration and other employment and working conditions;
    b. membership of trade unions and enjoyment of the benefits of
        collective bargaining;
    c. accommodation;

5. to secure for such workers lawfully within their territories treatment not less favourable than that of their own nationals with regard to employment taxes, dues or contributions payable in respect of employed persons;

6. to facilitate as far as possible the reunion of the family of a foreign worker permitted to establish himself in the territory;

7. to secure for such workers lawfully within their territories treatment not less favourable than that of their own nationals in respect of legal proceedings relating to matters referred to in this Article;

8. to secure that such workers lawfully residing within their territories are not expelled unless they endanger national security or offend against public interest or morality;

9. to permit, within legal limits, the transfer of such parts of the earnings and savings of such workers as they may desire;

10. to extend the protection and assistance provided for in this Article to self-employed migrants insofar as such measures apply.

PART III

Article 20

Undertakings

1. Each of the Contracting Parties undertakes:
   a. to consider Part I of this Charter as a declaration of the aims which it will pursue by all appropriate means, as stated in the introductory paragraph of that Part;
   b. to consider itself bound by at least five of the following Articles of Part II of this Charter: Articles 1, 5, 6, 12, 13, 16 and 19;
   c. in addition to the Articles selected by it in accordance with the preceding sub-paragraph, to consider itself bound by such a number of Articles or numbered paragraphs of Part II of the Charter as it may select, provided that the total number of Articles or numbered paragraphs by which it is bound is not less than 10 Articles or 45 numbered paragraphs.

2. The Articles or paragraphs selected in accordance with sub-paragraphs (*b*) and (*c*) of paragraph 1 of this Article shall be notified to the Secretary-General of the Council of Europe at the time when the instrument of ratification or approval of the Contracting Party concerned is deposited.

3. Any Contracting Party may, at a later date, declare by notification to the Secretary-General that it considers itself bound by any Articles or any numbered paragraphs of Part II of the Charter which it has not already accepted under the terms of paragraph 1 of this Article.

Such undertakings subsequently given shall be deemed to be an integral part of the ratification or approval, and shall have the same effect as from the thirtieth day after the date of the notification.

4. The Secretary-General shall communicate to all the signatory Governments and to the Director-General of the International Labour Office any notification which he shall have received pursuant to this Part of the Charter.

5. Each Contracting Party shall maintain a system of labour inspection appropriate to national conditions.

PART IV

ARTICLE 21

Reports concerning accepted provisions

The Contracting Parties shall send to the Secretary-General of the Council of Europe a report at two-yearly intervals, in a form to be determined by the Committee of Ministers, concerning the application of such provisions of Part II of the Charter as they have accepted.

ARTICLE 22

Reports concerning provisions which are not accepted

The Contracting Parties shall send to the Secretary-General, at appropriate intervals as requested by the Committee of Ministers, reports relating to the provisions of Part II of the Charter which they did not accept at the time of their ratification or approval or in a subsequent notification. The Committee of Ministers shall determine from time to time in respect of which provisions such reports shall be requested and the form of the reports to be provided.

ARTICLE 23

Communication of copies

1. Each Contracting Party shall communicate copies of its reports referred to in Articles 21 and 22 to such of its national organisations as are members of the international organisations of employers and trade unions to be invited under Article 27, paragraph 2, to be represented at meetings of the Sub-committee of the Governmental Social Committee.

2. The Contracting Parties shall forward to the Secretary-General any comments on the said reports received from these national organisations, if so requested by them.

ARTICLE 24

Examination of the reports

The reports sent to the Secretary-General in accordance with Articles 21 and 22 shall be examined by a Committee of Experts, who shall have also before them any comments forwarded to the Secretary-General in accordance with paragraph 2 of Article 23.

ARTICLE 25

Committee of Experts

1. The Committee of Experts shall consist of not more than seven members appointed by the Committee of Ministers from a list of independent experts of the highest integrity and of recognised competence in international social questions, nominated by the Contracting Parties.

2. The Members of the Committee shall be appointed for a period of six years. They may be reappointed. However, of the members first appointed, the terms of office of two members shall expire at the end of four years.

3. The members whose terms of office are to expire at the end of the initial period of four years shall be chosen by lot by the Committee of Ministers immediately after the first appointment has been made.

4. A member of the Committee of Experts appointed to replace a member whose term of office has not expired shall hold office for the remainder of his predecessor's term.

ARTICLE 26

Participation of the International Labour Organisation

The International Labour Organisation shall be invited to nominate a representative to participate in a consultative capacity in the deliberations of the Committee of Experts.

ARTICLE 27

Sub-committee of the Governmental Social Committee

1. The reports of the Contracting Parties and the conclusions of the Committee of Experts shall be submitted for examination to a Sub-committee of the Governmental Social Committee of the Council of Europe.

2. The Sub-committee shall be composed of one representative of each of the Contracting Parties. It shall invite no more than two international organisations of employers and no more than two international

trade union organisations as it may designate to be represented as observers in a consultative capacity at its meetings. Moreover, it may consult no more than two representatives of international non-governmental organisations having consultative status with the Council of Europe, in respect of questions with which the organisations are particularly qualified to deal, such as social welfare, and the economic and social protection of the family.

3. The Sub-committee shall present to the Committee of Ministers a report containing its conclusions and append the report of the Committee of Experts.

ARTICLE 28

Consultative Assembly

The Secretary-General of the Council of Europe shall transmit to the Consultative Assembly the conclusions of the Committee of Experts. The Consultative Assembly shall communicate its views on these Conclusions to the Committee of Ministers.

ARTICLE 29

Committee of Ministers

By a majority of two-thirds of the members entitled to sit on the Committee, the Committee of Ministers may, on the basis of the report of the Sub-committee, and after consultation with the Consultative Assembly, make to each Contracting Party any necessary recommendations.

PART V

ARTICLE 30

Derogations in time of war or public emergency

1. In time of war or other public emergency threatening the life of the nation any Contracting Party may take measures derogating from its obligations under this Charter to the extent strictly required by the exigencies of the situation, provided that such measures are not inconsistent with its other obligations under international law.

2. Any Contracting Party which has availed itself of this right of derogation shall, within a reasonable lapse of time, keep the Secretary-General of the Council of Europe fully informed of the measures taken and of the reasons therefor. It shall likewise inform

the Secretary-General when such measures have ceased to operate and the provisions of the Charter which it has accepted are again being fully executed.

3. The Secretary-General shall in turn inform other Contracting Parties and the Director-General of the International Labour Office of all communications received in accordance with paragraph 2 of this Article.

ARTICLE 31

Restrictions

1. The rights and principles set forth in Part I when effectively realised, and their effective exercise as provided for in Part II, shall not be subject to any restrictions or limitations not specified in those Parts, except such as are prescribed by law and are necessary in a democratic society for the protection of the rights and freedoms of others or for the protection of public interest, national security, public health, or morals.

2. The restrictions permitted under this Charter to the rights and obligations set forth herein shall not be applied for any purpose other than that for which they have been prescribed.

ARTICLE 32

Relations between the Charter and domestic law or international agreements

The provisions of this Charter shall not prejudice the provisions of domestic law or of any bilateral or multilateral treaties, conventions or agreements which are already in force, or may come into force, under which more favourable treatment would be accorded to the persons protected.

ARTICLE 33

Implementation by collective agreements

1. In member States where the provisions of paragraphs 1, 2, 3, 4 and 5 of Article 2, paragraphs 4, 6 and 7 of Article 7 and paragraphs 1, 2, 3 and 4 of Article 10 of Part II of this Charter are matters normally left to agreements between employers or employers' organisations and workers' organisations, or are normally carried out otherwise than by law, the undertakings of those paragraphs may be given and compliance with them shall be treated as effective if their provisions are applied through such agreements or other means to the great majority of the workers concerned.

2. In member States where these provisions are normally the subject of legislation, the undertakings concerned may likewise be given, and compliance with them shall be regarded as effective if the provisions are applied by law to the great majority of the workers concerned.

ARTICLE 34

Territorial application

1. This Charter shall apply to the metropolitan territory of each Contracting Party. Each signatory Government may, at the time of signature or of the deposit of its instrument of ratification or approval, specify, by declaration addressed to the Secretary-General of the Council of Europe, the territory which shall be considered to be its metropolitan territory for this purpose.

2. Any Contracting Party may, at the time of ratification or approval of this Charter or at any time thereafter, declare by notification addressed to the Secretary-General of the Council of Europe, that the Charter shall extend in whole or in part to a non-metropolitan territory or territories specified in the said declaration for whose international relations it is responsible or for which it assumes international responsibility. It shall specify in the declaration the Articles or paragraphs of Part II of the Charter which it accepts as binding in respect of the territories named in the declaration.

3. The Charter shall extend to the territory or territories named in the aforesaid declarations as from the thirtieth day after the date on which the Secretary-General shall have received notification of such declaration.

4. Any Contracting Party may declare at a later date by notification addressed to the Secretary-General of the Council of Europe, that, in respect of one or more of the territories to which the Charter has been extended in accordance with paragraph 2 of this Article, it accepts as binding any Articles or any numbered paragraphs which it has not already accepted in respect of that territory or territories. Such undertakings subsequently given shall be deemed to be an integral part of the original declaration in respect of the territory concerned, and shall have the same effect as from the thirtieth day after the date of the notification.

5. The Secretary-General shall communicate to the other signatory Governments and to the Director-General of the International Labour Office any notification transmitted to him in accordance with this Article.

ARTICLE 35

Signature, ratification and entry into force

1. This Charter shall be open for signature by the Members of the Council of Europe. It shall be ratified or approved. Instruments of ratification or approval shall be deposited with the Secretary-General of the Council of Europe.

2. This Charter shall come into force as from the thirtieth day after the date of deposit of the fifth instrument of ratification or approval.

3. In respect of any signatory Government ratifying subsequently, the Charter shall come into force as from the thirtieth day after the date of deposit of its instrument of ratification or approval.

4. The Secretary-General shall notify all the Members of the Council of Europe and the Director-General of the International Labour Office, of the entry into force of the Charter, the names of the Contracting Parties which have ratified or approved it and the subsequent deposit of any instruments of ratification or approval.

ARTICLE 36

Amendments

Any Member of the Council of Europe may propose amendments to this Charter in a communication addressed to the Secretary-General of the Council of Europe. The Secretary-General shall transmit to the other Members of the Council of Europe any amendments so proposed, which shall then be considered by the Committee of Ministers and submitted to the Consultative Assembly for opinion. Any amendments approved by the Committee of Ministers shall enter into force as from the thirtieth day after all the Contracting Parties have informed the Secretary-General of their acceptance. The Secretary-General shall notify all the Members of the Council of Europe and the Director-General of the International Labour Office of the entry into force of such amendments.

ARTICLE 37

Denunciation

1. Any Contracting Party may denounce this Charter only at the end of a period of five years from the date on which the Charter entered into force for it, or at the end of any successive period of two years, and, in each case, after giving six months' notice to the Secretary-General of the Council of Europe, who shall inform the

other Parties and the Director-General of the International Labour Office accordingly. Such denunciation shall not affect the validity of the Charter in respect of the other Contracting Parties provided that at all times there are not less than five such Contracting Parties.

2. Any Contracting Party may, in accordance with the provisions set out in the preceding paragraph, denounce any Article or paragraph of Part II of the Charter accepted by it provided that the number of Articles or paragraphs by which this Contracting Party is bound shall never be less than 10 in the former case and 45 in the latter and that this number of Articles or paragraphs shall continue to include the Articles selected by the Contracting Party among those to which special reference is made in Article 20, paragraph 1, sub-paragraph (b).

3. Any Contracting Party may denounce the present Charter or any of the Articles or paragraphs of Part II of the Charter, under the conditions specified in paragraph 1 of this Article in respect of any territory to which the said Charter is applicable by virtue of a declaration made in accordance with paragraph 2 of Article 34.

ARTICLE 38

Appendix

The Appendix to this Charter shall form an integral part of it.

In witness whereof, the undersigned, being duly authorised thereto, have signed this Charter.

Done at Turin, this 18th day of October 1961, in English and French, both texts being equally authoritative, in a single copy which shall be deposited within the archives of the Council of Europe. The Secretary-General shall transmit certified copies to each of the Signatories.

APPENDIX TO THE SOCIAL CHARTER

Scope of the Social Charter in terms of persons protected:

1. Without prejudice to Article 12, paragraph 4 and Article 13, paragraph 4, the persons covered by Articles 1 to 17 include foreigners only insofar as they are nationals of other Contracting Parties lawfully resident or working regularly within the territory of the Contracting Party concerned, subject to the understanding that these Articles are to be interpreted in the light of the provisions of Articles 18 and 19.

This interpretation would not prejudice the extension of similar facilities to other persons by any of the Contracting Parties.

2. Each Contracting Party will grant to refugees as defined in the Convention relating to the Status of Refugees, signed at Geneva on

28 July 1951, and lawfully staying in its territory, treatment as favourable as possible, and in any case not less favourable than under the obligations accepted by the Contracting Party under the said Convention and under any other existing international instruments applicable to those refugees.

PART I		PART II
Paragraph 18	and	*Article* 18, *paragraph* 1

It is understood that these provisions are not concerned with the question of entry into the territories of the Contracting Parties and do not prejudice the provisions of the European Convention on Establishment, signed at Paris on 13 December 1955.

PART II
Article 1, *paragraph* 2

This provision shall not be interpreted as prohibiting or authorising any union security clause or practice.

Article 4, *paragraph* 4

This provision shall be so understood as not to prohibit immediate dismissal for any serious offence.

Article 4, *paragraph* 5

It is understood that a Contracting Party may give the undertaking required in this paragraph if the great majority of workers are not permitted to suffer deductions from wages either by law or through collective agreements or arbitration awards, the exceptions being those persons not so covered.

Article 6, *paragraph* 4

It is understood that each Contracting Party may, insofar as it is concerned, regulate the exercise of the right to strike by law, provided that any further restriction that this might place on the right can be justified under the terms of Article 31.

Article 7, *paragraph* 8

It is understood that a Contracting Party may give the undertaking required in this paragraph if it fulfils the spirit of the undertaking by providing by law that the great majority of persons under 18 years of age shall not be employed in night work.

Article 12, paragraph 4

The words 'and subject to the conditions laid down in such agreements' in the introduction to this paragraph are taken to imply *inter alia* that with regard to benefits which are available independently of any insurance contribution a Contracting Party may require the completion of a prescribed period of residence before granting such benefits to nationals of other Contracting Parties.

Article 13, paragraph 4

Governments not Parties to the European Convention on Social and Medical Assistance may ratify the Social Charter in respect of this paragraph provided that they grant to nationals of other Contracting Parties a treatment which is in conformity with the provisions of the said Convention.

Article 19, paragraph 6

For the purpose of this provision, the term 'family of a foreign worker' is understood to mean at least his wife and dependent children under the age of 21 years.

PART III

It is understood that the Charter contains legal obligations of an international character, the application of which is submitted solely to the supervision provided for in Part IV thereof.

Article 20, paragraph 1

It is understood that the 'numbered paragraphs' may include Articles consisting of only one paragraph.

PART V

Article 30

The term 'in time of war or other public emergency' shall be so understood as to cover also the *threat* of war.

APPENDIX 7

ADDITIONAL PROTOCOLS

A. *Protocol Conferring upon the European Court of Human Rights Competence to give Advisory Opinions*[1]

The member States of the Council of Europe signatory hereto:

Having regard to the provisions of the Convention for the Protection of Human Rights and Fundamental Freedoms signed at Rome on 4 November 1950 (hereinafter referred to as 'the Convention'), and in particular Article 19 instituting, among other bodies, a European Court of Human Rights (hereinafter referred to as 'the Court');

Considering that it is expedient to confer upon the Court competence to give advisory opinions subject to certain conditions;

Have agreed as follows:

ARTICLE 1

1. The Court may, at the request of the Committee of Ministers, give advisory opinions on legal questions concerning the interpretation of the Convention and the Protocols thereto.

2. Such opinions shall not deal with any question relating to the content or scope of the rights or freedoms defined in Section 1 of the Convention and in the Protocols thereto, or with any other question which the Commission, the Court or the Committee of Ministers might have to consider in consequence of any such proceedings as could be instituted in accordance with the Convention.

3. Decisions of the Committee of Ministers to request an advisory opinion of the Court shall require a two-thirds majority vote of the representatives entitled to sit on the Committee.

ARTICLE 2

The Court shall decide whether a request for an advisory opinion submitted by the Committee of Ministers is within its consultative competence as defined in Article 1 of this Protocol.

---

[1] Opened for signature on 6 May 1963, and signed by Austria, Denmark, Germany, Ireland, Italy, Luxembourg, Netherlands, Norway, Sweden, Turkey and the United Kingdom.

ARTICLE 3

1. For the consideration of requests for an advisory opinion, the Court shall sit in plenary session.

2. Reasons shall be given for advisory opinions of the Court.

3. If the advisory opinion does not represent in whole or in part the unanimous opinion of the judges, any judge shall be entitled to deliver a separate opinion.

4. Advisory opinions of the Court shall be communicated to the Committee of Ministers.

ARTICLE 4

The powers of the Court under Article 55 of the Convention shall extend to the drawing up of such rules and the determination of such procedure as the Court may think necessary for the purposes of this Protocol.

ARTICLE 5

1. This Protocol shall be open to signature by Member States of the Council of Europe, signatories to the Convention, who may become Parties to it by:

   a. signature without reservation in respect of ratification or acceptance;

   b. signature with reservation in respect of ratification or acceptance, followed by ratification or acceptance.

   Instruments of ratification or acceptance shall be deposited with the Secretary-General of the Council of Europe.

2. This Protocol shall enter into force as soon as all the States Parties to the Convention shall have become Parties to the Protocol in accordance with the provisions of paragraph 1 of this Article.

3. From the date of the entry into force of this Protocol, Articles 1 to 4 shall be considered an integral part of the Convention.

4. The Secretary-General of the Council of Europe shall notify the Member States of the Council of:

   a. any signature without reservation in respect of ratification or acceptance;

   b. any signature with reservation in respect of ratification or acceptance;

   c. the deposit of any instrument of ratification or acceptance;

   d. the date of entry into force of this Protocol in accordance with paragraph 2 of this Article.

In witness whereof the undersigned, being duly authorised thereto, have signed this Protocol.

S

B.   *Protocol, Amending Articles* 29, 30 *&* 34 *of the Convention.*[1]

The member States of the Council of Europe, signatories to this Protocol,

Considering that it is advisable to amend certain provisions of the Convention for the Protection of Human Rights and Fundamental Freedoms signed at Rome on 4 November 1960 (hereinafter referred to as 'the Convention') concerning the procedure of the European Commission of Human Rights,

Have agreed as follows:

ARTICLE 1

1. Article 29 of the Convention is deleted.

2. The following provision shall be inserted in the Convention: 'Article 29

After it has accepted a petition submitted under Article 25, the Commission may nevertheless decide unanimously to reject the petition if, in the course of its examination, it finds that the existence of one of the grounds for non-acceptance provided for in Article 27 has been established.

In such a case, the decision shall be communicated to the parties'.

ARTICLE 2

In Article 30 of the Convention, the word 'Sub-Commission' shall be replaced by the word 'Commission'.

ARTICLE 3

1. At the beginning of Article 34 of the Convention, the following shall be inserted:

'Subject to the provisions of Article 29 . . .'

2. At the end of the same Article, the sentence 'the Sub-commission shall take its decisions by a majority of its members' shall be deleted.

ARTICLE 4

1. This Protocol shall be open to signature by the member States of the Council of Europe, who may become Parties to it either by:

[1] Opened for signature on 6 May 1963, and signed by Austria, Denmark, Germany, Ireland, Italy, Luxembourg, Netherlands, Norway, Sweden, Turkey and the United Kingdom.

a. signature without reservation in respect of ratification or acceptance, or

b. signature with reservation in respect of ratification or acceptance, followed by ratification or acceptance.

Instruments of ratification or acceptance shall be deposited with the Secretary-General of the Council of Europe.

2. This Protocol shall enter into force as soon as all States Parties to the Convention shall have become Parties to the Protocol, in accordance with the provisions of paragraph 1 of this Article.

3. The Secretary-General of the Council of Europe shall notify the Member States of the Council of:

a. any signature without reservation in respect of ratification or acceptance;

b. any signature with reservation in respect of ratification or acceptance;

c. the deposit of any instrument of ratification or acceptance;

d. the date of entry into force of this Protocol in accordance with paragraph 2 of this Article.

In witness whereof the undersigned, being duly authorised thereto, have signed this Protocol.

C. *Protocol Protecting Certain Additional Rights*[1]

Preamble

The Governments signatory hereto, being Members of the Council of Europe

Being resolved to take steps to ensure the collective enforcement of certain rights and freedoms other than those already included in Section I of the Convention for the Protection of Human Rights and Fundamental Freedoms signed at Rome on 4 November 1950 (hereinafter referred to as 'the Convention') and in Articles 1 to 3 of the First Protocol to the Convention, signed at Paris on 20 March 1952,

Have agreed as follows:

ARTICLE 1

No one shall be deprived of his liberty merely on the ground of inability to fulfil a contractual obligation.

---

[1] Opened for signature in September 1963.

S*

ARTICLE 2

1. Everyone lawfully within the territory of a State shall, within that territory, have the right to liberty of movement and freedom to choose his residence.

2. Everyone shall be free to leave any country, including his own.

3. No restrictions shall be placed on the exercise of these rights other than such as are in accordance with law and are necessary in a democratic society in the interests of national security or public safety for the maintenance of 'ordre public', for the prevention of crime, for the protection of health or morals, or for the protection of the rights and freedoms of others.

4. The rights set forth in paragraph 1 may also be subject, in particular areas, to restrictions imposed in accordance with law and justified by the public interest in a democratic society.

ARTICLE 3

1. No one shall be expelled, by means either of an individual or of a collective measure, from the territory of the State of which he is a national.

2. No one shall be deprived of the right to enter the territory of the State of which he is a national.

ARTICLE 4

Collective expulsion of aliens is prohibited.

ARTICLE 5

1. Any High Contracting Party may, at the time of signature or ratification of this Protocol, or at any time thereafter, communicate to the Secretary-General of the Council of Europe a declaration stating the extent to which it undertakes that the provisions of this Protocol shall apply to such of the territories for the international relations of which it is responsible as are named therein.

2. Any High Contracting Party which has communicated a declaration in virtue of the preceding paragraph may, from time to time, communicate a further declaration modifying the terms of any former declaration or terminating the application of the provisions of this Protocol in respect of any territory.

3. A declaration made in accordance with this Article shall be deemed to have been made in accordance with paragraph 1 of Article 63 of the Convention.

4. The territory of any State to which this Protocol applies by virtue

of ratification or acceptance by that State, and each territory to which this Protocol is applied by virtue of a declaration by that State under this Article, shall be treated as separate territories for the purpose of the references in Article 2 and 3 to the territory of a State.

ARTICLE 6

1. As between the High Contracting Parties the provisions of Articles 1 to 5 of this Protocol shall be regarded as additional articles to the Convention, and all the provisions of the Convention shall apply accordingly.

2. Nevertheless, the right of individual recourse recognised by a declaration made under Article 25 of the Convention, or the acceptance of the compulsory jurisdiction of the Court by a declaration made under Article 46 of the Convention, shall not be effective in relation to this Protocol unless the High Contracting Party concerned has made a statement recognising such right, or accepting such jurisdiction, in respect of all or any of Articles 1 to 4 of the Protocol.

ARTICLE 7

1. This Protocol shall be open for signature by the members of the Council of Europe who are the signatories of the Convention; it shall be ratified at the same time as or after the ratification of the Convention. It shall enter into force after the deposit of five instruments of ratification. As regards any signatory ratifying subsequently, the Protocol shall enter into force at the date of the deposit of its instrument of ratification.

2. The instruments of ratification shall be deposited with the Secretary-General of the Council of Europe, who will notify all members of the names of those who have ratified.

SELECT BIBLIOGRAPHY

Author's Note

There is now a vast amount of literature about the European Convention, the Commission and the Court. Three of my colleagues have written books on the subject:

GOLSONG H., *Das Rechts-schutz system der Europäischen Menschenrechtskonvention*, Karlsruhe, 1958.

WIEBRINGPAUS H., *Die Rom-Konvention für Menschenrechte in der Praxis der Strassburger Menschenrechtskommission*, Saarbrücken, 1959.

VASAK K., *La Convention Européenne des Droits de l' Homme*, Paris, 1963.

The law Faculty of the University of Strasbourg published in 1961 a book entitled *La Protection Internationale des Droits de l' Homme dans le Cadre Européen*, containing the proceedings of a symposium which it had organised, in collaboration with the Directorate of Human Rights of the Council of Europe, in November 1960; it includes many valuable papers. A book in English entitled *The European Convention on Human Rights: Background, Development and Prospects* by Mr. Gordon Lee Weil was published at Leyden in 1963, but was received too late for reference to be made to it in the text of this book.

More than two hundred articles have now appeared and the bibliography which follows makes no attempt to be comprehensive. It omits, in particular, many valuable articles in German which I am unfortunately unable to read. More comprehensive bibliographies are to be found in each volume of the *Yearbook of the European Convention on Human Rights*. The works listed below are those which I have been able to consult in preparing my manuscript.

ABBREVIATIONS

B.Y.I.L.:	*British Yearbook of International Law.*
I.C.L.Q.:	*International and Comparative Law Quarterly.*
Annuaire Français:	*Annuaire Français de Droit International.*
Strasbourg Recueil:	*La Protection Internationale des Droits de l' Homme dans le Cadre Européen*, Paris, 1961.
J.Int.Com.Jur.	*Journal of the International Commission of Jurists.*

BOOKS AND ARTICLES

ADAM, H. T. 'Le Droit de Propriété dans la Convention Européenne des Droits de l'Homme', *Revue du Droit Publique et de la Science Politique*, 1953, pp. 317–66.

BEBR, G. 'International Protection of Human Rights and Freedoms', 29 *Philippine Law Journal*, 1954, p. 307.

BROWNLEE, I. 'The Individual before Tribunals exercising International Jurisdiction', *I.C.L.Q.*, 1962, pp. 701–20.

CASSIN, R. 'La Cour Européenne des Droits de l'Homme', *European Yearbook*, Vol. VII, 1959, pp. 75–92.

CASTANOS, S., AND SIDJANSKI, D. 'La Convention Européenne des Droits de l'Homme', *Journal du Droit International*, 1955, pp. 580–603.

COHEN, M. 'Bill C-60 and International Law', *Canadian Bar Review*, March 1959, pp. 228–33.

COMTE, PHILIPPE. 'The Application of the European Convention on Human Rights in Municipal Law', *J.Int.Com.Jur.*, Vol. IV, 1962, p. 95.

COUNCIL OF EUROPE. *The Convention for the Protection of Human Rights and Fundamental Freedoms and Protocol*, European Treaty Series No. 5.
European Commission of Human Rights—Documents and Decisions, 1955–7.
Yearbook of the European Convention on Human Rights, Vol. II, 1958–9; Vol. III, 1960; Vol. IV, 1961.
Recommendations and Resolutions Adopted by the Assembly, 1950.
Texts Adopted by the Assembly, 1949, and annually since 1951.
'Fifth Anniversary of the Coming into Force of the European Convention on Human Rights', 1959.
'The Rights of the European Citizen', (Preface by Lord McNair), 1961.

EISSEN, M.-A. 'La Cour Européenne des Droits de l'Homme—de la Convention au Réglement', *Annuaire Français*, 1959, pp. 618–58.
'Le Premier Arrêt de las Cour Européenne des Droits de l'Homme', *Annuaire Français*, 1960, pp. 444–97.
'Le Nouveau Réglement Interieur de la Commission Européenne des Droits de l'Homme', *Annuaire Français*, 1960, pp. 774–90.
'La Convention et les Devoirs de l'Individu', *Strasbourg Recueil*, 1961, pp. 167–94.
'The European Convention on Human Rights and the Duties of the Individual', *Nordisk Tidsskrift for International Ret*, 1962, pp. 230–46.

EISSEN, M.-A., AND McNULTY, A. B. 'The European Commission of Human Rights—Procedure and Jurisdiction', *J.Int.Com.Jur.*, Vol. I, No. 2, pp. 198–219.

ELIAS, T. O. 'The New Constitution of Nigeria and the Protection of Human Rights and Fundamental Freedoms', *J.Int.Com.Jur.*, Vol. II, 1960, pp. 30–46.

EUROPEAN COMMISSION OF HUMAN RIGHTS. *Rules of Procedure of the Commission*, Strasbourg, 1962.

EUROPEAN COURT OF HUMAN RIGHTS. *Publications of the Court*, Series A, Judgments and Decisions:
>   Lawless Case—Preliminary Objections, Judgment of 14 November, 1960.
>   Lawless Case—Judgment of 7 April, 1961.
>   Lawless Case (Merits),—Judgment of 1 July, 1961.
>   De Becker Case—Judgment of 27 March, 1962.
>   Rules of Court, 1962.

EUROPEAN MOVEMENT. *The European Movement and the Council of Europe*, London, 1949.

EUSTATHIADES, C. TH. 'La mise en oeuvre des Droits de l'Homme sur le plan international', *Strasbourg Recueil*, 1961, pp. 217–30.

FACULTÉ DE DROIT DE STRASBOURG. *La Protection Internationale des Droits de l'Homme dans le cadre européen*, Paris, 1961.

GANJI, M. *International Protection of Human Rights*, Geneva, 1962.

GOLSONG, H. 'The European Convention on Human Rights in a German Court', *B.Y.I.L.*, 1957, p. 317.
'The European Convention on Human Rights before Domestic Courts', *B.Y.I.L.*, 1962.

HERAUD, G. 'Les Droits garantis par la Convention', *Strasbourg Recueil*, 1961, pp. 107–26.

INTERNATIONAL COMMISSION OF JURISTS. 'The Rule of Law in a Free Society', *Report on the Congress at New Delhi*, 1959.
'African Conference on the Rule of Law', *Report on the Conference at Lagos*, 1961.

JANSSEN-PEVTSCHIN, G., VELU, J., AND VANWELKENHUYZEN, A. 'La Convention de Sauvegarde des Droits de l'Homme et des Libertés Fondamentales et le Fonctionnement des Juridictions Belges', *Chronique de Politique Etrangère*, Brussels, 1962, pp. 199–264.

JENKS, C. W. *The International Protection of Trade Union Freedoms*, London, 1957.
Human Rights and International Labour Standards, London, 1960.

KELSEN, H. *The Law of the United Nations*, London, 1950.

LALIVE, J. F., AND VASAK, K. 'Chronique de la Jurisprudence de la Commission et de la Cour Européenne des Droits de l'Homme', *Journal du Droit International,* janviers-mars 1962, pp. 238–89.

LASKIN, B. 'Canada's Bill of Rights: A Dilemma for the Courts?', *I.C.L.Q.,* 1962, pp. 519–36.

LAUTERPACHT, H. *International Law and Human Rights,* London, 1950. 'The proposed European Court of Human Rights', *Transactions of the Grotius Society,* 1950, p. 25.

MCNAIR, LORD. *The Expansion of International Law,* 1962.

MCNULTY, A. B. 'Influences Directes exercées hors d'Europe par la Convention Européenne', *Strasbourg Recueil,* 1961, pp. 377–86.

MCNULTY, A. B., AND EISSEN, M.-A. 'The European Commission of Human Rights—Procedure and Jurisdiction', *J.Int.Com.Jur.,* Vol. I, No. 2. pp. 198–219.

MODINOS, P. 'La Convention européenne des Droits de l'Homme', *European Yearbook,* Vol. I, 1955, pp. 141–70.
'Les Enseignements de la Convention', *Strasbourg Recueil,* 1961, pp. 337–59.
'Effects and Repercussions of the European Convention', *I.C.L.Q.,* 1962, pp. 1097–1108.

MOSKOWITZ, M. *Human Rights and World Order,* New York, 1958.

MOUSKHELY, M. 'Les fondements philosophiques et sociologiques des Droits de l'Homme', *Strasbourg Recueil,* 1961, pp. 35–57.

NIETO SALO, J. 'La Convencion Europea de los Derechos del Hombre', *Instituciones Europeas,* Saragossa, 1960, pp. 43–61.

OPPENHEIM, L. *Treatise on International Law,* Vol. I. Peace, 1st edn., 1905.

PARDOS PEREZ, J. L. *Derechos del Hombre en el Consejo de Europa,* Murcia, 1960.

PINTO, R. *Les Organisations Européennes,* Paris, 1963.

ROBERTSON, A. H. 'The European Convention on Human Rights', *B.Y.I.L.,* 1950, pp. 145–63.
'The European Convention on Human Rights—Recent Developments', *B.Y.I.L.,* 1951, pp. 359–65.
The Council of Europe, 2nd edn., London, 1961. (French edn., Leyden, 1962).

ROLIN, H. 'Le Rôle du Requérant dans la Procédure prevue par la Commission Européenne des Droits de l'Homme', *Revue Hellénique de Droit International,* 1956, pp. 3–14.
'Les Conclusions du Colloque sur la Protection Internationale des Droits de l'Homme dans le Cadre Européen', *Strasbourg Recueil,* 1961, pp. 405–17.

SCHWEBEL, S. M. *The Secretary-General of the United Nations*, Harvard, 1952.

SCHWELB, EGON. 'International Conventions on Human Rights', *I.C.L.Q.*, 1960, p. 654.

SIDJANSKI, D. *See* Castanos, S.

SMITH, DE S. A. 'Fundamental Rights in the New Commonwealth', *I.C.L.Q.*, 1961, pp. 83–102 and 215–37.

SUSTERHENN, A. 'L'Application de la Convention sur le plan du Droit Interne', *Strasbourg Recueil*, 1961, pp. 303–20.

TENNFJORD, F. 'The European Social Charter—an Instrument of Social Collaboration in Europe', *European Yearbook*, Vol. IX, 1961, pp. 71–83.

VANWELKENHUYZEN, A. *See* Janssen-Pevtschin.

VARANDA, R. SAINZ DE R. *Convencion Europea de los Derechos del Hombre*, Saragossa, 1959.

VASAK, K. 'Cour et Commission des Droits de l'Homme', *Juris-Classeur de Droit International*, 1961, Fascicule 155 F.
'De la Convention Européenne à la Convention Africaine des Droits de l'Homme', *Revue Juridique et Politique d'Outre-Mer*, janviers-mars 1962, pp. 59–76.
See also Lalive, J. F.

VELU, J. 'Le Problème de l'Application aux Juridictions Administratives des Régles de la Convention Européenne des Droit de l'Homme relatives à la publicité des Audiences et des Jugements', *Revue de Droit International et de Droit Comparé*, Brussels, 1961, pp. 129–71.
See also Janssen-Pevtschin.

VIS, W. 'La Réparation des Violations de la Convention Européenne des Droits de l'Homme', *Strasbourg Recueil*, 1961, p. 279.

WALDOCK, C. H. M. 'The Decline of the Optional Clause', *B.Y.I.L.*, 1955, pp. 244–87.
'The European Convention on Human Rights', *B.Y.I.L.*, 1958, pp. 356–63.

WEIL, G. L. *The European Convention on Human Rights*, Leyden, 1963.

WEIS, PAUL. 'The Convention relating to the Status of Stateless Persons', *I.C.L.Q.*, 1961, p. 255.
'The United Nations Convention on the Reduction of Statelessness, 1961', *I.C.L.Q.*, 1962, pp. 1073–96.

WIEBRINGHAUS, H. 'La Regle de l'épuisement préalable des voies de recours internes dans la jurisprudence de la Commission Européenne des Droits de l'Homme', *Annuaire Français*, 1959, p. 685. 'La Protection Internationale des Droits de l'Homme dans le cadre du Conseil de l'Europe', *Rivista di Diritto Europeo*, 1961, pp. 48–62.

INDEX

acceleration of procedure, need for, 139, 164

accusation, right to information re, 25

advisory opinions, 123, 163ff, 167

Africa, human rights in, 175f

agents, for parties to Court cases, 102

agricultural workers, 144

aliens: expulsion of, 27, 151, 153; political activities of, 40

Allan, Robert, 90f

America, human rights in, 174f

American States, Organisation of, 174

appreciation, margin of, 133ff

arbitration, 88

Arik, Fikret, 96

Arnaldo, Einard, 94, 95

Arnhem, 28

arraignment, of State before Commission, 49, 50

arrest, arbitrary, 19

Assembly, Consultative, of Council of Europe, 75

assembly, freedom of, 19, 30

assistance, social and medical, 147f, 167; European Convention on, 148

association, freedom of, 19, 30

asylum, right of, 152, 154f

Austria, 16, 21, 54, 72ff, 92, 166, 171; v. Italy, 60ff, 99

autonomy, local, 152

Azara, Antonio, 9

Azikiwe, Dr., 176

ballot, secret, 10, 36, 37

bargaining, collective, 146, 148, 150

Bartin, —, 167

Bebr, G., 9n

Belgium, 16, 37, 54, 92, 109, 166; see also de Becker

beneficiaries, of Convention, 15

Berlin, blockade of, 4

Bill of Rights: American, 177; English, 177; international, 2n

British Guiana, 78

Brussels Exhibition (1958), 92

Brussels Treaty (1948), 3

Canada, 177f

capital: levy, 33; taxes on, 33f

Cassin, René, 94, 95, 97n

children, protection of, 146, 147

Church, and education, 13

churches, construction of, 28n

Churchill, (Sir) Winston S., 7

Civil and Political Rights, draft Covenant on, 152, 172n

'closed shop', 30

Collective Bargaining, Convention on, 9n

Colonial Clause, 109f

colonial territories: Court and, 161f; human rights in, 110, 172

Commission for Human Rights, European, 10, 43ff; and Court, relations, 102ff, 116ff; functions, 43; judges, 44, 77ff; list of members, 48; membership, 43f; — qualifications for, 44, 45, 46, 47n; — election, 44f, 77; procedure, 49, 55ff; summary of work, 58f

Communism, 4; and education, 13

Communist Party, German, 40, 129

compensation, for expropriation, 32

Comte, Philippe, 16n, 28n, 50n

conciliation, 10

conscience, freedom of, 28

constitutions, State, and Convention, 111

Consultative Assembly, 10–11

Convention on Human Rights: breaches of, 10; drafting technique, 17ff; implementation, 107; origin of, 4; ratifications, 14, 111; signature, 4f

275